The Vale of C

Or, The Martyr

GW01159082

Grace Aguilar

Alpha Editions

This edition published in 2024

ISBN : 9789362092939

Design and Setting By
Alpha Editions
www.alphaedis.com
Email - info@alphaedis.com

As per information held with us this book is in Public Domain.
This book is a reproduction of an important historical work. Alpha Editions uses the
best technology to reproduce historical work in the same manner it was first
published to preserve its original nature. Any marks or number seen are left
intentionally to preserve its true form.

Contents

MEMOIR OF GRACE AGUILAR.

Grace Aguilar was born at Hackney, June 2nd, 1816. She was the eldest child, and only daughter of Emanuel Aguilar, one of those merchants descended from the Jews of Spain, who, almost within the memory of man, fled from persecution in that country, and sought and found an asylum in England.

The delicate frame and feeble health observable in Grace Aguilar throughout her life, displayed itself from infancy; from the age of three years, she was almost constantly under the care of some physician, and, by their advice, annually spending the summer months by the sea, in the hope of rousing and strengthening a naturally fragile constitution. This want of physical energy was, however, in direct contrast to her mental powers, which developed early, and readily. She learned to read with scarcely any trouble, and when once that knowledge was gained, her answer when asked what she would like for a present, was invariably "A book," which, was read, re-read, and preserved with a care remarkable in so young a child. With the exception of eighteen months passed at school, her mother was her sole instructress, and both parents took equal delight in directing her studies, and facilitating her personal inspection of all that was curious and interesting in the various counties of England to which they resorted for her health.

From the early age of seven she commenced keeping a journal, which was continued with scarce any intermission throughout her life. In 1825 she visited Oxford, Cheltenham, Gloucester, Worcester, Ross, and Bath, and though at that time but nine years old, her father took her to Gloucester and Worcester cathedrals, and also to see a porcelain and pin manufactory, &c., the attention and interest she displayed on these occasions, affording convincing proof that her mind was alive to appreciate and enjoy what was thus presented to her observation. Before she had completed her twelfth year she ventured to try her powers in composition, and wrote a little drama, called Gustavus Vasa, never published, and only here recorded as being the first germ of what was afterwards to become the ruling passion.

In September, 1828, the family went to reside in Devonshire for the health of Mr. Aguilar, and there a strong admiration for the beauties and wonders of nature manifested itself: she constantly collected shells, stones, seaweed, mosses, &c., in her daily rambles; and not satisfied with admiring their beauty, sedulously procured whatever little catechisms or other books on those subjects she could purchase, or borrow, eagerly endeavoring by their study, to increase her knowledge of their nature and properties.

When she had attained the age of fourteen, her father commenced a regular course of instruction for his child, by reading aloud, while she was employed in drawing, needlework, &c. History was selected, that being the study which now most interested her, and the first work chosen was Josephus.

It was while spending a short time at Tavistock, in 1830, that the beauty of the surrounding scenery led her to express her thoughts in verse. Several small pieces soon followed her first essay, and she became extremely fond of this new exercise and enjoyment of her opening powers, yet her mind was so well regulated, that she never permitted herself to indulge in original composition until her duties, and her studies, were all performed.

Grace Aguilar was extremely fond of music; she had learned the piano from infancy, and in 1831 commenced the harp. She sang pleasingly, preferring English songs, and invariably selecting them for the beauty or sentiment of the words; she was also passionately fond of dancing, and her cheerful lively manners in the society of her young friends, would scarcely have led any to imagine how deeply she felt and pondered upon the serious and solemn subjects which afterwards formed the labor of her life. She seemed to enjoy all, to enter into all, but a keen observer would detect the hold that sacred and holy principle ever exercised over her lightest act, and gayest hour. A sense of duty was apparent in the merest trifle, and her following out of the divine command of obedience to parents, was only equalled by the unbounded affection she felt for them. A wish was once expressed by her mother that she should not waltz, and no solicitation could afterwards tempt her. Her mother also required her to read sermons, and study religion and the Bible regularly; this was readily submitted to, first as a task, but afterwards with much delight; for evidence of which we cannot do better than quote her own words in one of her religious works.

"This formed into a habit, and persevered in for a life, would in time, and without labor or weariness, give the comfort and the knowledge that we seek; each year it would become lighter, and more blest, each year we should discover something we knew not before, and in the valley of the shadow of death, feel to our heart's core that the Lord our God is Truth."—*Women of Israel*, Vol. II, page 43.

Nor did Grace Aguilar only study religion for her own personal observance and profit. She embraced its *principles* (the principles of all creeds) in a widely extended and truly liberal sense. She carried her practice of its holy and benevolent precepts into every minutiae of her daily life, doing all the good her limited means would allow, finding time, in the midst of her own studies, and most varied and continual occupations, to work for, and instruct her poor neighbors in the country, and while steadily venerating and adhering to her own faith, neither inquiring nor heeding the religious opinions of the needy whom she succored or consoled. To be permitted to help and comfort, she considered a privilege and a pleasure; she left the rest to God; and thus bestowing and receiving blessings and smiles from all who had the opportunity of knowing her, her young life flowed on, in an almost uninterrupted stream of enjoyment, until she had completed her nineteenth year.

Alas! the scene was soon to change, and trials awaited that spirit which, in the midst of sunshine, had so beautifully striven to prepare itself a shelter from the storm. The two brothers of Miss Aguilar, whom she tenderly loved, left the paternal roof to be placed far from their family at school. Her mother's health necessitated a painful and dangerous operation, and from that time for several years, alternate hopes and fears through long and dreary watchings beside the sick bed of that beloved mother, became the portion of her gifted child. But even this depressing and arduous change in the duties of her existence did not suspend her literary pursuits and labors. She profited by all the intervals she could command, and wrote the tale of the "Martyr," the "Spirit of Judaism," and "Israel Defended;" the latter translated from the French, at the earnest request of a friend, and printed only for private circulation. The "Magic Wreath," a little poetical work, and the first our authoress ever published, dedicated to the Right Honorable the Countess of Munster, also appeared about this time.

In the Spring of 1835, Grace Aguilar was attacked with measles, and never afterwards recovered her previous state of health, suffering at intervals with such exhausting feelings of weakness, as to become without any visible disease really alarming.

The medical attendants recommended entire rest of mind and body; she visited the sea, and seemed a little revived, but anxieties were gathering around her horizon, to which it became evidently impossible her ardent and active mind could remain passive or indifferent, and which recalled every feeling, every energy of her impressible nature into action. Her elder brother, who had long chosen music as his profession, was sent to Germany to pursue his studies; the younger determined upon entering the sea service. The excitement of these changes, and the parting with both, was highly injurious to their affectionate sister, and her delight a few months after, at welcoming the sailor boy returned from his first voyage, with all his tales of danger and adventure, and his keen enjoyment of the path of life he had chosen, together with her struggles to do her utmost to share his walks and companionship, contributed yet more to impair her inadequate strength.

The second parting was scarcely over ere her father, who had long shown symptoms of failing health, became the victim of consumption. He breathed his last in her arms, and the daughter, while sorrowing over all she had lost, roused herself once more to the utmost, feeling that she was the sole comforter beside her remaining parent. Soon after, when her brother again returned, finding the death of his father, he resolved not to make his third voyage as a midshipman, but endeavor to procure some employment sufficiently lucrative to prevent his remaining a burthen upon his widowed mother. Long and anxiously did he pursue this object, his sister, whose acquaintance with literary and talented persons had greatly increased, using all her energy and influence in his behalf, and concentrating all the enthusiastic feelings of her nature in inspiring him with patience, comfort, and hope, as often as they failed him under his repeated disappointments. At length his application was taken up by a powerful friend, for her sake, and she had the happiness of succeeding, and saw him depart at the very summit of his wishes. Repose, which had been so long necessary, seemed now at hand; but her nerves had been too long and too repeatedly overstrung, and when this task was done, the worn and weary spirit could sustain no more, and sank under the labor that had been imposed upon it.

Severe illness followed, and though it yielded after a time to skilful remedies and tender care, her excessive languor and severe headaches, continued to give her family and friends great uneasiness.

During all these demands upon her time, her thoughts, and her health, however, the ruling passion neither slumbered nor slept. She completed the Jewish Faith, and also prepared Home Influence for the press, though very unfit to have taxed her powers so far. Her medical attendant became urgent for total change of air and scene, and again strongly interdicted *all* mental exertion—a trip to Frankfort, to visit her elder brother, was therefore decided on. In June, 1847, she set out, and bore the journey without suffering nearly so much as might have been expected. Her hopes were nigh, her spirits raised—the novelty and interest of her first travels on the Continent gave her for a very transient period a gleam, as it were, of strength. For a week or two she appeared to rally, then again every exertion became too much for her, every stimulating remedy to exhaust her. She was ordered from Frankfort to try the baths and mineral waters of Schwalbach, but without success. After a stay of six weeks, and persevering with exemplary patience in the treatment prescribed, she was one night seized with alarming convulsive spasms, so terrible that her family removed her next morning with all speed back to Frankfort, to the house of a family of most kind friends, where every attention and care was lavishly bestowed.

In vain. She took to her bed the very day of her arrival, and never rose from it again; she became daily weaker, and in three weeks from that time her sufferings ceased for ever. She was perfectly conscious to within less than two hours before her death, and took an affectionate leave of her mother and brother. Speech had been a matter of difficulty for some time previous, her throat being greatly affected by her malady; but she had, in consequence, learned to use her fingers in the manner of the deaf and dumb, and almost the last time they moved, it was to spell upon them feebly, "Though He slay me, yet will I trust in Him."

She was buried in the cemetery of Frankfort, one side of which is set apart for the people of her faith. The stone which marks the spot bears upon it a butterfly and five stars, emblematic of the soul in heaven, and beneath appears the inscription—

> "Give her of the fruit of her hands, and let her own works praise her in the gates."—Prov. ch. xxxi, v. 31.

And thus, 16th September, 1847, at the early age of thirty-one, Grace Aguilar was laid to rest—the bowl was broken, the silver cord was loosed. Her life was short and checkered with pain and anxiety, but she strove hard to make it useful and valuable, by employing diligently and faithfully the talents with which she had been endowed. Nor did the serious view with which she ever regarded earthly existence, induce her to neglect or despise any occasion of enjoyment, advantage, or sociality which presented itself. Her heart was ever open to receive, her hand to give.

Inasmuch as she succeeded to the satisfaction of her fellow beings, let them be grateful; inasmuch as she failed, let those who perceive it deny her not the meed of praise, for her endeavor to open the path she believed would lead mankind to practical virtue and happiness, and strive to carry out the pure philanthropic principles by which she was actuated, and which she so earnestly endeavored to diffuse.

OCTOBER, 1849.

CHAPTER I.

"They had met, and they had parted;
Time had closed o'er each again,
Leaving lone the weary hearted
Mournfully to wear his chain."—MS.

A deliciously cool, still evening, had succeeded the intense heat of a Spanish summer day, throwing rich shadows and rosy gleams on a wild, rude mountain pass in central Spain. Massive crags and gigantic trees seemed to contest dominion over the path, if path it could be called; where the traveller, if he would persist in going onwards, could only make his way by sometimes scrambling over rocks, whose close approach from opposite sides presented a mere fissure covered with flowers and brushwood, through which the slimmest figure would fail to penetrate; sometimes wading through rushing and brawling streams, whose rapid currents bore many a jagged branch and craggy fragment along with them; sometimes threading the intricacies of a dense forest, recognizing the huge pine, the sweet acorn oak, the cork tree, interspersed with others of lesser growth, but of equally wild perplexing luxuriance. On either side—at times so close that two could not walk abreast, at others so divided that forests and streams intervened—arose mountain walls seeming to reach the very heavens, their base covered with trees and foliage, which gradually thinning, left their dark heads totally barren, coming out in clear relief against the deep blue sky.

That this pass led to any inhabited district was little probable, for it grew wilder and wilder, appearing to lead to the very heart of the Sierra Toledo— a huge ridge traversing Spain. By human foot it had evidently been seldom trod; yet on this particular evening a traveller there wended his solitary way. His figure was slight to boyishness, but of fair proportion, and of such graceful agility of movement, that the obstacles in his path, which to others of stouter mould and heavier step might have been of serious inconvenience, appeared by him as unnoticed as unfelt. The deep plume of his broad-rimmed hat could not conceal the deep blue restless eyes, the delicate complexion, and rich brown clustering hair; the varying expression of features, which if not regularly handsome, were bright with intelligence and truth, and betraying like a crystal mirror every impulse of the heart—characteristics both of feature and disposition wholly dissimilar to the sons of Spain.

His physiognomy told truth. Arthur Stanley was, as his name implied, an Englishman of noble family; one of the many whom the disastrous wars of the Roses had rendered voluntary exiles. His father and four brothers had fallen in battle at Margaret's side. Himself and a twin brother, when scarcely fifteen, were taken prisoners at Tewkesbury, and for three years left to languish in prison. Wishing to conciliate the still powerful family of Stanley, Edward offered the youths liberty and honor if they would swear allegiance to himself. They refused peremptorily; and with a refinement of cruelty more like Richard of Gloucester than himself, Edward ordered one to the block, the other to perpetual imprisonment. They drew lots, and Edwin Stanley perished. Arthur, after an interval, succeeded in effecting his escape, and fled from England, lingered in Provence a few months, and then unable to bear an inactive life, hastened to the Court of Arragon; to the heir apparent of which, he bore letters of introduction, from men of rank and influence, and speedily distinguished himself in the wars then agitating Spain. The character of the Spaniards—impenetrable and haughty reserve—occasioned, in general, prejudice and dislike towards all foreigners. But powerful as was their pride, so was their generosity; and the young and lonely stranger, who had thrown himself so trustingly and frankly on their friendship, was universally received with kindness and regard. In men of lower natures, indeed, prejudice still lingered; but this was of little matter; Arthur speedily took his place among the noblest chivalry of Spain; devoted to the interests of the King of Sicily, but still glorying in the name and feeling of an Englishman, he resolved, in his young enthusiasm, to make his country honored in himself.

He had been five years in Spain, and was now four and twenty; but few would have imagined him that age, so frank and free and full of thoughtless mirth and hasty impulse was his character. These last fifteen months, however, a shadow seemed to have fallen over him, not deep enough to create remark, but *felt* by himself. His feelings, always ardent, had been all excited, and were all concentrated, on a subject so wrapt in mystery, that the wish to solve it engrossed his whole being. Except when engaged in the weary stratagem, the rapid march, and actual conflict, necessary for Ferdinand's interest, but one thought, composed of many, occupied his mind, and in solitude so distractingly, that he could never rest; he would traverse the country for miles, conscious indeed of what he *sought*, but perfectly unconscious where he *went*.

It was in one of these moods he had entered the pass we have described, rejoicing in its difficulties, but not thinking where it led, or what place he sought, when a huge crag suddenly rising almost perpendicularly before him, effectually roused him from his trance. Outlet there was none. All around him towered mountains, reaching to the skies. The path was so winding, that, as he looked round bewildered, he could not even imagine how he came there. To retrace his steps, seemed quite as difficult as to proceed. The sun too had declined, or was effectually concealed by the towering rocks, for sudden darkness seemed around him. There was but one way, and Stanley prepared to scale the precipitous crag before him with more eagerness than he would a beaten path. He threw off his cloak, folded it in the smallest possible compass, and secured it like a knapsack to his shoulders, slung his sword over his neck, and, with a vigorous spring, which conquered several paces of slippery rock at once, commenced the ascent. Some brushwood, and one or two stunted trees, gave him now and then a hold for his hands; and occasional ledges in the rock, a resting for his foot; but still one false step, one failing nerve, and he must have fallen backwards and been dashed to pieces; but to Arthur the danger was his safety. Where he was going, indeed he knew not. He could see no further than the summit of the crag, which appeared like a line against the sky; but any bewilderment were preferable to the strange stagnation towards outward objects, which had enwrapped him ten minutes before.

Panting, breathless, almost exhausted, he reached the summit, and before him yawned a chasm, dark, fathomless, as if nature in some wild convulsion had rent the rock asunder. The level ground on which he stood was barely four feet square; behind him sloped the most precipitous side of the crag, devoid of tree or bush, and slippery from the constant moisture that formed a deep black pool at its base. Stanley hazarded but one glance behind, then looked steadily forward, till his eye seemed accustomed to the width of the chasm, which did not exceed three feet. He fixed his hold firmly on a blasted trunk growing within the chasm; It shook—gave way—another moment and he would have been lost; but in that moment he loosed his hold, clasped both hands above his head, and successfully made the leap—aware only of the immense effort by the exhaustion which followed compelling him to sink down on the grass, deprived even of energy to look around him.

So marvellous was the change of scenery on which his eyes unclosed, that he started to his feet, bewildered. A gradual hill, partly covered with rich meadow grass, and partly with corn, diversified with foliage, sloped downwards, leading by an easy descent to a small valley, where orange and lime trees, the pine and chestnut, palm and cedar, grew in beautiful luxuriance. On the left was a small dwelling, almost hidden in trees. Directly beneath him a natural fountain threw its sparkling showers on beds of sweet-scented and gayly-colored flowers. The hand of man had very evidently aided nature in forming the wild yet chaste beauty of the scene; and Arthur bounded down the slope, disturbing a few tame sheep and goats on his way, determined on discovering the genius of the place.

No living object was visible, however; and with his usual reckless spirit, he resolved on exploring further, ere he demanded the hospitality of the dwelling. A narrow path led into a thicker wood, and in the very heart of its shade stood a small edifice, the nature of which Arthur vainly endeavored to understand. It was square, and formed of solid blocks of cedar; neither carving nor imagery of any kind adorned it; yet it had evidently been built with skill and care. There was neither tower nor bell, the usual accompaniments of a chapel, which Stanley had at first imagined it; and he stood gazing on it more and more bewildered. At that moment, a female voice of singular and thrilling beauty sounded from within. It was evidently a hymn she chanted, for the strain was slow and solemn, but though *words* were distinctly intelligible, their language was entirely unknown. The young man listened at first, conscious only of increasing wonderment, which was quickly succeeded by a thrill of hope, so strange, so engrossing, that he stood, outwardly indeed as if turned to stone; inwardly, with every pulse so throbbing that to move or speak was impossible. The voice ceased; and in another minute a door, so skilfully constructed as when closed to be invisible in the solid wall, opened noiselessly; and a female figure stood before him.

CHAPTER II.

"Farewell! though in that sound be years
Of blighted hopes and fruitless tears—
Though the soul vibrate to its knell
Of joys departed—yet farewell."

MRS. HEMANS.

To attempt description of either face or form would be useless. The exquisite proportions of the rounded figure, the very perfection of each feature, the delicate clearness of the complexion—brunette when brought in close contact with the Saxon, blonde when compared with the Spaniard—all attractions in themselves, were literally forgotten, or at least unheeded, beneath the spell which dwelt in the *expression* of her countenance. Truth, purity, holiness, something scarcely of this nether world, yet blended indescribably with all a woman's nature, had rested there, attracting the most unobservant, and riveting all whose own hearts contained a spark of the same lofty attributes. Her dress, too, was peculiar—a full loose petticoat of dark blue silk, reaching only to the ankle, and so displaying the beautifully-shaped foot; a jacket of pale yellow, the texture seeming of the finest woven wool, reaching to the throat; with sleeves tight on the shoulders, but falling in wide folds as low as the wrist, and so with every movement displaying the round soft arm beneath. An antique brooch of curiously wrought silver confined the jacket at the throat. The collar, made either to stand up or fall, was this evening unclosed and thrown black, its silver fringe gleaming through the clustering tresses that fell in all their native richness and raven blackness over her shoulders, parted and braided on her brow, so as to heighten the chaste and classic expression of her features.

On a stranger that beautiful vision must have burst with bewildering power: to Arthur Stanley she united *memory* with *being*, the *past* with the *present*, with such an intensity of emotion, that for a few minutes his very breath was impeded. She turned, without seeing him, in a contrary direction; and the movement roused him.

"Marie!" he passionately exclaimed, flinging himself directly in her path, and startling her so painfully, that though there was a strong and visible effort at self-control, she must have fallen had he not caught her in his arms. There was an effort to break from his hold, a murmured exclamation, in which terror, astonishment, and yet joy, were painfully mingled, and then the heroine gave place to the woman, for her head sunk on his shoulder and she burst into tears.

Time passed. Nearly an hour from that strange meeting, and still they were together; but no joy, nor even hope was on the countenance of either. At first, Arthur had alluded to their hours of happy yet unconfessed affection, when both had felt, intuitively, that they were all in all to each other, though not a syllable of love had passed their lips; on the sweet memories of those blissful hours, so brief, so fleeting, but still Marie wept: the memory seemed anguish more than joy. And then he spoke of returned affection, as avowed by her, when his fond words had called it forth; and shuddered at the recollection that that hour of acknowledged and mutual love, had proved the signal of their separation. He referred again to her agonized words, that a union was impossible, that she dared not wed him; it was sin even to love him; that in the tumultuary, yet delicious emotions she had experienced, she had forgotten, utterly forgotten in what it must end—the agony of desolation for herself, and, if he so loved her, for Stanley also—and again he conjured her to explain their meaning. They had been separated, after that fearful interview, by a hasty summons for him to rejoin his camp; and when he returned, she had vanished. He could not trace either her or the friend with whom she had been staying. Don Albert had indeed said, his wife had gone to one of the southern cities, and his young guest returned to her father's home; but where that home was, Don Albert had so effectually evaded, that neither direct questionings nor wary caution could obtain reply. But he had found her now; they had met once more, and oh, why need they part again? Why might he not seek her father, and beseech his blessing and consent?

His words were eloquent, his tone impassioned, and hard indeed the struggle they occasioned. But Marie wavered not in the repetition of the same miserable truth, under the impression of which they had separated before. She conjured him to leave her, to forget the existence of this hidden valley, for danger threatened her father and herself if it was discovered. So painful was her evident terror, that Arthur pledged his honor never to reveal it, declaring that to retrace the path by which he had discovered it, was even to himself impossible. But still he urged her, what was this fatal secret? Why was it sin to love him? Was she the betrothed of another? and the large drops starting to the young man's brow denoted the agony of the question.

"No, Arthur, no," was the instant rejoinder: "I never could love, never could be another's, this trial is hard enough, but it is all I have to bear. I am not called upon to give my hand to another, while my heart is solely thine."

"Then wherefore join that harsh word 'sin,' with such pure love, my Marie? Why send me from you wretched and most lonely, when no human power divides us?"

"No human power!—alas! alas!—a father's curse—an offended God—these are too awful to encounter, Arthur. Oh do not try me more; leave me to my fate, called down by my own weakness, dearest Arthur. If you indeed love me, tempt me not by such fond words; they do but render duty harder. Oh, wherefore have you loved me!"

But such suffering tone, such broken words, were not likely to check young Stanley's solicitations. Again and again he urged her, at least to say what fatal secret so divided them; did he but know it, it might be all removed. Marie listened to him for several minutes, with averted head and in unbroken silence; and when she did look on him again, he started at her marble paleness and the convulsive quivering of her lips, which for above a minute prevented the utterance of a word.

"Be it so," she said at length; "you shall know this impassable barrier. You are too honorable to reveal it. Alas! it is not that fear which restrained me; my own weakness which shrinks from being to thee as to other men, were the truth once known, an object of aversion and of scorn."

"Aversion! scorn! Marie, thou ravest," impetuously exclaimed Stanley; "torture me not by these dark words: the worst cannot be more suffering."

But when the words were said, when with blanched lips and cheeks, and yet unfaltering tone, Marie revealed the secret which was to separate them for ever, Arthur staggered back, relinquishing the hands he had so fondly clasped, casting on her one look in which love and aversion were strangely and fearfully blended, and then burying his face in his hands, his whole frame shook as with some sudden and irrepressible anguish.

"Thou knowest all, now," continued Marie, after a pause, and she stood before him with arms folded on her bosom, and an expression of meek humility struggling with misery on her beautiful features. "Señor Stanley, I need not now implore you to leave me; that look was sufficient, say but you forgive the deception I have been compelled to practise—and—and forget me. Remember what I am, and you will soon cease to love."

"Never, never!" replied Stanley, as with passionate agony he flung himself before her. "Come with me to my own bright land; who shall know what thou art there? Marie, my own beloved, be mine. What to me is race or blood? I see but the Marie I have loved, I shall ever love. Come with me. Edward has made overtures of peace if I would return to England. For thy sake I will live beneath his sway; be but mine, and oh, we shall be happy yet."

"And my father," gasped the unhappy girl, for the generous nature of Arthur's love rendered her trial almost too severe. "Wilt thou protect him too? wilt thou for my sake forget what he is, and be to him a son?" He turned from her with a stifled groan. "Thou canst not—I knew it—oh bless thee for thy generous love; but tempt me no more, Arthur; it cannot be; I dare not be thy bride."

"And yet thou speakest of love. 'Tis false, thou canst not love me," and Stanley sprung to his feet disappointed, wounded, till he scarce knew what he said. "I would give up Spain and her monarch's love for thee. I would live in slavery beneath a tyrant's rule to give thee a home of love. I would forget, trample on, annihilate the prejudices of a life, unite the pure blood of Stanley with the darkened torrent running through thy veins, forget thy race, descent, all but thine own sweet self. I would do this, all this for love of thee. And for me, what wilt thou do?—reject me, bid me leave thee—and yet thou speakest of love: 'tis false, thou lovest another better!"

"Ay!" replied Marie, in a tone which startled him, "ay, thou hast rightly spoken; thy words have recalled what in this deep agony I had well nigh forgotten. There is a love, a duty stronger than that I bear to thee. I would resign all else, but not my father's God."

The words were few and simple; but the tone in which they were spoken recalled Arthur's better nature, and banished hope at once. A pause ensued, broken only by the young man's hurried tread, as he traversed the little platform in the vain struggle for calmness. On him this blow had fallen wholly unprepared; Marie had faced it from the moment they had parted fifteen months before, and her only prayer had been (a fearful one for a young and loving heart), that Stanley would forget her, and they might never meet again. But this was not to be; and though she had believed herself prepared, one look on his face, one sound of his voice had proved how vain had been her dream.

"I will obey thee, Marie," Stanley said, at length, pausing before her. "I will leave thee now, but not—not for ever. No, no; if indeed thou lovest me time will not change thee, if thou hast one sacred tie, when nature severs that, and thou art alone on earth, thou shalt be mine, whatever be thy race."

"Hope it not, ask it not! Oh, Arthur, better thou shouldst hate me, as thy people do my race: I cannot bear such gentle words," faltered poor Marie, as her head sunk for a minute on his bosom, and the pent-up tears burst forth. "But this is folly," she continued, forcing back the choking sob, and breaking from his passionate embrace. "There is danger alike for my father and thee, if thou tarriest longer. Not that way," she added, as his eye glanced inquiringly towards the hill by which he had descended; "there is another and an easier path; follow me—thou wilt not betray it?"

"Never!" was the solemn rejoinder, and not a word more passed between them. He followed her through what seemed to be an endless maze, and paused before a towering rock, which, smooth and perpendicular as a wall built by man, ran round the vale and seemed to reach to heaven. Pushing aside the thick brushwood, Marie stood beside the rock, and by some invisible movement, a low door flew open and disclosed a winding staircase.

"Thou wilt trust me, Arthur?"

"Ay, unto death," he answered, springing after her up the rugged stair. Narrow loopholes, almost concealed without by trees and brushwood, dimly lighted the staircase, as also a low, narrow passage, which branched off in zig-zag windings at the top, and terminated, as their woody path had done, in a solid wall. But again an invisible door flew open, closing behind them; and after walking about a hundred yards through prickly shrubs and entangled brushwood that obscured his sight, Marie paused, and Arthur gazed round bewildered. A seemingly boundless plain stretched for miles around him, its green level only diversified by rocks scattered about in huge masses and wild confusion, as if hurled in fury from some giant's hand. The rock whence he had issued was completely invisible. He looked around again and again, but only to bewilder himself yet more.

"The way looks more dreary than it is. Keep to the left: though it seems the less trodden path thou wilt find there a shelter for the night, and to-morrow's sun will soon guide thee to a frontier town; thy road will be easy then. Night is falling so fast now, thou hadst best not linger, Arthur."

But he did linger, till once more he had drawn from her a confession of her love, that none other could take his place, even while she conjured him never to seek her again—and so they parted. Five minutes more, and there was not a vestige of a human form on the wide-extended plain.

CHAPTER III.

"Now History unfolds her ample page,
Rich with the spoils of Time."

Clearly to comprehend the internal condition of Spain at the period of our narrative (1479)—a condition which, though apparently purely national, had influence over every domestic hearth—it is necessary to glance back a few years. The various petty Sovereignties into which Spain had been divided never permitted any lengthened period of peace; but these had at length merged into two great kingdoms, under the names of Arragon and Castile. The *form* of both governments was monarchical; but the *genius* of the former was purely republican, and the power of the sovereign so circumscribed by the Junta, the Justicia, and the Holy Brotherhood, that the vices or follies of the monarch were of less consequence, in a national point of view, in Arragon, than in any other kingdom. It was not so with Castile. From the death of Henry the Third, in 1404, a series of foreign and civil disasters had plunged the kingdom in a state of anarchy and misery. John the Second had some virtues as an individual, but none as a king; and his son Henry, who succeeded him in 1450, had neither the one nor the other. Governed as his father had been, entirely by favorites, the discontent of all classes of his subjects rapidly increased; the people were disgusted and furious at the extravagance of the monarch's minion; the nobles, fired at his insolence; and an utter contempt of the king, increased the virulence of the popular ferment. Unmindful of the disgrace attendant on his divorce from Blanche of Navarre, Henry sought and obtained the hand of Joanna, Princess of Portugal, whose ambition and unprincipled intrigues heightened the ill-favor with which he was already regarded. The court of Castile, once so famous for chastity and honor, sank to the lowest ebb of infamy, the shadow of which, seeming to extend over the whole land, affected nobles and people with its baleful influence. All law was at an end: the people, even while they murmured against the King, followed his evil example; and history shrinks from the scenes of debauchery and licentiousness, robbery and murder, which desecrated the land. But this state of things could not last long, while there still remained some noble hearts amongst the Castilians. Five years after their marriage, the Queen was said to have given birth to a daughter, whom Henry declared should be his successor, in lieu of his young brother Alfonso (John's son, by a second wife, Isabella of Portugal). This child the nobles refused to receive, believing and declaring that she was not Henry's daughter, and arrogated to themselves the right of trying and passing sentence on their Sovereign, who, by his weak, flagitious conduct had, they unanimously declared, forfeited all right even to the present possession of the crown.

The confederates, who were the very highest and noblest officers of the realm, assembled at Avita, and with a solemnity and pomp which gave the whole ceremony an imposing character of reality, dethroned King Henry in effigy, and proclaimed the youthful Alfonso sovereign in his stead. All present swore fealty, but no actual good followed: the flame of civil discord was re-lighted, and raged with yet greater fury; continuing even after the sudden and mysterious death of the young prince, whose extraordinary talent, amiability, and firmness, though only fourteen, gave rise to the rumor that he had actually been put to death by his own party, who beheld in his rising genius the utter destruction of their own turbulence and pride. Be this as it may, his death occasioned no cessation of hostilities, the confederates carrying on the war in the name of his sister, the Infanta Isabella. Her youth and sex had pointed her out as one not likely to interfere or check the projects of popular ambition, and therefore the very fittest to bring forward as an excuse for their revolt. With every appearance of humility and deference, they offered her the crown; but the proudest and boldest shrank back abashed, before the flashing eye and proud majesty of demeanor with which she answered, "The crown is not yours to bestow; it is held by Henry, according to the laws alike of God and man; and till his death, you have no right to bestow, nor I to receive it."

But though firm in this resolution, Isabella did not refuse to coincide in their plans for securing her succession. To this measure Henry himself consented, thus appearing tacitly to acknowledge the truth of the reports that Joanna was a surreptitious child, and for a brief period Castile was delivered from the horrors of war. Once declared heiress of Castile and Leon, Isabella's hand was sought by many noble suitors, and her choice fell on Ferdinand, the young King of Sicily, and heir-apparent to the crown of Arragon. Love was Isabella's incentive. Prudence, and a true patriotic ambition, urged the Archbishop of Toledo not only to ratify the choice, but to smooth every difficulty in their way; he saw at once the glory which might accrue to Spain by this peaceful union of two rival thrones. Every possible and impossible obstacle was privately thrown by Henry to prevent this union, even while he gave publicly his consent; his prejudice against Ferdinand being immovable and deadly. But the manoeuvres of the Archbishop were more skilful than those of the King. The royal lovers—for such they really were—were secretly united at Valladolid, to reach which place in safety Ferdinand had been compelled to travel in disguise, and attended only by four cavaliers; and at that period so straitened were the circumstances of the Prince and Princess, who afterwards possessed the boundless treasures of the new world, that they were actually compelled to borrow money to defray the expenses of their wedding!

The moment Henry became aware of this marriage, the civil struggle recommenced. In vain the firm, yet pacific Archbishop of Toledo recalled the consent he had given, and proved that the union not only secured the after-glory of Spain, but Henry's present undisturbed possession of his throne. Urged on by his wife, and his intriguing favorite, the Marquis of Villena, who was for ever changing sides, he published a manifesto, in which he declared on oath that he believed Joanna to be his daughter, and proclaimed her heiress of Castile. Ferdinand and Isabella instantly raised an array, regardless of the forces of Portugal (to whose monarch Joanna had been betrothed), who were rapidly advancing to the assistance of Henry. Ere, however, war had regularly commenced, a brief respite was obtained by the death of Henry, and instantly and unanimously Isabella was proclaimed Queen of Leon and Castile. Peace, however, was not instantly regained; the King of Portugal married Joanna, and resolved on defending her rights. Some skirmishing took place, and at length a long-sustained conflict near Fero decided the point—Ferdinand and the Castilians were victorious; the King of Portugal made an honorable retreat to his own frontiers, and the Marquis of Villena, the head of the malcontents, and by many supposed to be the real father of Joanna, submitted to Isabella. Peace thus dawned for Castile; but it was not till three years afterwards, when Ferdinand had triumphed over the enemies of Arragon, and succeeded his father as Sovereign of that kingdom, that any vigorous measures could be taken for the restoration of internal order.

The petty Sovereignties of the Peninsular, with the sole exception of the mountainous district of Navarre, and the Moorish territories in the south, were now all united; and it was the sagacious ambition of Ferdinand and Isabella to render Spain as important in the scale of kingdoms as any other European territory; and to do this, they knew, demanded as firm a control over their own subjects, as the subjection of still harassing foes.

Above a century had elapsed since Spain had been exposed to the sway of weak or evil kings, and all the consequent miseries of misrule and war. Rapine, outrage, and murder had become so frequent and unchecked, as frequently to interrupt commerce, by preventing all communication between one place and another. The people acknowledged no law but their own passions. The nobles were so engrossed with hatred of each other, and universal contempt of their late sovereign, with personal ambition and general discontent, that they had little time or leisure to attend to any but their own interest. But a very brief interval convinced both nobles and people that a new era was dawning for them. In the short period of eighteen months, the wise administration of Isabella and Ferdinand, had effected a sufficient change to startle all ranks into the conviction that their best interests lay in prompt obedience, and in exerting themselves in their several spheres, to second the sovereign's will. The chivalric qualities of Ferdinand, his undoubted wisdom and unwavering firmness, excited both love and fear; while devotion itself is not too strong a term to express the national feeling entertained toward Isabella. Her sweet, womanly gentleness, blended as it was with the dignity of the sovereign; her ready sympathy in all that concerned her people—for the lowest of her subjects; doing justice, even if it were the proud noble who injured, and the serf that suffered—all was so strange, yet fraught with such national repose, that her influence every year increased; while every emotion of chivalry found exercise, and yet rest in the heart of the aristocracy for their Queen; her simple word would be obeyed, on the instant, by men who would have paused, and weighed, and reasoned, if any other—even Ferdinand himself—had spoken. Isabella knew her power; and if ever sovereign used it for the good, the happiness of her people, that proud glory was her own.

In spite of the miserable condition of the people during the civil struggles, the wealth of Spain had not decreased. It was protected and increased by a class of people whose low and despised estate was, probably, their safeguard—these were the Jews, who for many centuries had, both publicly and secretly, resided in Spain. There were many classes of this people in the land, scattered alike over Castile, Leon, Arragon, Navarre, and also in the Moorish territories; some there were confined to the mystic learning and profound studies of the schools, whence they sent many deeply learned men to other countries, where their worth and wisdom gained them yet greater regard than they received in Spain: others were low and degraded in outward seeming, yet literally holding and guiding the financial and commercial interests of the kingdom;—whose position was of the lowest—scorned and hated by the very people who yet employed them, and exposed to insult from every class; the third, and by far the largest body of Spanish Jews, were those who, Israelites in secret, were so completely Catholic in seeming, that the court, the camp, the council, even the monasteries themselves, counted them amongst them. And this had been the case for years—we should say for centuries—and yet so inviolable was the faith pledged to each other, so awful the dangers around them, were even suspicion excited, that the fatal secret never transpired; offices of state, as well as distinctions of honor, were frequently conferred on men who, had their faith or race been suspected, would have been regarded as the scum of the earth, and sentenced to torture and death, for daring to pass for what they were not. At the period of which we write, the fatal enemy to the secret Jews of more modern times, known as the Holy Office, did not exist; but a secret and terrible tribunal there was, whose power and extent were unknown to the Sovereigns of the land.

The Inquisition is generally supposed to have been founded by Ferdinand and Isabella, about the year 1480 or '82; but a deeper research informs us that it had been introduced into Spain several centuries earlier, and obtained great influence in Arragon. Confiding in the protection of the papal see, the Inquisitors set no bounds to their ferocity: secret informations, imprisonments, tortures, midnight assassinations, marked their proceedings; but they overreached themselves. All Spain, setting aside petty rivalships, rose up against them. All who should give them encouragement or assistance were declared traitors to their country; the very lives of the Inquisitors and their families were, in the first burst of fury, endangered; but after a time, imagining they had sunk into harmless insignificance, their oppressors desisted in their efforts against them, and were guilty of the unpardonable error of not exterminating them entirely.[A]

[Footnote A: Stockdale's History of the Inquisition.]

According to the popular belief, the dreaded tribunal slept, and so soundly, they feared not, imagined not its awakening. They little knew that its subterranean halls were established near almost all the principal cities, and that its engines were often at work, even in the palaces of kings. Many a family wept the loss of a beloved member, they knew not, guessed not how— for those who once entered those fatal walls were never permitted to depart; so secret were their measures, that even the existence of this fearful mockery of justice and Religion was not known, or at that time it would have been wholly eradicated. Superstition had not then gained the ascendency which in after years so tarnished the glory of Spain, and opened the wide gates to the ruin and debasement under which she labors now. The fierce wars and revolutions ravaging the land had given too many, and too favorable opportunities for the exercise of this secret power; but still, regard for their own safety prevented the more public display of their office, as ambition prompted. The vigorous proceedings of Ferdinand and Isabella rendered them yet more wary; and little did the Sovereigns suspect that in their very courts this fatal power held sway. The existence of this tribunal naturally increased the dangers environing the Israelites who were daring enough to live amongst the Catholics as one of them; but of this particular danger they themselves were not generally aware, and their extraordinary skill in the concealment of their faith (to every item of which they yet adhered) baffled, except in a very few instances, even these ministers of darkness.

CHAPTER IV.

"In war did never lion rage more fierce—
In peace was never gentle lamb more mild,
Than was that young and princely gentleman."

SHAKSPEARE.

The wars ravaging Spain had nursed many a gallant warrior, and given ample opportunities for the possession and display of those chivalric qualities without which, in that age, no manly character was considered perfect. The armies of Ferdinand and Isabella counted some of the noblest names and most valiant knights of Christendom. The Spanish chivalry had always been famous, and when once organized under a leader of such capacity and firmness as Ferdinand; when the notice and regard of the Queen they idolized could only be obtained by manly virtue as well as the warrior's ardor, a new spirit seemed to wake within them; petty rivalships and jealousies were laid aside, all they sought was to become distinguished; and never had chivalry shone with so pure and glorious a lustre in the court of Spain as then, when, invisibly and unconsciously, it verged on its decline.

It was amongst all this blaze of chivalry that Arthur Stanley had had ample opportunity to raise, in his own person, the martial glory of his own still much loved and deeply regretted land. Ferdinand had honored him with so large a portion of his coveted regard, that no petty feelings on the part of the Spaniards, because he was a stranger, could interfere with his advancement; his friends, however, were mostly among the Arragonese; to Isabella, and the Castilians, he was only known as a valiant young warrior, and a marked favorite of the king. There was one person, however, whom the civil contentions of Spain had so brought forward, that his name was never spoken, either in council, court, or camp, palace or hut—by monarch or captive, soldier or citizen—without a burst of such warm and passionate attachment that it was almost strange how any single individual, and comparatively speaking, in a private station, could so have won the hearts of thousands. Yet it had been gradually that this pre-eminence had been attained—gradually, and entirely by the worth of its object. At the early age of sixteen, and as page to Gonzalos de Lara, Ferdinand Morales had witnessed with all the enthusiasm of a peculiarly ardent, though outwardly quiet nature, the exciting proceedings at Avila. His youth, his dignified mien, his earnestness, perhaps even his striking beauty, attracted the immediate attention of the young Alfonso, and a bond of union of reciprocal affection from that hour linked the youths together. It is useless arguing on the folly and frivolity of such rapid attachments; there are those with whom one day will be sufficient, not only to awaken, but to rivet, those mysterious sympathies which are the undying links of friendship; and others again, with whom we may associate intimately for months—nay, years—and yet feel we have not one thought in common, nor formed one link to sever which is pain.

During Alfonso's brief career, Ferdinand Morales displayed personal qualities, and a wisdom and faithfulness in his cause, well deserving not only the prince's love, but the confidence of all those who were really Alfonso's friends. His deep grief and ill-concealed indignation at the prince's mysteriously sudden death might, for the time, have obtained him enemies, and endangered his own life; but the favor of Isabella, whom it was then the policy of the confederates to conciliate in all things possible, protected and advanced him. The love borne by the Infanta for her young brother surpassed even the tenderest affection of such relatives; all who had loved and served him were dear to her; and at a time when so much of treachery and insidious policy lurked around her, even in the garb of seeming devotion to her cause, the unwavering fidelity and straightforward conduct of Morales, combined as it was with his deep affection for Alfonso, permitted her whole mind to rest on him, secure not only of his faithfulness, but of vigilance which would discover and counteract every evil scheming of seeming friends. Her constantly chosen messenger to Ferdinand, he became known and trusted by both that prince and his native subjects. His wealth, which, seemed exhaustless, independent of his preferments, was ever at the service of either Isabella or her betrothed; he it was from whom the necessary means for her private nuptials were borrowed. At that scene he was, of course, present, and, at his own desire, escorted Ferdinand back to his own domains—an honorable but most dangerous office, performed with his usual unwavering fidelity and skill. That one so faithful in adversity should advance from post to post as soon as dawning prosperity permitted Isabella and Ferdinand to reward merit as well as to evince gratitude, was not surprising; but no royal favor, no coveted honors, no extended power, could alter one tittle of his single-hearted truth—his unrestrained intercourse with and interest in his equals, were they of the church, court, or camp—his gentle and unassuming manner to his inferiors. It was these things that made him so universally beloved. The coldest natures, if thrown in contact with him, unconsciously to themselves kindled into warmth; vice itself could not meet the glance of that piercing eye without shrinking, for the moment, in loathing from itself.

Until Isabella and Ferdinand were firmly established on the throne, and Arragon and Castile united, there had been little leisure amongst their warriors to think of domestic ties, otherwise it might perhaps have been noticed as somewhat remarkable that Ferdinand Morales appeared to stand alone; kindred, indeed, he claimed with four or five of the noblest amongst the Castilians, but he seemed to have no near relative; and though he mingled courteously, and to some young hearts far too pleasingly, amongst Isabella's court, it seemed as if he would never stoop to love. The Queen often jested him on his apparent insensibility, and entreating him to wed. At first he had smiled away such words; but two or three months after the commencement of our tale, he acknowledged that his affections had been for some years engaged to one living so completely in retirement as to be unknown to all; he had but waited till peace had dawned for Spain, and he might offer her not only his love, but a secure and quiet home. He spoke in confidence, and Isabella, woman-like, had listened with no little interest, giving her royal approval of his choice, without knowing more than his own words revealed; but feeling convinced, she said, that Ferdinand Morales would never wed one whose birth or lineage would tarnish his pure Castilian blood, or endanger the holy faith of which he was so true a member. A red flush might have stained the cheek of the warrior at these words, but the deep obeisance with which he had departed from the royal presence concealed the unwonted emotion. Ere a year from that time elapsed, not only the ancient city of Segovia, where his large estates lay, but all Castile were thrown into a most unusual state of excitement by the marriage of the popular idol, Don Ferdinand Morales, with a young and marvellously lovely girl, whom few, if any, had ever seen before, and whose very name, Donna Marie Henriquez, though acknowledged as essentially Castilian, was yet unfamiliar. The mystery, however, as to who she was, and where he could have found her, was speedily lost in the universal admiration of her exceeding and remarkable loveliness, and of the new yet equally attractive character which, as a devoted husband, Morales thenceforward displayed. Many had imagined that he was too grave, too wrapt in his many engrossing duties, alike as statesman and general, ever to play the lover; and he had seemed resolved that this impression should remain, and shrunk from the exposure of such sacred feelings; for none, save Isabella, knew he loved until they saw his bride.

CHAPTER V.

"And we have won a bower of refuge now
In this fresh waste."

MRS. HEMANS.

The Vale of Cedars, as described in our first chapter, had been originally the work of a single individual, who had found there a refuge and concealment from the secret power of the Inquisition, from whose walls he had almost miraculously escaped: this individual was Julien Henriquez, the grandfather of Marie. For five years he remained concealed, working unaided, but successfully, in forming a comfortable home and concealed retreat, not only for himself but for his family. Nature herself appeared to have marked the spot as an impenetrable retreat, and Julien's skill and energy increased and strengthened the natural barriers. During these five years the secret search for his person, at first carried on so vigilantly that his enemies supposed nothing but death could have concealed him, gradually relaxed, and then subsided altogether. Foes and friends alike believed him dead, and when he did re-appear in the coarse robe, shrouding cowl, and hempen belt, of a wandering friar, he traversed the most populous towns in safety, unrecognized and unsuspected. It was with some difficulty he found his family, and a matter of no little skill to convey them, without exciting suspicion by their disappearance, to his retreat; but all was accomplished at length, and years of domestic felicity crowned every former effort, and inspired and encouraged more.

Besides his own immediate family, consisting of his wife, a son, and daughter, Henriquez had the charge of two nephews and a niece, children of his sister, whose husband had perished by the arm of the same secret power from which Henriquez had escaped; their mother had died of a broken heart, from the fearful mystery of her husband's fate, and the orphans were to Julien as his own.

As years passed, the Vale of Cedars became not only a safe, but a luxurious home. Every visit to the world Julien turned to profit, by the purchase first of necessaries, then of luxuries. The little temple was erected by the active aid of the young men, and the solemn rites of their peculiar faith adhered to in security. Small as the family was, deaths, marriages, and births took place, and feelings and sympathies were excited, and struggles secretly endured, making that small spot of earth in very truth a world. The cousins intermarried. Ferdinand and Josephine left the vale for a more stirring life; Manuel, Henriquez's own son, and Miriam, his niece, preferred the quiet of the vale. Julien, his nephew, too, had loved; but his cousin's love was given to his brother, and he departed, unmurmuringly indeed, but he dared not yet trust himself to associate calmly with the object of his love: he had ever been a peculiarly sad and silent boy; the fate of his father never for an instant seemed to leave his mind, and he had secretly vowed to avenge him. Love, for a while, had banished these thoughts; but when that returned in all the misery of isolation to his own breast, former thoughts regained dominion, and he tried to conquer the one feeling by the encouragement of the other. His brother and his wife constantly visited the vale; if at no other time, almost always at those solemn festivals which generally fell about the period of the Catholic Easter and Michaelmas; often accompanied by faithful friends, holding the same mysterious bond of brotherhood, and to whom the secret of that vale was as precious and secure as to its natural inmates. Its aged founder had frequently the happiness of gathering around him from twenty to thirty of his secret race, and of feeling that his work would benefit friends as well as offspring. Julien alone never returned to the vale, and his family at length mourned him as one amongst the dead.

The career of his brother was glorious but brief; he fell fighting for his country, and his widow and young son returned to the parental retreat. Though the cousins had married the same day, the son of Ferdinand was ten years older than his cousin Marie; Manuel and Miriam having lived twelve years together ere the longed-for treasure was bestowed. At first, therefore, she had been to the youthful Ferdinand but as a plaything, to pet and laugh with: he left the vale as page to his father's companion in arms, Gonzalos de Lara, when Marie was little more than five years old; but still his love for her and his home was such that whenever it was possible, he would snatch if it were but half a day to visit them. Gradually, and to him it seemed almost strangely, the plaything child changed into the graceful girl, and then again into the lovely woman; and dearer than ever became his boyhood's home, though years had snatched away so many of its beloved inmates, that, at the period of our story, its sole occupants were Marie and her father.

Had her mother lived, perchance Marie had never been exposed to the dangers of an introduction to the world. Betrothed, in the secret hearts of not only her own parents, but of Ferdinand's mother, to her cousin, if she lived to attain sufficient age, Miriam would not have thought it so impossible as Manuel did, that the affections of his child might be sought for by, and given to another, if she mingled with the world; she would at least have waited till she was Ferdinand's wedded wife, and then sent her forth secure. But such subtle fears and feelings are peculiarly *woman's*; not the tenderest, most devoted father, could of himself have either thought of, or understood them. He might perhaps have owned their justice had they been presented to him by the affectionate warnings of an almost idolized wife; but that voice was hushed, her sweet counsels buried in the grave; and the fond, proud father, only thought of his child's brilliant beauty, and how she would be admired and beloved, could she be but generally known. And so, for her sake, he actually did violence to his own love for the quiet retirement of the vale, and bore her to the care of Donna Emilie de Castro; seeing nothing, feeling nothing, but the admiration she excited, and that she was indeed the loveliest there. One wish he had, and that was, that his nephew could have been there likewise; but being engaged at that time on some important private business for the Queen, Ferdinand did not even know that his cousin had ever left the vale.

That his child's affections could be excited towards any but those of her own race was a circumstance so impossible, and moreover a sin so fearful, that it never entered Manuel's mind: he knew not woman's nature, dreamed not of its quick impulses, its passionate yearnings, its susceptibility towards all gentle emotions, or he could not have so trustingly believed in the power of her peculiar faith and creed to guard her from the danger. Even his dearest desire that she should become the wife of her cousin she knew not; for the father shrunk from revealing it to either his child or nephew, unless Ferdinand loved and sought her himself. What therefore had she to warn her from the precipice on which she stood, when new, strange, yet most exquisitely sweet emotions gradually obtained possession of her heart in her daily intercourse with Arthur Stanley? What they were indeed she knew not; the word love was never uttered by either; she only knew that his presence, his voice, the pressure of his hand, brought with it a thrilling sensation of intense happiness, such as she had never known, never imagined before. It was indeed but a brief dream, for when he spoke, when he besought her to be his, then indeed she woke to consciousness, not only that she loved, but of the dark and fatal barrier between them, which no human effort could o'erleap. The sacrifice of race, of faith, of family, indeed might be made; but to do this never entered the mind and heart of Marie, so utterly was it impossible. To her peculiar feelings it was sin enough thus to have loved.

Manuel Henriquez bore his child back to the vale, little dreaming of the anguish to which his unguarded love had exposed her. She had ever been rather a pensive and gentle girl, and therefore that she should be still serious was no matter of surprise. For fifteen months she had sought to banish every dream of Arthur, every thought but that in loving him she had sinned against her God. Time and prayer had in some measure softened the first acute agony of her feelings; she thought she was conquering them altogether, when his unexpected appearance excited every feeling anew. Yet in that harrowing interview still she had been firm. She had even told him a secret, which it was almost death to reveal, that he might forget her; for how could he wed with her? And yet even that barrier he would have passed, and his generous, his determined love, would linger on her memory spite of every effort to think of him no more.

It was a fearful struggle, and often and often she yearned to confess all to her father, whom she loved with no common love; but she knew too well, not only the grief such tidings would be to him, but what his judgment must be, and she shrunk in agony from the condemnation of her feelings by another, constantly as she was condemning them herself.

Henriquez had been absent from the vale during Stanley's unexpected visit, and he tarried long enough to excite the alarm, not only of his child but of their domestics; nor was its cause when explained likely to ease Marie's anxiety. He had been attacked on the day of his intended return by a strange sensation of giddiness, followed by insensibility, which appeared to have weakened him more than he had thought compatible with so brief an illness. He made light of it, but still he was uneasy, not that he feared death himself, but that it might take him from his Marie ere his wishes were accomplished, and her earthly happiness, as he thought, secured. The first attack was but the forerunner of others, sometimes very slight and brief, at others longer and more alarming, rendering Marie more and more determined to keep her fatal secret from him; for it appeared to her that any stronger emotion than customary would be followed by those attacks; and as her love for him seemed to increase in intensity with the anxiety his precarious health occasioned, so did her dread of occasioning him aught of grief. But how fruitless are our best and wisest resolutions! One little hour, and every thought was changed.

CHAPTER VI.

"Oh! praise me not—
Look gently on me, or I sink to earth
Not thus."

DE CHATILLON.

It was the custom of the inmates of the Vale of Cedars, once in every year, and generally about the season of Michaelmas, to celebrate a festival, which ordained the erection of a booth or tent of "branches of thick trees," in which for seven days every meal was taken, and greater part of the day (except the time passed in the little Temple) was spent. Large branches of the palm and cedar, the willow, acacia, and the oak, cut so as to prevent their withering for the seven days, formed the walls of the tent; their leaves intermingling over head, so as to form a shelter, and yet permit the beautiful blue of the heavens to peep within. Flowers of every shade and scent formed a bordering within; and bouquets, richly and tastefully arranged, placed in vases filled with scented earth, hung from the branches forming the roof. Fruit, too, was there—the purple grape, the ripe red orange, the paler lemon, the lime, the pomegranate, the citron, all of which the vale afforded, adorned the board (which for those seven days was always spread within the tent), intermingled with cakes made by Marie.

This was one of the festivals for which many of the secret race would visit the vale; but it so happened that, this year, Manuel, his child, and their retainers, kept it alone—a source of disappointment and anxiety to the former, whose health was rapidly (but still to his child almost invisibly) failing. At the close of the solemn fast which always preceded by five days this festival of rejoicing, he had had a recurrence of his deathlike fits of insensibility, longer and more alarming than usual; but he had rallied, and attributed it so naturally to his long fast, that alarm once more gave place to hope in the heart of his daughter. Not thus, however, felt her father—convinced that death could not be long delayed, he but waited for his nephew's appearance and acknowledged love for his cousin, at once to give her to him, and prepare her for the worst. Parental anxiety naturally increased with every hour that passed, and Ferdinand appeared not.

It was the eve of the Sabbath; one from which in general all earthly cares and thoughts were banished, giving place to tranquil and spiritual joy. The father and daughter were alone within their lovely tent, but both so wrapt in evidently painful thought, that a strange silence usurped the usual cheerful converse. So unwonted was the anxious gloom on Manuel's brow, that his child could bear it no longer, and flinging her arms round his neck, she besought him in the tenderest accents to confide in her, as he had ever done, since her mother's death, to tell her what so pained him—might she not remove it? Henriquez could not resist that fond yet mournful pleading. He told her, that he felt health was departing, that death seemed ever hovering near, but that its pain, its care, would all depart, could he behold his long-cherished wish fulfilled, and his Marie the wife of Ferdinand, whose every look and tone during his last visit had betrayed his devoted love.

Marie heard; and her cheek and lips blanched to such ashy whiteness, that her father in alarm folded her to his breast; and sought to soothe a grief, which he believed was occasioned merely by the sudden and fearful thought of his approaching death; and sought to soothe, by a reference to the endearing love, the cherished tenderness which would still be hers; how Ferdinand would be to her all, aye more than all that he had been, and how, with love like his, she would be happier than she had been yet. Much he said, and he might have said still more, for it was long ere the startled girl could interrupt him. But when he conjured her to speak to him, not to look upon his death so fearfully, the beautiful truth of her nature rose up against the involuntary deceit. It was not his death which thus appalled her; alas—alas!—and she hated herself for the fearful thought—she had almost lost sight of that, in the words which followed. Breaking from his embrace, she sunk down on her knees before him, and buying her face upon his hand, in broken accents and with choking sobs, revealed the whole. How could she do her noble kinsman such fearful wrong as to wed him, when her whole heart, thoughts, nay, life itself, seemed wrapt in the memory of another? And that other! Oh! who, what was he? Once she looked up in her father's face, but so fearful were the emotions written there—wrath struggling with love, grief, pity, almost terror—that hastily she withdrew her glance, and remained kneeling, bent even to the dust, long after the confession had been poured forth, waiting in fear and anguish for his words.

"Marie, Marie! is it my Marie, my sainted Miriam's, child, who thus speaks? who hath thus sinned sole representative of a race of ages, in whose pure thoughts such fearful sin hath never mingled. My child so to love the stranger as to reject, to scorn her own! Oh God, my God, why hast thou so forsaken me? Would I had died before!" And the heavy groan which followed, confirmed the anguish breathed in those broken words.

"Father!" implored the unhappy girl, clasping his knees in an agony of supplication, though she raised not her head—"Oh my father! in mercy do not speak thus! Words of wrath, of reproach, fearful as they are from thee, yet I can bear them, but not such woe! Oh, think what I have borne, what I must still bear. If I have sinned, my sin will bring, nay, it has already brought its own chastisement. Speak to me but one word of love—or, if it must be, wrath.—but not, not such accents of despair!"

Her father struggled to reply; but the conflux of strong emotion was too powerful, and Marie sprung up to support him as he fell. She had often seen him insensible before, when there appeared no cause for such attacks; but was it strange that at such a moment she should feel that *she* had caused it?— that her sin perchance had killed her father; he might never wake more to say he forgave, he blessed her,—or that in those agonized moments of suspense she vowed, if he might but speak again, that his will should be hers, even did it demand the annihilation of every former treasured thought! And the vow seemed heard. Gradually and, it appeared, painfully life returned. His first action was to clasp her convulsively to his heart; his next, to put her gently yet firmly from him, and bury his face in his hands, and weep.

No sight is more terrible, even to an indifferent spectator, than to behold tears wrung from the eyes of man—and to his child it was indeed torture. But she controlled the choking anguish—calmly and firmly she spoke, and gradually the paroxysm subsided.

"That I have sinned in loving a stranger thus, I have long felt," she said; "and had I been aware of the nature of these feelings, they should never have gained ascendency. But I awoke too late—my very being was enchained. Still I may break from these engrossing thoughts—I would do so—pain shall be welcome, if it may in time atone for the involuntary sin of loving the stranger, and the yet more terrible one of grieving thee. Oh, my father, do what thou wilt, command me as thou wilt—I am henceforth wholly thine."

"And thou wilt wed Ferdinand, my child?"

"Would he still wish it, father, if he knew the whole? And is it right, is it just, to wed him, and the truth still unrevealed? Oh, if he do love me, as you say, how can I requite him by deceit?"

"Tell him not, tell him not," replied Henriquez, again fearfully agitated; "let none other know what has been. What can it do, save to grieve him beyond thy power to repair? No, no. Once his, and all these fearful thoughts will pass away, and their sin be blotted out, in thy true faithfulness to one who loves thee. His wife, and I know that thou wilt love him, and be true, as if thou hadst never loved another—"

"Ay, could I not be true, I would not wed," murmured Marie, more to herself than to her father; "and if suffering indeed, atone for sin, terribly will it be redeemed. But oh, my father, tell me—I have sworn to be guided by thee, and in all things I will be—tell me, in wedding him whom thou hast chosen, do I not still do foul wrong, if not to him (her voice faltered), unto another, whose love is mine as well?"

"Better for him, as for thee, to wed another, Marie! Would'st thou wed the stranger, wert thou free?"

She buried her face in his bosom, and murmured, "Never!"

"Then in what can this passion end, but in misery for both? In constant temptation to perjure thy soul, in forsaking all for him. And if thou didst, would it bring happiness? My child, thou art absolved, even had aught of promise passed between you. Knowest thou not that a maiden of herself hath no power to vow? Her father's will alone absolves it or confirms. Thou doest him no wrong. Be Ferdinand's bride, and all shall be forgiven, all forgotten—thou art my child, my Miriam's child once more!"

He pressed her again fondly to him; but though she made no reply, his arguments could not convince her. She had indeed told Arthur that she never could be his, but yet avowed that she loved him; and if he did meet her as the wife of another, what must he believe her? And Ferdinand, if he did so love her, that preoccupied heart was indeed a sad requital. She had, however, that evening but little time to think, for ere either spoke again, the branches at the entrance of the tent were hastily pushed aside, and a tall manly form stood upon the threshold. Marie sprang to her feet with a faint cry—could it be that the vow of an hour was already called upon to be fulfilled?—but the intruder attributed her alarm to a different cause, and hastily flinging off his wrapping mantle and deep plumed morion, he exclaimed, "What! alarmed by me, my gentle cousin? dearest Marie! am I forgotten?" And Henriquez, forgetting all of bodily exhaustion, all of mental suffering, in the deep joy his sudden appearance caused, could only fold the warrior in his feeble arms, and drooping his head on his shoulder, sob forth expressively, "My son! my son!"

CHAPTER VII.

"And thus how oft do life and death
 Twine hand in hand together;
And the funeral shroud, and bridal wreath,
 How small a space may sever!"

MS.

One little week did Ferdinand spend within the home of his boyhood; and in that brief interval the earthly fate of Marie Henriquez was decided. He had deferred his visit till such peace and prosperity had dawned for Spain, that he could offer his bride not only a home suited to his rank, but the comfort of his presence and protection for an indeterminate time. He had come there purposely to reveal his long-cherished love; to conjure Marie to bless him with the promise of her hand; and, if successful, to return, in two short months, for the celebration of their marriage, according to their own secret rites, ere the ceremony was performed in the sight of the whole Catholic world. The intermarriages of first cousins had been so common an occurrence in his family, that Ferdinand, in spite of some tremblings, as a lover, had regarded his final union with Marie with almost as much certainty, and as a thing of course, as his uncle himself.

The effects of that agitating interview between father and daughter had been visible to Ferdinand; but he attributed it, very naturally, to the cause privately assigned for it by his kinsman—Marie's first conviction that her father's days were numbered. He had been greatly shocked at the change in Henriquez's appearance, and deeply affected at the solemn and startling earnestness with which he consigned his child to his care, beseeching him, under all circumstances, to love and cherish her. His nephew could scarcely understand, then, such earnest pleadings. Alas! ere his life closed, their cause was clear enough.

Unconscious that her father and cousin were together, or of the nature of their conversation, Marie had joined them, unexpectedly, ere the interview was over. From her father's lips, and in a tone of trembling agitation, she heard that his long-cherished prayer was granted, and that she was his nephew's plighted, bride. He joined their hands, blessed them, and left them alone together, ere she had had power to utter a single word; and when voice was recalled by the tender, earnest accents of her cousin, beseeching her to ratify her father's consent—to say she would learn to love him, if she did not then; that she would not refuse the devotedness he proffered—what could she answer? She had so long loved him, venerated him, gloried in his achievements, his honors, as of an elder and much-loved brother, that, had she followed the impulse of her nature, she would have thrown herself as a sister on his neck, and poured forth her tale of sorrow. But she had sworn to be guided by her father, and he had besought her to reveal nothing; and therefore she promised to be his, even while with tears she declared herself unworthy. But such words were of little meaning to her enraptured lover save to bid him passionately deny them, and excite his ardent affection more than ever—satisfied that she could be not indifferent, listening as she did, with such flushed cheek and glistening eye, to the theme of his life since they had parted—the favor of the sovereigns, and the station he had won.

During the two months which intervened between Don Ferdinand's departure and promised return, Marie strained every nerve to face her destiny, and so meet it with calmness. Had she not loved, it would have been impossible to feel herself the cherished object of her cousin's love without returning it, possessing, as he did, alike inward and outward attraction to win regard. She studiously and earnestly banished every thought of Arthur as it rose; she prayed only for strength to be faithful, not only in outward seeming but in inward thought; that Stanley might never cross her path again, or, if he did, that his very affections might be estranged from her; that the secret she had revealed might alone be thought upon, till all of love had gone. The torture of such prayer, let those who love decide; but it was the thought of his woe, did he ever know she was another's bride, that haunted her. Her own suffering it was comparitively easy to bear, believing as she did, that they were called for by her involuntary sin: but his—so successfully had she conquered herself; that it was only when his countenance of reproach would flit before her, that the groan burst from her heart, and she felt bowed unto the earth.

Infirmity itself seemed conquered in the rejoicing thankfulness with which Henriquez regarded this fulfilment of his wishes. He appeared actually to regain strength and energy; his alarming fainting fits had not recurred since his nephew's visit, and Marie hoped he would be spared her longer than he believed. He never recurred to her confession, but lavished on her, if possible, yet more endearing love, and constantly alluded to the intense happiness which her consent to be her cousin's bride had given him. Once he left the vale, despite his precarious health, taking with him his old retainer, Reuben, and returned, laden with the richest gems and costliest silks, to adorn his child, on her bridal day, as befitted the bride of Ferdinand.

Time passed: the day specified by Ferdinand rapidly approached. He was there to meet it—and not alone. Thoughtful of his Marie's feeling, he had resolved that she should not stand beside the altar without one female friend; and he brought one, the sight of whom awakened associations with such overpowering strength, that Marie could only throw herself upon her bosom, almost convulsed with tears. It was Donna Emelie de Castro, at whose house she had joined the world; but her emotion, supposed natural to the agitating ceremony impending, and her father's precarious health, happily for her, passed without further notice than sympathy and love.

Henriquez, for once, was indifferent alike to the agitation of Marie, or the presence of Ferdinand. His glance was fixed on one of a little group, all of whom, with the exception of this individual, were familiar to his home and heart. He was clothed as a monk; but his cowl was thrown back, and his gaze so fixed on Marie that she blushed beneath it, and turned away.

"Do not turn from me, my child," he said; and Henriquez started at the voice, it was so fraught with memories of the departed. "Stranger as I must be, save in name, to thee—thou art none such to me. I seem to feel thy mother once again before me—and never was sister more beloved!—Manuel, hast thou, indeed, forgotten Julien?"

Almost ere he ceased to speak, the long separated relatives were clasped in each, other's arms. The five-and-twenty years, which had changed the prime of manhood into advancing age, and blanched the hair of each, had had no power to decrease the strong ties of kindred, so powerful in their secret race. The agitation and excitement of Henriquez was so excessive, not only then, but during the few days intervening before the celebration of the bridal, that Marie, in spite of the near approach of the dreaded day, could only think of him.

Ferdinand was no exacting lover: his affection for her was so intense, so true; his confidence in her truth so perfect, that, though he might at times have fancied that she loved not then with fervor equal to his own, he was contented to believe that his devotion would in time create in her as powerful a feeling. He had so watched, so tended her from infancy: she had so clung to and reverenced him, so opened her young heart, without one reservation, to his view—so treated him as her most cherished, most loved friend, that how could he dream she had aught to conceal, or believe that, did she know there was, she could have hesitated, one moment, to refuse his hand, preferring even the misery of so grieving him, to the continued agony of deceit? It was this perfect confidence, this almost childish trust, so beautiful in one tried, as he had been, in the ordeal of the world, that wrung Marie's heart with deepest torture. He believed her other than she was;—but it was too late—she dared not undeceive him.

The nuptial morning dawned. The party, not more than twelve or fourteen in all, assembled within the little edifice, whose nature had so puzzled Arthur. Its interior was as peculiar as its outward appearance: its walls, of polished cedar, were unadorned with either carving, pictures, or imagery. In the centre, facing the east, was a sort of raised table or desk, surrounded by a railing, and covered with a cloth of the richest and most elaborately worked brocade. Exactly opposite, and occupying the centre of the eastern wall, was a sort of lofty chest, or ark; the upper part of which, arched, and richly painted, with a blue ground, bore in two columns, strange hieroglyphics in gold: beneath this were portals of polished cedar, panelled, and marked out with gold, but bearing no device; their hinges set in gilded pillars, which supported the arch above. Before these portals were generally drawn curtains, of material rich and glittering as that upon the reading-desk. But this day not only were the curtains drawn aside, but the portals themselves flung open, as the bridal party neared the steps which led to it, and disclosed six or seven rolls of parchment, folded on silver pins, and filled with the same strange letters, each clothed in drapery of variously colored brocade, or velvet, and surmounted by two sets of silver ornaments, in which the bell and pomegranate were, though small, distinctly discernible. A superb lamp, of solid silver, was suspended from the roof; and one of smaller dimensions, but of equally valuable material, and always kept lighted, hung just before the ark.

Julien Morales, at his own particular request, was to read the ceremony; and three hours after noon he stood within the portals, on the highest step; a slab of white marble divided him from the bride and bridegroom, over whom a canopy was raised, supported by four silver poles. The luxuriant hair of the bride had been gathered up, and, save two massive braids, shading her brow and cheek, was concealed under a head-dress, somewhat resembling an eastern turban, but well suited to her countenance. Her dress, of the fashion before described, was all of white—the jacket or bodice richly woven with gold threads; but so thick a veil enveloped face and form, that her sweet face was concealed, until, at one particular part of the mysterious rite (for such, to the Spaniards, this ceremony must have been), the veil was uplifted for her to taste the sacred wine, and not allowed to fall again. Neither the bridegroom (agitated himself, for his was not a nature to think lightly of the nuptial rite), nor Henriquez (whose excitement was extreme) was conscious of the looks of alarm, blended with admiration, which the raising of the veil attracted towards Marie. Lovely she was; but it was the loveliness of a marble statue, not of life—her very lips were blanched, and every feature still, indeed; but a stillness of so peculiar an expression, so inexpressibly, so thrillingly sad, that admiration appeared indefinably and strangely transformed to pain. The wedding ring was placed upon her hand—a thin crystal goblet broken by Ferdinand, on the marble at his feet—and the rites were concluded. An almost convulsive embrace from her father—the unusual wildness of his voice and manner, as he blessed, and called her his own precious child, who this day had placed the seal upon his happiness, and confirmed twenty years of filial devotedness and love—awoke her from that stagnating trance. She folded her arms round his neck, and burst into passionate tears; and there were none, not even Ferdinand, to chide or doubt that emotion—it was but natural to her character, and the solemn service of the day.

Gay and joyous was the meal which followed the bridal. No appurtenances of modern pomp and luxury, indeed, decorated the board: its only ornaments were the loveliest flowers, arranged in alabaster vases, and silver baskets filled with blushing fruit. The food was simple, and the wines not choice; but the guests thought not of mere sensual enjoyment. In these secret meetings, each felt there was something holy; richer homes, more gorgeous feasts, were theirs in the world, whenever they so willed; but such intercourse of brotherhood seldom occurred, and when it came, was consequently hallowed.

Some time they sat around the board; and so unrestrained, so full of varied interest was their eager converse, that sunset came unheeded; and the silver lamps, fed with sweet incense, were placed upon the table. Julien then arose, and solemnly pronounced the usual blessing, or rather thanksgiving, after the bridal feast. Marie did not look up during its continuance; but as it concluded, she arose, and was about to retire with Donna Emilie, when her eye caught her father, and a cry of alarm broke from her. The burning flush had given place to a livid paleness—the glittering of the eye to a fixed and glassy gaze. The frame was, for a moment, rigid as stone, then fearfully convulsed; and Reuben, starting forward, caught his master as he fell. There was something so startling and unusual in the seizure, that even those accustomed to his periods of insensibility were alarmed; and vain was every effort of Ferdinand to awaken hope and comfort in the seemingly frozen spirit of his bride.

Henriquez was conveyed to his room, and every restorative applied; but even the skill of Julien, well versed as he was in the healing art, was without effect. More than an hour passed, and still he lay like death; and no sound, no sob, broke from the torn heart of his hapless child, who knelt beside his couch; her large dark eyes, distended to even more than their usual size, fixed upon his face; her hands clasped round one of his; but had she sought thus to give warmth she would have failed, for the hand of the living was cold and damp as that of the seeming dead.

A slight, almost imperceptible flush floated over that livid cheek—the eyes unclosed, but so quickly closed again that it was more like the convulsive quivering of the muscle than the effort of the will; and Marie alone had marked the change.

"Father!" she almost shrieked in agony, "in mercy speak to me again—say but you forgive—bless—"

"Forgive" feebly repeated the dying man; and the strong feeling of the father, for a brief interval, conquered even death—"Forgive?—my beautiful—my own!—the word is meaningless, applied to thee. Art thou not my Ferdinand's bride, and hast thou not so taken the sting, the trial even from this dread moment? My precious one!—would I could see that face once more—but it is dark—all dark—kiss me, my child!"

She threw herself upon his bosom, and covered his cheek with kisses. He passed his hand feebly over her face, as if the touch could once more bring her features to his sight; and then extending his left hand, feebly called—"Ferdinand!"

His nephew caught the withered hand, and kneeling down, pressed it reverentially and fondly to his lips.

Henriquez's lips moved, but there came no word.

"Doubt me not, my more than father! From boyhood to youth, from youth to manhood, I have doted on thy child. Shall I love and cherish her less now, that she has only me? Oh, trust me!—if devotion can give joy, she will know no grief, that man can avert, again!"

A strange but a beautiful light for a single minute dispersed the fearful shadow creeping over Henriquez's features.

"My son! my son!—I bless thee—and thou, too, my drooping flower. Julien! my brother—lay me beside my Miriam. Thou didst not come for this—but it is well. My children—my friends—send up the hymn of praise—the avowal of our faith; once more awake the voice of our fathers!"

He was obeyed; a psalm arose, solemn and sweet, in accents familiar as their mother tongue, to those who chanted; but had any other been near, not a syllable would have been intelligible. But the voice which in general led to such solemn service—so thrilling in its sweetness, that the most indifferent could not listen to it unmoved—now lay hushed and mute, powerless even to breathe the sobs that crushed her heart. And when the psalm ceased, and the prayer for the dying followed, with one mighty effort Henriquez raised himself, and clasping his hands, uttered distinctly the last solemn words ever spoken by his race, and then sunk back—and there was silence. Minutes, many minutes, rolled by—but Marie moved not. Gently, and tenderly, Don Ferdinand succeeded in disengaging the convulsive hold with which she still clasped her parent, and sought to bear her from that sad and solemn room. Wildly she looked up in his face, and then on those beloved features, already fixed and gray in death;—with frantic strength she pushed aside her husband, and sunk down by her father's side.

CHAPTER VIII.

"Slight are the outward signs of evil thought:
Within, within—'twas there the spirit wrought.
Love shows all changes: hate, ambition, guile,
Betray no further than the bitter smile."

BYRON.

Our readers must imagine that nearly a year and a half has elapsed since the conclusion of our last chapter. During that interval the outward life of Marie had passed in a calm, even stream; which, could she have succeeded in entirely banishing thoughts of the past, would have been unalloyed enjoyment. Her marriage, as we hinted in our fourth chapter, had been solemnized in public, with all the form and ceremony of the Catholic Church, and with a splendor incumbent on the high rank and immense wealth of the bridegroom. In compliance with Marie's wishes, however, she had not yet been presented to the Queen; delicate health (which was the fact, for a terrible fever had succeeded the varied emotions of her wedding day) and her late bereavement, was her husband's excuse to Isabella for her non-appearance—an excuse graciously accepted; the rather that the Queen of Castile was then much engrossed with political changes and national reforms, than from any failing of interest in Don Ferdinand's bride.

Changed as was her estate, from her lovely home in the Vale of Cedars, where she had dwelt as the sole companion of an ailing parent, to the mistress of a large establishment in one of the most populous cities of Castile; the idolized wife of the Governor of the town—and, as such, the object of popular love and veneration, and called upon, frequently, to exert influence and authority—still Marie did not fail performing every new duty with a grace and sweetness binding her more and more closely to the doting heart of her husband. For her inward self, Marie was calm—nay, at intervals, almost happy. She had neither prayed nor struggled in vain, and she felt as if her very prayer was answered in the fact that Arthur Stanley had been appointed to some high and honorable post in Sicily, and they were not therefore likely yet to meet again. The wife of such a character as Morales could not have continued wretched unless perversely resolved so to be. But his very virtues, while they inspired the deepest reverence towards him, engendered some degree of fear. Could she really have loved him as—he believed she did—this feeling would not have had existence; but its foundation was the constant thought that she was deceiving him—the remorse, that his fond confidence was so utterly misplaced—the consciousness, that there was still something to conceal, which, if discovered, must blight his happiness for ever, and estrange him from her, were it only for the past deceit. Had his character been less lofty—his confidence in her less perfect—his very love less fond and trusting—she could have borne her trial better; but to one true, ingenuous, open as herself, what could be more terrible than the unceasing thought that she was acting a part—and to her husband? Often and often she longed, with an almost irresistible impulse, to fling herself at his feet, and beseech him not to pierce her heart with such fond trust; but the impulse was forcibly controlled. What would such confession avail her now?—or him, save to wound?

Amongst the many Spaniards of noble birth who visited Don Ferdinand's, was one Don Luis Garcia, whose actual rank and office no one seemed to know; and yet, in affairs of church or state, camp or council, he was always so associated, that it was impossible to discover to which of these he was allied; in fact, there was a mystery around him, which no one could solve. Notwithstanding his easy—nay, it was by some thought fascinating manners, his presence generally created a restraint, felt intuitively by all, yet comprehended by none. That there is such, an emotion as antipathy mercifully placed within us, often as a warning, we do most strenuously believe; but we seldom trace and recognize it as such, till circumstances reveal its truth.

The real character of Don Luis, and the office he held, our future pages will disclose; suffice it here to state, that there was no lack of personal attractions or mental graces, to account for the universal, yet unspoken and unacknowledged dislike which he inspired. Apparently in the prime of life, he yet seemed to have relinquished all the pleasures and even the passions of life. Austere, even rigid, in those acts of piety and personal mortifications enjoined by his religion—voluntary fasts, privations, nights supposed to be past in vigil and in penance; occasional rich gifts to patron saints, and their human followers; an absence of all worldly feeling, even ambition; some extraordinary deeds of benevolence—all rendered him an object of actual veneration to the priests and monks with which the goodly city of Segovia abounded; and even the populace declared him faultless, as a catholic and a man, even while their inward shuddering belied the words.

Don Ferdinand Morales alone was untroubled with these contradictory emotions. Incapable of hypocrisy himself, he could not imagine it in others: his nature seemed actually too frank and true for the admission even of a prejudice. Little did he dream that his name, his wealth, his very favor with the Queen, his influence with her subjects, had already stamped him, in the breast of the man to whom his house and heart alike were open, as an object of suspicion and espial; and that ere a year had passed over his wedded life, these feelings were ripened, cherished—changed from the mere thought of persecution, to palpable resolve, by personal and ungovernable hate.

Don Luis had never known love; not even the fleeting fancy, much less the actual passion, of the sensualist, or the spiritual aspirings of true affection. Of the last, in fact, he was utterly incapable. No feeling, with him, was of an evanescent nature: under the cold austerity of the ordinary man, lay coals of living fire. It mattered not under what guise excited—hate, revenge, ambition, he was capable of all. At love, alone, he had ever laughed—exulting in his own security.

The internal condition of Spain, as we have before said, had been, until the accession of Isabella and Ferdinand, one of the grossest license and most fearful immorality. Encouraged in the indulgence of every passion, by the example of the Court, no dictates of either religion or morality ever interfered to protect the sanctity of home; unbridled desires were often the sole cause of murderous assaults; and these fearful crimes continually passing unpunished, encouraged the supposition that men's passions were given to be their sole guide, before which, honor, innocence, and virtue fell powerless.

The vigorous proceedings of Ferdinand and Isabella had already remedied these terrible abuses. Over the public safety and reform they had some power; but over the hearts of individuals they had none; and there were still some with whom past license was far more influencing than present restraint and legal severity; still some who paused at no crime so that the gratification of their passions was ensured; and foremost amongst these, though by his secret office pledged to the annihilation of all domestic and social ties, as regarded his own person, was Don Luis Garcia.

For rather more than a year, Don Ferdinand Morales had enjoyed the society of his young wife uninterruptedly, save by occasional visits, of brief duration, to Valladolid and Leon, where Isabella alternately held her court. He was now, however, summoned to attend the sovereigns, on a visit to Ferdinand's paternal dominions, an office which would cause his absence for a much longer interval. He obeyed with extreme reluctance—nor did Marie feel the separation less. There was, in some measure, a feeling of security in his presence, which, whenever he was absent, gave place to fearful tremblings as to what might transpire to shake her faith in her, ere he returned.

Resolved that not the very faintest breath of scandal should touch *his* wife, Marie, during the absence of Morales, always kept herself secluded. This time her retirement was stricter than ever; and great, then, was her indignation and astonishment, when about a fortnight before her husband's expected return, and in direct contradiction to her commands, Don Luis Garcia was admitted to her presence; and nothing but actual flight, for which she was far too proud and self-possessed, could have averted the private interview which followed. The actual words which passed we know not, but, after a very brief interval of careless converse on the part of Garcia—something he said earnestly, and in the tones of pitying sympathy, which caused the cheek and lips of Marie to blanch to marble, and her whole frame to shiver, and then grow rigid, as if turned to stone. Could it be that the fatal secret, which she believed was known only to herself and Arthur, that she had loved another ere she wedded Ferdinand, had been penetrated by the man towards whom she had ever felt the most intense abhorrence? and that he dared refer to it as a source of sympathy—as a proof that he could feel for her more than her unsuspecting husband? Why was speech so frozen up within her, that she could not, for the moment, answer, and give him back the lie? But that silence of deadly terror lasted not long: he had continued to speak; at first she was unconscious of his change of tone, words, and even action; but when his actual meaning flashed upon her, voice, strength, energy returned in such a burst of womanly indignation, womanly majesty, that Garcia himself, skilled in every art of evil as he was, quailed beneath it, and felt that he was powerless, save by violence and revenge.

While that terrible interview lasted, the wife of Morales had not failed; but when once more alone, the most deadly terror took possession of her. She had, indeed, so triumphed as to banish Garcia, defeated, from her presence; but fearful threats of vengeance were in that interview divulged—allusions to some secret power, over which he was the head, armed with authority even greater than that of the sovereign's—mysteriously spoken, but still almost strangely intelligible, that in her betrayal or her silence lay the safety or the danger of her husband—all compelled the conviction that her terror and her indignation at the daring insult must be buried deep in her own breast; even while the supposition that Don Luis knew all the past (though how, her wildest imagination could not discover), and that therefore she was in his power, urged her yet more to a full confession to her husband. Better if his heart must be wrung by her, than by a foe; and yet she shrunk in anguish from the task.

She was, however, deceived as to the amount of Garcia's knowledge of her past life. Accustomed to read human nature under all its varied phases—employing an unusually acute penetration so to know his fellows as to enable him, when needed, to create the greatest amount of misery—he had simply perceived that Marie's love for her husband was of a different nature to his for her, and that she had some secret to conceal. On this he had based his words: his suspicions were, unhappily, confirmed by the still, yet expressive agony they had occasioned. Baffled, as in some measure he had been, his internal rage that he should have so quailed before a woman, naturally increased the whirlwind of contending passions: but schooled by his impenetrable system of hypocrisy to outward quietness and control, he waited, certain that circumstances would either of themselves occur, or be so guided by him as to give him ample means of triumph and revenge.

CHAPTER IX.

"You would have thought the very windows spake;
So many greedy looks of young and old
Through casements darted their desiring eyes."

SHAKSPEARE.

In an apartment, whose pale, green hangings, embroidered with richly-colored flowers, and whose furniture and ornaments, all of delicate material and refined taste, marked it as a meet boudoir for gentle blood, sat Marie and her husband. She occupied her favorite seat—a cushion at his feet, and was listening with interest to his animated history of the Sovereign's welcome to Saragossa, the popular ferment at their appearance, the good they had accomplished, and would still accomplish, as their judicious plans matured. It was clear, he said, that they had resolved the sovereign power should not be merely nominal, as it had been. By making himself proclaimed and received as grand master of the three great orders of knighthood—Saint Iago, Compostella, and Alcantara—the immense influence of those associations must succumb to, and be guided by, Ferdinand alone; the power of the nobles would thus be insensibly diminished, and the mass of the kingdom—the PEOPLE—as a natural consequence, become of more importance, their position more open to the eyes of the sovereigns, and their condition, physically and morally, ameliorated and improved.

"I feel and acknowledge this, dearest; though one of the class whose power must be diminished to accomplish it;" he continued, "I am too anxious for the internal prosperity of my country to quarrel with any measures which minds so enlightened as its present sovereigns may deem requisite. But this is but a grave theme for thee, love. Knowest thou that her Grace reproached me with not bringing thee to join the Arragonese festivities? When Donna Emilie spoke of thee, and thy gentle worth and feminine loveliness, as being such as indeed her Grace would love, my Sovereign banished me her presence as a disloyal cavalier for so deserting thee; and when I marked how pale and thin thou art, I feel that she was right; I should have borne thee with me."

"Or not have left me. Oh, my husband, leave me not again!" she replied, with sudden and involuntary emotion, which caused him to throw his arm round her, and fondly kiss her brow.

"Not for the court, dearest; but that gentle heart must not forget thou art a warrior's wife, and as such, for his honor's sake, must sometimes bear the pang of parting. Nay, thou tremblest, and art still paler! Ere such summons come, thou wilt have learned to know and love thy Queen, and in her protecting favor find some solace, should I be called to war."

"War! talk they of war again? I thought all was now at peace?"

"Yes, love, in our sovereign's hereditary dominions; but there can be no lasting peace while some of the fairest territory of Spain still dims the supremacy of Castile, and bows down to Moorish masters. It is towards Grenada King Ferdinand looks, yearning for the day when, all internal commotions healed, he can head a gallant army to compel subjection; and sad as it will be to leave thee, sweet, thou wilt forgive thy soldier if he say, would that the day were come!"

"And will not their present extent of kingdom suffice the sovereigns? When they recall their former petty domains, and compare them with the present, is it not enough?"

Morales smiled. "Thou speakest as a very woman, gentle one, to whom the actual word 'ambition' is unknown. Why, the very cause thou namest urges our sovereigns to the conquest of these Moors. They are the blot upon a kingdom otherwise as fair and great as any other European land. They thirst to raise it in the scale of kingdoms—to send down their names to posterity, as the founders of the Spanish monarchy—the builders and supporters of a united throne, and so leave their children an undivided land. Surely this is a glorious project, one which every Spanish warrior must rejoice to aid. But fear not a speedy summons, love; much must be accomplished first. Isabella will visit this ancient city ere then, and thou wilt learn to love and reverence her as I do."

"In truth, my husband, thou hast made me loyal as thyself; but say they not she is severe, determined, stern?"

"To the guilty, yes; even the weak crafty will not stand before her repelling glance: but what hast thou to fear, my love? Penetrative as she is, seeming to read the heart through the countenance, she can read nought in thee save qualities to love. I remember well the eagle glance she fixed on King Ferdinand's young English favorite, Senor Stanley, the first time he was presented to her. But she was satisfied, for he ranks as deservedly high in her favor as in her husband's. Thou hast heard me speak of this young Englishman, my Marie?"

Her face was at that moment turned from him, or he might have started at its sudden flush; but she assented by a sign.

"He was so full of joyousness and mirth, that to us of graver nature it seemed almost below his dignity as man; and now they tell me he is changed so mournfully; grave, sad, silent, maturity seems to have descended upon him ere he has quite passed boyhood; or he has some secret sorrow, too sacred to be revealed. There is some talk of his recall from Sicily, he having besought the king for a post of more active and more dangerous service. Ferdinand loves such daring spirits, and therefore no doubt will grant his boon. Ha! Alberic, what is it?" he continued, eagerly, as a page entered, and delivered a packet secured with floss silk, and sealed with the royal signet, adding that it had been brought by an officer of the royal guard, attended by some men at arms. "Give him welcome suited to his rank, boy: I will but peruse these, and attend him instantly."

The page withdrew, and Don Ferdinand, hastily cutting the silk, was speedily so engrossed in his despatches, as to forget for the time even the presence of his wife; and well it was so; for it enabled her with a strong effort to conquer the deadly sickness Morale's careless words had caused—the pang of dread accompanying every thought of Arthur's return to Spain—to still the throbbing pulse and quivering lip, and, outwardly unmoved, meet his joyous glance once more.

"'Tis as I thought and hoped," he said, with animation: "the sovereigns hold their court for some months in this city; coeval, in antiquity, associations, and loyalty, with Valladolid and Leon, Isabella, with her characteristic thought for all her subjects, has decided on making it occasionally the seat of empire alternately with them, and commissions me, under her royal seal, to see the castle fittingly prepared. Listen, love, what her Grace writes further—'Take heed, my good lord, and hide not in a casket the brightest gem which we have heard adorns thy home. We would ourselves judge the value of thy well-hoarded jewel—not that we doubt its worth; for it would be strange, indeed, if he who hath ever borne off the laurel wreath from the competitors for glory, should not in like manner seek and win the prize of beauty. In simple language, let Donna Marie be in attendance.' And so thou shalt, love; and by thy gentle virtues and modest loveliness, add increase of honor to thy husband. Ha! what says Gonzalo de Lara?" he added, as his eye glanced over another paper—"'Tumults in Sicily—active measures—Senor Stanley— enough on which to expend his chivalric ardor, and evince his devotedness to Ferdinand; but Sicily quieted—supposed the king will still grant his request—assign him some post about his person, be at hand for military service against the Moors.' Good! then the war is resolved on. We must bestir ourselves, dearest, to prepare fit reception for our royal guests; there is but brief time."

He embraced and left her as he spoke; and for several minutes Marie remained without the power even to rise from her seat: one pang conquered, another came. Arthur's recall appeared determined; would it be so soon that he would join this sovereigns before they reached Segovia? She dared not think, save to pray, with wild and desperate fervor, that such might not be.

Magnificent, indeed, were Don Ferdinand's preparations for the banquet with which he intended to welcome his sovereigns to Segovia. The castle was to be the seat of their residence, and the actual *locale* of their court; but it was at his own private dwelling he resolved, by a sumptuous entertainment, to evince how deeply and reverentially he felt the favor with which he was regarded by both monarchs, more especially by Isabella, his native Sovereign.

In the many struggles which were constantly occurring between the Spaniards and Moors, the former had become acquainted with the light yet beautiful architecture and varied skill in all the arts peculiar to the latter, and displayed their improved taste in both public and private buildings. Morales, in addition to natural taste, possessed great affluence, which enabled him to evince yet greater splendor in his establishment than was usual to his countrymen.

There was one octangular room, the large panels forming the walls of which were painted, each forming a striking picture of the principal events in the history of Spain, from the descent of Don Palayo, and the mountaineers of Asturias, who struck the first blow for Spanish freedom, to the accession of Ferdinand and Isabella. The paintings were not detached pictures, but drawn and colored on the wall itself, which had been previously prepared for the reception of the colors by a curious process, still in use among the Orientals.[A] The colors, when dry, were rubbed, till the utmost brilliancy was attained; and this, combined as it was with a freedom and correctness of drawing, produced an effect as striking then as it would be novel to modern eyes. One side, divided into three compartments, contained in one a touching likeness of the young Alfonso. His figure, rather larger than life, was clothed in armor, which shone as inlaid with gold. His head was bare, and his bright locks flowed over his shoulders as he wore them in life. His brilliant eye, his lofty brow, and peculiarly sweet expression of mouth, had been caught by the limner, and transferred to his painting in all their original beauty. Round him were grouped some of the celebrated cavaliers of his party; and the background, occupied by troops not in regular battalions, but as impelled by some whelming feeling of national excitement, impossible to be restrained. Answering to this was a full length of the infanta Isabella I., in the act of refusing the crown offered by the confederates. The centre compartment represented the union of Castile and Arragon by the nuptials of their respective sovereigns in the cathedral church of Valladolid. Over these pictures were suspended golden lamps, inlaid with gems; so that, day or night, the effect should remain the same. Opposite the dais, huge folding-doors opened on an extensive hall, where the banquets were generally held, and down which Don Ferdinand intended to range the tables for his guests of lesser rank, leaving the octangular apartment for the royal tables, and those of the most distinguished nobles; the one, however, so communicating with the other, as to appear one lengthened chamber. On the right hand of the dais, another large door opened on a withdrawing-room, the floor of which was of marble, curiously tinted; and the walls hung with Genoa velvet, ruby-colored, and bordered by a wide fringe of gold. Superb vases of alternate crystal and frosted silver, on pedestals of alabaster and of aqua-marine, were ranged along the walls, the delicate beauty of their material and workmanship coming out well against the rich coloring of the hangings behind. The roof, a lofty dome, displayed the light Arabesque workmanship, peculiar to Moorish architecture, as did the form and ornaments of the windows. This apartment opened into another, much smaller, each side of which, apparently formed of silver plate, reflected as mirrors every object; and the pillars supporting the peculiarly light roof of the same glittering material. Some parts of the extensive gardens Morales intended to illuminate; and others, for the effect of contrast, to be left in deepest shadow.

[Footnote A: See Art Union Journal, August, 1845.]

Nothing was omitted which could do honor to the royal guests, or cast a reproach upon the magnificent hospitality of their hosts. The preparations were but just completed, when an advance guard arrived at Segovia with the tidings of the rapid approach of the sovereigns; and Morales, with a gallant troop of his own retainers, and a procession of the civil and military officers of Segovia, hastened to meet and escort them to the town.

With an uncontrollable impulse, Marie had followed the example of almost every female in Segovia, and, wrapt in her shrouding veil, had stationed herself, with some attendants at a casement overlooking the long line of march. The city itself presented one scene of gladsome bustle and excitment: flags were suspended from every "turret, dome, and tower," rich tapestries hung over balconies, which were filled with females of every rank and grade, vying in the richness and elegance of their apparel, and their coquettish use of the veil and fan, so as to half-hide and half-display their features, more or less beautiful—for beautiful as a nation, the Spanish women undoubtedly are. Bells were ringing from every church; ever and anon came a burst of warlike music, as detached troops galloped in the town, welcomed with shouts as the officer at their head was recognized. Even the priests themselves, with their sober dresses and solemn countenances, seemed touched with the universal excitement, relaxing into smiles and hearty greeting with the laymen they encountered. As the hours waned, popular excitement increased. It was the first visit of Isabella to the city; and already had her character been displayed in such actions as to kindle the warmest love towards the woman, in addition to the enthusiastic loyalty towards the Queen.

At length the rumor rose that the main body was approaching—in little more than a hour the sovereigns would pass the gates, and excitement waxed wilder and wilder, and impatience was only restrained by the interest excited towards the gallant bodies of cavalry, which now in slow and measured march approached, forming the commencement of a line, which for three hours continued to pour within the city in one unbroken strain.

Even Marie herself, pre-occupied as she was in the dread search for one object, could not glance down on the moving multitude beneath her without in some degree sharing the enthusiasm of her countrymen. There were gallant warriors of every age, from the old man to the beardless youth; chargers, superb in form and rich in decoration; a field of spears glittering in the broad sunshine, some bearing the light gay pennoncelle, others absolutely bending beneath the heavy folds of banners, which the light breeze at times extended so as to display their curious heraldic bearings, and then sunk heavily around their staffs. Esquires bearing their masters' shields, whose spotless fields flung back a hundred-fold the noonday sun—plumes so long and drooping, as to fall from the gilded crest till they rested on the shoulder—armor so bright as to dazzle the eyes of the beholders, save when partly concealed under the magnificent surcoats and mantles, amongst which the richest velvets, slashed with gold or silver, distinguished the highest nobles. Pageantry like this mingled with such stirring sounds as the tramp of the noble horse, curveting, prancing, rearing, as if disdaining the slow order of march—the thrilling blast of many trumpets, the long roll, or short, sharp call of the drum; and the mingled notes of martial instruments, blending together in wild yet stirring harmony, would be sufficient even in this prosaic age to bid the heart throb and the cheek burn, recognizing it, as perhaps we should, merely as the *symbol*, not the *thing*. What, then, must it have been, when men felt such glittering pageant and chivalric seeming, the *realities* of life?

At length came the principal group; the pressure of the crowds increased, and human hearts so throbbed, that it seemed as if they could not breathe, save in the stunning shouts, bidding the very welkin ring. Surrounded by a guard of honor, composed indiscriminately of Castilians and Arragonese, mounted on a jet black steed, which pawed the ground, and shook his graceful head, as conscious of his princely burden, magnificently attired, but in the robes of peace, with a circlet of gold and gems enwreathing his black velvet cap, his countenance breathing this day but the kindly emotions of his more youthful nature, unshadowed by the wile and intrigue of after-years, King Ferdinand looked the mighty monarch, whose talents raised his country from obscurity, and bade her stand forth among the first of European nations. But tumultuary as were the shouts with which he was recognized, they were faint in comparison to those which burst forth at sight of the Princess at his side.

Isabella had quitted her litter on re-entering her own dominions, and now rode a cream-colored charger, which she managed with the grace and dignity of one well accustomed to the exercise, alike in processions of peace and scenes of war.

The difference of age between the sovereigns was not perceivable,[A] for the grave and thoughtful character of Ferdinand gave him rather the appearance of seniority; while the unusual fairness of Isabella's complexion, her slight and somewhat small stature, produced on her the contrary effect. The dark gray eye, the rich brown hair and delicate skin of the Queen of Castile deprived her, somewhat remarkably, of all the characteristics of a Spaniard, but, from their very novelty attracted the admiration of her subjects. Beautiful she was not; but her charm lay in the variable expression of her features. Peculiarly and sweetly feminine, infused, as Washington Irving observes, with "a soft, tender melancholy," as was their general expression, they could yet so kindle into indignant majesty, so flash with reproach or scorn, that the very color of the eye became indistinguishable, and the boldest and the strongest quailed beneath the mighty and the holy spirit, which they could not but feel, that frail woman form enshrined.

[Footnote A: Isabella was eight or ten years Ferdinand's senior.]

Round the sovereigns were grouped, in no regular order of march, but forming a brilliant *cortége*, many of the celebrated characters of their reign— men, not only of war, but of literature and wisdom, whom both monarchs gloried in distinguishing above their fellows, seeking to exalt the honor of their country, not only in extent of dominion, but by the shining qualities of her sons. It was to this group the strained gaze of Marie turned, and became riveted on the Queen, feeling strangely and indefinably a degree of comfort as she gazed; to explain wherefore, even to herself, was impossible; but she felt as if she no longer stood alone in the wide world, whose gaze she dreaded; a new impulse rose within her, urging her, instead of remaining indifferent, as she thought she should, to seek and win Isabella's regard. She gazed and gazed, till she could have fancied her very destiny was in some way connected with the Queen's visit to Segovia—that some mysterious influences were connecting her, insignificant as she was, with Isabella's will. She strove with the baseless vision; but it would gain ground, folding up her whole mind in its formless imaginings. The sight of her husband, conversing eagerly with the sovereign, in some degree startled her back to the present scene. His cheek was flushed with exercise and excitement; his large dark eyes glittering, and a sunny smile robbing his mouth of its wonted expression of sternness. On passing his mansion he looked eagerly up, and with proud and joyous greeting doffed his velvet cap, and bowed with as earnest reverence as if he had still to *seek* and win her. The chivalry of Don Ferdinand Morales was proved, yet more *after* marriage than *before.*

It was over: the procession had at length passed: she had scanned every face and form whose gallant bearing proclaimed him noble; but Arthur Stanley was not amongst them, and inexpressibly relieved, Marie Morales sunk down on a low seat, and covering her face with her hands, lifted up her whole soul in one wild—yet how fervent!—burst of thanksgiving.

CHAPTER X.

"Yet was I calm. I knew the time
  My breast would thrill before thy look;
But now, to tremble were a crime:
  We met, and not a nerve was shook."

BYRON.

The excitement of the city did not subside with the close of the procession. The quiet gravity and impressive appearance of age, which had always marked Segovia, as a city more of the past than present, gave place to all the bustling animation peculiar to a provincial residence of royalty. Its central position gave it advantages over Valladolid, the usual seat of the monarchs of Castile and Leon, to sovereigns who were seeking the internal peace and prosperity of their subjects, and were resolved on reforming abuses in every quarter of their domains. The deputation from the city was graciously received; their offering—a golden vase filled with precious stones—accepted, and the seal put to their loyal excitement by receiving from Isabella's own lips, the glad information that she had decided on making Segovia her residence for the ensuing year, and that she trusted the loyalty which the good citizens of Segovia had so warmly proffered would be proved, by their endeavors in their own households to reform the abuses which long years of misrule and misery had engendered. She depended on them, her people, to aid her with heart and hand, and bade them remember, no individual was so insignificant as to remove his shoulder from the wheel on plea of uselessness. She trusted to her citizen subjects to raise the internal glory of her kingdom, as she did to her nobles to guard their safety, elevate her chivalry, and by their untarnished honor and stainless valor, present an invincible front to foreign foes. Isabella knew human nature well; the citizens returned to their houses bound for ever to her service.

Don Luis Garcia had joined the train of Morales when he set forth to meet the sovereigns. His extraordinary austerity and semblance of lowly piety, combined as they were with universal talent, had been so much noised abroad as to reach the ears of Ferdinand and Isabella; and Morales, ever eager to promote the interests of a countryman, took the earliest opportunity of presenting him to them. He was graciously enough received: but, though neither spoke it, an indefinable feeling of disappointment took possession of their minds, the wherefore they knew not. Don Luis had conversed well, both as to the matter and the manner; but neither Ferdinand nor Isabella felt the smallest inclination to advance him to any post about themselves. In virtue of his supposed rank, however, he of course mingled with the courtly crowd, which on the appointed evening thronged the mansion of Don Ferdinand.

Tremblingly as Marie looked forward to that evening, she spared no pains to gratify her husband in the choice of her toilet. Sorrow had never made her indifferent, and she sought to please him even in the most trifling occurrences of life. Her beautiful hair still lay in soft, glossy bands against the delicate cheeks, and was gathered up behind in a massive plait, forming, as it were, a diadem at the back of the exquisitely shaped head, from which fell a white veil—rather, perhaps, a half mantle, as it shaded the shoulders, not the face—of silver tissue, so delicately woven as to resemble lace, save in its glittering material. A coronet of diamonds was wreathed in and out the plait, removing all semblance of heaviness from the headgear, and completely divesting it of gaudiness. Her robe, of blue brocade, so closely woven with silver threads as to glisten in the light of a hundred lamps almost like diamonds, had no ornament save the large pearls which looped up the loose sleeves above the elbow, buttoned the bodice or jacket down the front, and richly embroidered the wide collar, which, thrown back, disclosed the wearer's delicate throat and beautiful fall of the shoulders, more than her usual attire permitted to be visible. The tiny white silk slipper, embroidered in pearl, a collaret and bracelets of the same beautiful ornament, of very large size, completed her costume.

Not even the presence of royalty could restrain the burst of undisguised admiration which greeted Marie, as, led forward by her eager husband, she was presented to the sovereigns, and knelt to do them homage. Ferdinand himself gazed on her a moment astonished; then with animated courtesy hastily raised her, and playfully chid the movement as unmeet from a hostess to her guests.

A strange moisture had risen to the eyes of the Queen as she first beheld Marie. It might have been that marvellous perfection of face and form which caused the emotion; for if all perfection, even from man's hand, is affecting even to tears, what must be the work of God? It might have been that on that young, sweet face, to the Queen's mental eye, a dim shadow from the formless realms of the future hovered—that, stealing from that outward form of loveliness, she beheld its twin sister, sorrow. Whatever it might have been, kind and gentle as Isabella's manner ever was, especially to her own sex, to Marie it was kinder and gentler still.

How false is the charge breathed from man's lips, that woman never admires woman!—that we are incapable of the lofty feeling of admiration of our own sex either for beautiful qualities or beauteous form! There is no object in creation more lovely, more fraught with intensest interest (if, indeed, we are not so wholly wrapt in the petty world of self as to have none for such lofty sympathies) than a young girl standing on the threshold of a new existence; beautiful, innocent, and true; offspring as yet of joy and hope alone, but before whom stretches the dim vista of graver years, and the yearning thoughts, unspoken griefs, and buried feelings, which even in the happiest career must still be woman's lot. There may be many who can see no charm and feel no interest in girlhood's beauty: but not in such is woman's best and holiest nature; and therefore not by such should she be judged.

"We will not chide thee, Senor, for thy jealous care of this most precious gem," said Isabella, addressing Don Ferdinand, while her eye followed Marie, who, re-assured by the Queen's manner, had conquered her painful timidity, and was receiving and returning with easy grace and natural dignity the greetings and gallantries of her guests: "she is too pure, too precious to meet the common eye, or breathe a courtly atmosphere."

Don Ferdinand's eye glistened. "And yet I fear her not," he rejoined: "she is as true, as loving, as she is loved and lovely."

"I doubt it not: nay, 'tis the spotless purity of soul breathing in that sweet face, which I would not behold tainted, by association with those less pure. No: let her rest within the sanctuary of thy heart and hearth, Don Ferdinand. We do not command her constant attendance on our person, as we had intended."

Conscious of the inexpressible relief which this assurance would be to his wife, Morales eagerly and gratefully expressed his thanks; and the Queen passed on, rejoicing in the power of so easily conferring joy.

We may not linger on the splendor of this scene, or attempt description of the varied and picturesque groups filling the gorgeous suite of rooms, pausing at times to admire the decorations of the domed chamber, or passing to and fro in the hall of mirrors, gayly reflected from the walls and pillars. The brilliant appearance of the extensive gardens; their sudden and dazzling illuminations as night advanced; their curious temples, and sparkling fountains sending up sheets of silver in the still air and darkening night, and falling in myriads of diamonds on innumerable flowers, whose brilliant coloring, illuminated by small lamps, concealed beneath their foliage, shone forth like gems; the groups of Moorish slaves, still as statues in their various attitudes; the wild, barbaric music, startling, yet delighting all who listened, and causing many an eager warrior to grasp his sword, longing even at such a moment to exchange that splendid scene for the clash and stir of war—we must leave all to the imagination of our readers, and bid them follow us to the banquet hall, where, summoned by the sound of the gong, the numerous guests sat down to tables, groaning beneath the profuse hospitality of their host, and the refined magnificence of the display.

All the warrior stirred the soul of the King, as, on taking his seat at the dais, he glanced round and beheld the glorious triumphs of his country so strikingly portrayed. But Isabella saw but one picture, felt but one thought;

and Marie never forgot the look she fixed on the breathing portrait of Alfonso, nor the tone with which she inquired—

"Hadst thou ever a brother, Marie?"

"Never, royal Madam."

"Then thou canst not enter into the deep love I bore yon princely boy, nor the feeling that picture brings. Marie, I would cast aside my crown, descend my throne without one regretful murmur, could I but hold him to my heart once more, as I did the night he bade me his glad farewell. It was for ever! Thy husband speaks of him sometimes?"

"Often, often, my gracious liege, till his lip has quivered and his eye has glistened!"

Isabella pressed her hand, and with even more than her wonted graciousness, turned to receive from the hand of her host the gemmed goblet of wine, which, in accordance with established custom, Don Ferdinand knelt down to present, having first drunk of it himself.

Inspiringly sounded the martial music during the continuance of the banquet. Brightly sparkled the brimming goblets of the far-famed Spanish wine. Lightly round the table ran the gay laugh and gayer jest. Soft and sweet were the whispers of many a gallant cavalier to his fair companion; for, in compliment to Isabella, the national reserve of the daughters of Spain was in some degree laid aside and a free intercourse with their male companions permitted. Each, indeed, wore the veil, which could be thrown off, forming a mantle behind, or drawn close to conceal every feature, as coquettish fancy willed; nor were the large fans wanting, with which the Spanish woman is said to hold as long and desperate a flirtation as the coquette of other lands can do with the assistance of voice and eye. Isabella's example had, however, already created reformation in her female train, and the national levity and love of intrigue, had in a great degree diminished.

The animation of the scene was at its height when suddenly the music ceased, a single gong was heard to sound, and Alberic, the senior page, brought tidings of the arrival of new guests; and his master, with native courtesy, hastened down the hall to give them welcome.

Marie had not heard, or, perhaps, had not heeded the interruption in the music; for, fascinated by the manner and conversation of the Queen, she had given herself up for the time wholly to its influence, to the forgetfulness even of her inward self. The sound of many footsteps and a rejoicing exclamation from the King, excited the attention at once of Isabella and her hostess. Marie glanced down the splendid hall; and well was it for her that she was standing behind the Queen's seat, and somewhat deep in shadow. Momentary as was all *visible* emotion, its effect was such as must have caused remark and wonder had it been perceived: on herself, that casual glance, was as if she had received some invisibly dealt, yet fearful blow. Her brain reeled, her eyes swam, a fearful, stunning sound awoke within her ears, and such failing of bodily power as compelled her, spite of herself, to grasp the Queen's chair for support. But how mighty—how marvellous is the power of *will* and *mind!* In less than a minute every failing sense was recalled, every slackened nerve restrung, and, save in the deadly paleness of lip, as well as cheek, not a trace of that terrible conflict remained.

Aware that it was at a gay banquet he was to meet the King, Arthur Stanley had arranged his dress with some care. We need only particularize his sword, which was remarkable for its extreme simplicity, the hilt being of the basket shape, and instead of being inlaid with precious stones, as was the general custom of this day, was composed merely of highly burnished steel. He had received it from his dying father: and it was his pride to preserve it unsullied, as it had descended to him. He heeded neither laughter at its uncouth plainness, nor even the malicious sneer as to the poor Englishman's incapacity to purchase a handsomer one; rejecting every offer of a real Toledo, and declaring that he would prove both the strength and brightness of English steel, so that none should gainsay it.

"Welcome, Don Arthur! welcome, Senor Stanley! By St. Francis, I shall never learn thy native title, youth!" exclaimed the monarch, frankly, as he extended his hand, which Stanley knelt to salute. "Returned with fresher laurels, Stanley? Why, man, thou wilt make us thy debtor in good earnest!"

"Nay, my gracious liege: that can never be!" replied Stanley, earnestly. "Grateful I am, indeed, when there is opportunity to evince fidelity and valor in your Grace's service; but believe me, where so much has been and is received, not a life's devotion on my part can remove the impression, that I am the debtor still."

"I believe thee, boy! I do believe thee! I would mistrust myself ere I mistrusted thee. We will hear of thy doings to-morrow. Enough now to know we are well satisfied with thy government in Sicily, and trust our native subject who succeeds thee will do his part as well. Away to thy seat, and rejoice that thou hast arrived ere this gay scene has closed. Yet stay: our lovely hostess hath not yet given thee welcome. Where is the Senora? Isabella, hast thou spirited her hence? She was here but now."

"Nay, good my Lord: she has vanished unwittingly," replied Isabella, as she turned towards the spot where Marie had been standing. "Don Ferdinand, we must entreat thee to recall her!"

"It needs not, royal Madam: I am here:" and Marie stepped forward from the deep shade of the falling drapery behind the royal seats which had concealed her, and stood calmly, almost proudly erect beside the Queen, the full light falling on her face and form. But there was little need for light to recognize her: the voice was sufficient; and even the vivid consciousness of where he stood, the hundred curious eyes upon him, could not restrain the sudden start—the bewildered look. Could that be Marie? Could that be the wife of Ferdinand Morales? If she were the one, how could she be the other, when scarcely eighteen months previous, she had told him that which, if it were true, must equally prevent her union with Morales as with himself? In what were they different save in the vast superiority of wealth and rank? And in the chaos of bewildering emotions, so trustful was he in the truth of her he loved, that, against the very evidence of his own senses, he for the moment disbelieved in the identity of the wife of Morales with the Marie Henriquez of the Cedar Vale. Perhaps it was well he did so, for it enabled him to still the tumultuous throbbing of his every pulse as her voice again sounded in his ear, saying he was welcome, most welcome as her husband's friend, and to retire without any apparent emotion to his seat.

He had merely bowed reverentially in reply. In any other person the silence itself would have caused remark: but for the last three years Stanley's reserve and silence in the company of women had been such, that a departure from his general rule even in the present case would have been more noticed than his silence. Thoughts of painful, almost chaotic bewilderment indeed, so chased each other across his mind as to render the scene around him indistinct, the many faces and eager voices like the phantasma of a dream. But the pride of manhood roused him from the sickening trance, and urged him to enter into the details, called for by his companions in arms, of the revolt of the Sicilians, with even more than usual animation.

One timid glance Marie had hazarded towards her husband, and it was met by such a look and smile of love and pride that she was re-assured to perform the duties of the evening unfalteringly to the end. Alas! she little knew that her momentary emotion and that of Arthur had alike been seen, commented upon, and welcomed with fiend-like glee, as the connecting link of an until then impalpable plot, by one individual in that courtly crowd, whose presence, hateful as it was, she had forgotten in the new and happier thoughts which Isabella's presence and notice had occasioned.

And who was there, the mere spectator of this glittering pageant, but would have pronounced that there, at least, all was joy, and good-will, and trust, and love? Who, even did they acknowledge the theory that one human heart, unveiled, would disperse this vain dream of seeming unalloyed enjoyment, would yet have selected the right individual for the proof, or would not have shrunk back awed and saddened had the truth been told? Surely it is well for the young, the hopeful, and the joyous, that in such scenes they see but life's surface—not its depths.

The festive scene lasted some time longer, nor did it conclude with the departure of the King and Queen: many still lingered, wandering at their own will about the rooms and gardens, and dispersing gradually, as was then the custom, without any set farewell.

Her attendance no longer required by the Queen, and aware that her presence was not needed by her guests, Marie sought the gardens; her fevered spirit and aching head yearning to exchange the dazzling lights and close rooms for the darkness and refreshing breeze of night. Almost unconsciously she had reached some distance from the house, and now stood beside a beautiful statue of a-water-nymph, overlooking a deep still pool, so clear and limpid, that when the moon cast her light upon it, it shone like a sheet of silver, reflecting every surrounding object. There were many paths that led to it, concealed one from the other by gigantic trees and overhanging shrubs. It was a favorite spot with. Marie, and she now stood leaning against the statue, quite unconscious that tears were falling faster and faster from her eyes, and mingling with the waters at her feet.

"Marie!" exclaimed the voice of Stanley at that moment: "Canst thou be Marie? so false, so—" but his words were checked, for the terror, the tumult of feeling, while it impelled her to start from him, deprived her of all power; and a rapid movement on his part alone prevented her from falling in the deep pool beneath their feet. It was but a moment: she withdrew herself from his supporting arms, and stood erect before him, though words she had none.

"Speak to me!" reiterated Arthur, his voice sounding hollow and changed; "I ask but one word. My very senses seem to play me false, and mock me with thy outward semblance to one I have so loved. Her name, too, was Marie; her voice soft and thrilling as thine own: and yet, yet, I feel that 'tis but semblance—'tis but mockery—the phantasy of a disordered brain. Speak, in mercy! Say that it is but semblance—that thou art not the Marie I have so loved."

"It is true—I am that Marie. I have wronged thee most cruelly, most falsely," she answered, in a tone low and collected indeed, but expressive of intense suffering. "It is too late now, either to atone or to explain. Leave me, Senor Stanley: I am another's!"

"Too late to explain? By heaven but thou shalt!" burst fiercely and wrathfully from Stanley. "Is it not enough, that thou hast changed my whole nature into gall, made truth itself a lie, purity a meaningless word, but thou wilt shroud thyself under the specious hood of duty to another, when, before heaven, thou wast mine alone. Speak!"

"Ay, I will speak—implore thee by the love thou didst once bear me, Arthur, leave me now! I can hear no more to-night."

"On condition thou wilt see me in private once again. Marie, thou darest not refuse me this! Thou canst not have so fallen as to give no reason for this most foul wrong—fancied weak, futile as it may be. We part now, but we meet again!" And with a strong effort at control he strode hastily from her.

The moon at that moment breaking from thick clouds, darted her full light upon the pool, till it shone like an illuminated mirror amidst the surrounding darkness; and though Arthur had disappeared, its clear surface distinctly reflected the outline of another closely shrouded figure. Marie turned in terror, and beheld, gleaming with the triumph of a fiend, the hated countenance of Don Luis Garcia. One look told her that he Lad seen all, heard all; but she had no power to speak or move. Keeping his basilisk gaze fixed on her, he withdrew backwards into the deep shade till he had entirely disappeared.

Summoning all her energy, Marie fled back towards the house, and at the moment she reached it, Don Ferdinand crossed the deserted hall.

"Marie, dearest, here and alone? Pale, too, and trembling! In heaven's name, what hath chanced?"

A moment more, and she would have flung herself at his feet and told him all—all, and beseeching his forgiveness, conjure him to shield her from Arthur, from herself; but as she looked up in his face, and met its beaming animation, its manly reflection of the pure gratification that evening had bestowed, how could she, how dared she be the one to dash it with woe? And, overpowered with this fearful contention of feeling, she threw her arms around him as he bent tenderly over her, and burying her head in his bosom, burst into tears.

"Thou art exhausted, mine own love! It has been too exciting, too wearying a scene for thee. Why, what a poor, weak girl thou art! How fortunate for thee that thy Queen demands not thy constant attendance, and that thy husband is not ambitious to behold thee shining in the court, as thy grace and beauty might! I am too glad to feel thee all, all my own. Smile on me, love, and then to thy couch. A few hours' quiet rest, and thou wilt be thyself again." And he bore her himself with caressing gentleness to her apartment.

CHAPTER XI.

"Then Roderick from the Douglas broke,
As flashes flame through sable smoke,
Kindling its wreaths long, dark, and low.
To one broad blaze of ruddy glow;
So the deep anguish of despair
Burst in fierce jealousy to air."

SIR WALTER SCOTT.

"Sure, now, Pedro, the poor young Senor cannot be entirely in his right mind; he does nothing but tramp, tramp, tramp, the whole night long, and mutters so fiercely to himself, and such dark words, it would make one tremble were they not belied by His sweet face and sad smile," was the observation of old Juana Lopez to her husband some ten days after Arthur Stanley had been domiciled in their dwelling. The old man muttered something about his being a foreigner from the Wild Island, where they had all been busy cutting one another's throats, and what could she expect otherwise?"

"Expect? why that he must have become Spanish born and bred since he has been in King Ferdinand's service so long, and was such a boy when he left England."

"Stuff, woman; there's no taking the foreign blood out of him, try as you will," growled the old man, who in common with many of his class, was exceedingly annoyed that a foreigner should possess so much of the King's confidence, and not a little displeased that his dwelling should have been fixed on for the young officer's quarters. "It would not have been Isabella, God bless her! to have chosen such a minion; she tolerates him for Ferdinand's sake; but they will find him out one day. Saint Iago forbid the evil don't fall first."

"Now that is all prejudice, Viego Pedro, and you know it. Bless his beautiful face! there is no thought of evil there, I'd stake my existence. He is tormented in his mind about something, poor youth; but his eyes are too bright and his smile too sad for any thing evil."

"Hold your foolish tongue: you women think if a man is better looking than his fellows, he is better in every respect—poor fools as ye are; but as for this Englisher, with such a white skin and glossy curls, and blue eyes—why I'd be ashamed to show myself amongst men—pshaw—the woman's blind."

"Nay, Viego Pedro, prejudice has folded her kerchief round your eyes, not mine," retorted the old dame; and their war of words concerning the merits and demerits of their unconscious lodger continued, till old Pedro grumbled himself off, and his more light-hearted helpmate busied herself in preparing a tempting meal for her guest, which, to her great disappointment, shared the fate of many others, and left his table almost untouched.

To attempt description of Stanley's feelings would be as impossible as tedious; yet some few words must be said. His peculiarly enthusiastic, perhaps romantic disposition, had caused him to cling tenaciously to the memory of Marie, even after the revelation of a secret which to other men would have seemed to place an impassable barrier between them. To Arthur, difficulties in pursuit of an object only rendered its attainment the more intensely desired. Perhaps his hope rested on the conviction not so much of his own faithful love as on the unchangeable nature of hers. He might have doubted himself, but to doubt her was impossible. Conscious himself that, wrong as it might be, he could sacrifice every thing for her—country, rank, faith itself, even the prejudice of centuries, every thing but honor—an ideal stronger in the warrior's mind than even creed—he could not and would not believe that her secret was to her sacred as his honor to him, and that she could no more turn renegade from the fidelity which that secret comprised, than he could from his honor. She had spoken of but one relation, an aged father; and he felt in his strong hopefulness, that it was only for that father's sake she had striven to conquer her love, and had told him they might never wed, and that when that link was broken he might win her yet.

Loving and believing thus, his anguish in beholding her the wife of another may be imagined. The more he tried to think, the more confused and mystifying his thoughts became. Every interview which he had with her, and more especially that in the Vale of Cedars, was written in indelible characters on his heart and brain; and while beholding her as the wife of Morales contradicted their every word, still it could not blot them from his memory; and he would think, and think, in the vain search for but one imaginary reason, however faint, however unsatisfactory, for her conduct, till his brain turned, and his senses reeled. It was not the mere suffering of unrequited love; it was the misery of having been deceived; and then, when racked and tortured by the impossibility of discovering some cause for this deceit, her secret would flash across him, and the wild thought arise that both he and Don Ferdinand were victims to the magic and the sorcery, by means of which alone her hated race could ever make themselves beloved.

Compelled as he was to mingle with the Court as usual, these powerful emotions were of course always under strong restraint, except when in the solitude of his own quarters. That when there he should give them vent, neither conscious of, nor caring for the remarks they excited from his host and hostess, was not very remarkable; perhaps he was scarcely aware how powerfully dislike towards Don Ferdinand shared his thoughts with his vain suggestions as to the cause of Marie's falsity. The reason for this suddenly aroused dislike he could not indeed have defined, except that Morales had obtained without difficulty a treasure, to obtain which he had offered to sacrifice so much. So fourteen days passed, and though firmly resolved to have one more interview with Marie, no opportunity had presented itself, nor in fact could he feel that he had as yet obtained the self-command necessary for the cold, calm tone which he intended to assume. It happened that once or twice the King had made Arthur his messenger to Don Ferdinand; but since the night of the entertainment he had never penetrated farther than the audience chamber, there performed his mission briefly, and departed. Traversing the principal street of Segovia one morning, he was accosted somewhat too courteously, he thought, for their slight acquaintance, by Don Luis Garcia.

"And whither so early, Senor Stanley?" he inquired so courteously that it could not give offence, particularly as it followed other queries of a graceful greeting, and was not put forth abruptly.

"To the mansion of Don Ferdinand Morales," replied the young Englishman, frankly.

"Indeed! from the King?"

Stanley answered in the affirmative, too deeply engrossed with his own thoughts, to attend much to his companion, whose interrogations he would undoubtedly in a more natural mood have felt inclined to resent.

"Don Ferdinand Morales ranks as high in the favor of the people as of the King—a marvellous conjunction of qualities, is it not, Senor Stanley?" continued Garcia, after walking by his side some minutes in silence. "A Monarch's favorite is seldom that of his subjects; but Morales is unusually deserving. I wonder not at the love he wins."

"Neither Ferdinand nor Isabella bestows favors on the undeserving," briefly, almost sternly answered Stanley, with an unconscious change of tone and manner, which did not escape his companion.

"And he is so singularly fortunate, every thing he touches seems to turn to gold—an universal idol, possessed too of such wealth and splendor, and, above all, with such a being to share them with him. Fortune has marked him favored in all things. Didst ever behold a creature equal in loveliness to Donna Marie, Senor Stanley?"

A momentary, and to any other but Don Luis, incomprehensible emotion, passed over the countenance of Stanley at these words; but though it was instantly recalled, and indifference both in expression of countenance and voice resumed, it passed not unobserved; and Don Luis, rejoicing in the pain he saw he was inflicting, continued an eloquent panegyric on the wife of Morales, the intense love she bore her husband, and the beautiful unity and harmony of their wedded life, until they parted within a short distance of the public entrance to Don Ferdinand's mansion, towards which Stanley turned.

Don Luis looked after his retreating form, and folding his arms in his mantle, bent down his head, assuming an attitude which to passers-by expressed the meek humility of his supposed character. There was a wild gleam of triumph, in his eyes which he knew, and therefore they were thus bent down, and there were thoughts in his heart which might thus be worded:—"I have it all, all. Waiting has done better for me than acting; but now the watch is over, and the coil is laid. There have been those who, standing on the loftiest pinnacle, have fallen by a touch to earth; none knew the how or wherefore." And shrouding himself closer in his wrapping mantle, he walked rapidly on till he reached a side entrance into the gardens, which stretched for many acres around Don Ferdinand's mansion. Here again he paused, looked cautiously around him, then swiftly entered, and softly closed the door behind him.

Already agitated by the effort to retain calmness during Garcia's artful words, it was no light matter for Stanley to compose himself for his interview with Morales. Vain was the gentle courtesy of the latter, vain his kindly words, vain his confidential reception of the young Englishman, to remove from Arthur's heart the wild torrent of passion called forth by Garcia's allusion to Marie's intense love for her husband. To any one but Morales, his abrupt and unconnected replies, his strange and uncourteous manners, must have excited irritation; but Don Ferdinand only saw that the young man was disturbed and pained, and for this very reason exerted his utmost kindliness of words and manner to draw him from, himself. They parted after an interval of about half an hour, Morales to go to the castle as requested; Arthur to proceed, as he thought, to the environs of the city. But in vain did he strive with himself. The window of the room in which he had met Don Ferdinand looked into the garden, and there, slowly pacing a shaded path, he had recognized the figure of Marie. The intense desire to speak with her once more, and so have the fatal mystery solved, became too powerful for control. Every feeling of honor and delicacy perished before it, and hardly knowing what he did, he retraced his steps, entered unquestioned, passed through the hall to the gardens beyond, and in less than ten minutes after he had parted from her husband, stood in the presence of Marie.

CHAPTER XII.

"If she be false, oh, then Heaven mock itself!
I'll not believe it."

SHAKSPEARE.

Don Ferdinand had scarcely quitted his mansion ere fleet steps resounded behind him, and turning, he beheld Don Luis Garcia, who greeted him with such a marked expression, both in voice and face, of sadness, that Morales involuntarily paused, and with much commiseration inquired what had chanced.

"Nothing of personal misfortune, my friend; but there are times when the spirit is tortured by a doubtful duty. To preserve silence is undoubtedly wrong, and may lead to wrong, yet greater; and yet, to speak, is so painfully distressing to my peace-loving disposition, that I am tossed for ever on conflicting impulses, and would gladly be guided by another."

"If you would be guided by my counsel, my good friend, I must entreat a clearer statement," replied Morales, half smiling. "You have spoken so mysteriously, that I cannot even guess your meaning. I cannot imagine one so straightforward and strong-minded as yourself hesitating and doubtful as to duty, of whatever nature."

"Not if it concerned myself: but in this case I must either continue to see wrong done, with the constant dread of its coming to light, without my interference; or inflict anguish where I would gladly give but joy; and very probably, in addition, have my tale disbelieved, and myself condemned, though for that matter, personal pain is of no consequence, could I but pursue the right."

"But how stands this important case, my good friend?"

"Thus: I have been so unfortunate as to discover that one is false, whom her doting husband believes most true—that the lover of her youth has returned, and still holds her imagination chained—that she meets him in secret, and has appointed another clandestine interview, from which who may tell the evil that may ensue? I would prevent this interview—would recall her to her better nature, or put her husband on his guard: but how dare I do this—how interfere thus closely between man and wife? Counsel me, my friend, in pity!"

"If you have good foundation for this charge, Don Luis, it is your duty to speak out," replied Morales, gravely.

"And to whom?"

"To the lawful guardian of this misguided one—her husband."

"But how can I excite his anguish—how turn his present heaven of joy to a very hell of woe, distrust, suspicion?"

"Does the leech heed his patient's anguish when probing a painful wound, or cutting away the mortified flesh? His office is not enviable, but it is necessary, and; if feelingly performed, we love him not the less. Speak out. Don Luis, openly, frankly, yet gently, to the apparently injured husband. Do more: counsel him to act as openly, as gently with his seemingly guilty wife; and that which now appears so dark, may be proved clear, and joy dawn again for both, by a few words of mutual explanation. But there must be no mystery on your part—no either heightening or smoothing what you may have learnt. Speak out the simple truth; insinuate nought, for that love is worthless, that husband false to his sacred charge, if he believes in guilt ere he questions the accused."

Don Luis looked on the open countenance before him for a few minutes without reply, thinking, not if he should spare him, but if his plans might not be foiled, did Morales himself act as he had said. But the pause was not long: never had he read human countenance aright, if Arthur Stanley were not at that moment with Marie. He laid his hand on Don Ferdinand's arm, and so peculiar was the expression on his countenance, so low and plaintively musical the tone in which be said, "God give you strength, my poor friend," that the rich color unconsciously forsook the cheek of the hardy warrior, leaving him pallid as death; and so sharp a thrill passed through his heart, that it was with difficulty he retained his feet; but Morales was not merely physically, he was mentally brave. With a powerful, a mighty effort of will, he called life, energy, courage back, and said, sternly and unfalteringly, "Don Luis Garcia, again I say, speak out! I understand you; it is I who am the apparently injured husband. Marie! Great God of heaven! that man should dare couple her pure name with ignominy! Marie! my Marie! the seemingly guilty wife! Well, put forth your tale: I am not the man to shrink from my own words. Speak truth, and I will hear you; and—and, if I can, not spurn you from me as a liar! Speak out!"

Don Luis needed not a second bidding: he had remarked, seen, and heard quite enough the evening of Don Ferdinand's banquet, to require nothing more than the simple truth, to harrow the heart of his hearer, even while Morales disbelieved his every word. Speciously, indeed, he turned his own mere suspicions as to Marie's unhappiness, and her early love for Arthur, into realities, founded on certain information, but with this sole exception—he told but the truth. Without moving a muscle, without change of countenance, or uttering a syllable of rejoinder, Don Ferdinand listened to Garcia's recital, fixing his large piercing eye on his face, with a gaze that none but one so hardened in hypocrisy could have withstood. Once only Morales's features contracted for a single instant, as convulsed by some spasm. It was the recollection of Marie's passionate tears, the night of the festival; and yet she had shed them on *his* bosom. How could she be guilty? And the spasm passed.

"I have heard you, Don Luis," he said, so calmly, as Garcia ceased, that the latter started. "If there be truth in this strange tale, I thank you for imparting it: if it be false—if you have dared pollute my ears with one word that has no foundation, cross not my path again, lest I be tempted to turn and crush you as I would a loathsome reptile, who in very wantonness has stung me."

He turned from him rapidly, traversed the brief space, and disappeared within his house. Don Luis looked after him with a low, fiendish laugh, and plunged once more into the gardens.

"Is the Senora within?" Inquired Don Ferdinand, encountering his wife's favorite attendant at the entrance of Marie's private suit of rooms; and though his cheek was somewhat pale, his voice was firm as usual. The reply was in the negative; the Senora was in the gardens. "Alone? Why are you not with her as usual, Manuella?"

"I was with her, my Lord; she only dismissed me ten minutes ago."

Without rejoinder, Don Ferdinand turned in the direction she had pointed out. It was a lovely walk, in the most shaded parts of the extensive grounds, walled by alternate orange and lemon trees; some with the blossom, germ, and fruit all on one tree; others full of the paly fruit; and others, again, as wreathed with snow, from the profusion of odoriferous flowers. An abrupt curve led to a grassy plot, from which a sparkling fountain sent up its glistening showers, before a luxurious bower, which Morales's tender care had formed of large and healthy slips, cut from the trees of the Vale of Cedars, and flowery shrubs and variegated moss from the same spot; and there he had introduced his Marie, calling it by the fond name of "Home!" As he neared the curve, voices struck on his ear—Marie's and another's. She was not alone! and that other!—could it be?—nay, it was—there was neither doubt nor hesitation—it was his—his—against whom Don Luis had warned him. Was it for this Marie had dismissed her attendant? It could not be; it was mere accident, and Don Ferdinand tried to go forward to address them as usual; but the effort even for him was too much, and he sunk down on a rustic bench near him, and burying his head in his hands, tried to shut out sight and sound till power and calmness would return. But though he could close his eyes on all outward things, he could not deaden hearing; and words reached him which, while he strove not to hear, seemed to be traced by a dagger's point upon his heart, and from very physical agony deprived him of strength to move.

"And thou wilt give me no reason—idle, weak as it must be—thou wilt refuse me even an excuse for thy perjury?" rung on the still air, in the excited tones of Arthur Stanley. "Wealth, beauty, power—ay, they are said to be omnipotent with thy false sex; but little did I dream that it could be so with thee; and in six short months—nay, less time, thou couldst conquer love, forget past vows, leap over the obstacle thou saidst must part us, and wed another! 'Twas short space to do so much!" And he laughed a bitter, jibing laugh.

"It was short, indeed!" faintly articulated Marie; "but long enough to bear."

"To bear!" he answered; "nay, what hadst thou to bear? The petted minion of two mighty sovereigns, the idol of a nation—came, and sought, and won—how couldst thou resist him? What were my claims to his—an exile and a foreigner, with nought but my good sword, and a love so deep, so faithful (his voice softened), that it formed my very being? But what was love to thee before ambition? Oh, fool, fool that I was, to believe a woman's tongue—to dream that truth could dwell in those sweet-sounding words— those tears, that seemed to tell of grief in parting, bitter as my own—fool, to believe thy specious tale! There could be no cause to part us, else wherefore art thou Morales's wife? Thou didst never love me! From the first deceived, thou calledst forth affection, to triumph in thy power, and wreck the slender joys left to an exile! And yet I love thee—oh, God, how deeply!"

"Arthur!" answered Marie, and her bloodless lips so quivered, they could scarcely frame the word—"wrong I have done thee, grievous wrong; but oh! blast not my memory with injuries I have not inflicted. Look back; recall our every interview. Had I intended to deceive, to call forth the holiest feelings of the human heart, to make them a mock and scorn, to triumph in a power, of whose very existence till thou breathed love I was unconscious—should I have said our love was vain—was so utterly hopeless, we could never be other than strangers—should I have conjured thee to leave—aye, and to forget me, had I not felt that I loved too well, and trembled for myself yet more than for thee? Oh, Arthur, Arthur, do not add to the bitterness of this moment by unjust reproaches! I have injured thee enough by my ill-fated beauty, and too readily acknowledged love: but more I have not done. From the first I said that there was a fate around us—thine I might never be!"

"Then wherefore wed Morales? Is he not as I am, and therefore equally unmeet mate for thee—if, indeed, thy tale be true? Didst thou not tell me, when I implored thee to say if thy hand was pledged unto another, that such misery was spared thee—thou wert free, and free wouldst remain while thy heart was mine?"

"Ay," faltered Marie, "thou rememberest all too well."

"Then didst thou not deceive? Art thou not as perjured now as I once believed thee true—as false as thou art lovely? How couldst thou love, if so soon it was as nought?"

"Then believe me all thou sayest," replied Marie, more firmly—"believe me thus false and perjured, and forget me, Senor Stanley; crush even my memory from thy heart, and give not a thought to one so worthless! Mystery as there was around me when we first met, there is a double veil around me now, which I may not lift even to clear myself with thee. Turn thy love into the scorn which my perjury deserves, and leave me."

"I will not!" burst impetuously from Arthur, as he suddenly flung himself at her feet. "Marie, I will not leave thee thus; say but that some unforeseen circumstances, not thine own will, made thee the wife of this proud Spaniard; say but that neither thy will nor thy affections were consulted, that no word of thine could give him hope he was beloved—that thou lovest me still; say but this, and I will bless thee!"

"Ask it not, Senor Stanley. The duty of a wife would be of itself sufficient to forbid such words; with me gratitude and reverence render that duty more sacred still. Wouldst thou indeed sink me so low as, even as a wife, to cease to respect me? Rise, Senor Stanley! such posture is unsuited to thee or me; rise, and leave me; we must never meet alone again."

Almost overpowered with contending emotions, as he was, there was a dignity, the dignity of truth in that brief appeal, which Arthur vainly struggled to resist. She had not attempted a single word of exoneration, and yet his reproaches rushed back into his own heart as cruel and unjust, and answer he had none. He rose mechanically, and as he turned aside to conceal the weakness, a deep and fearful imprecation suddenly broke from him; and raising her head, Marie beheld her husband.

Every softened feeling fled from Stanley's breast; the passionate anger which Marie's words had calmed towards herself, now burst fourth unrestrained towards Morales. His sudden appearance bringing the conviction that he had played the spy upon their interview, roused his native irritation almost into madness. His sword flew from its scabbard, and in fearful passion he exclaimed—"Tyrant and coward! How durst thou play the spy? Is it not enough that thou hast robbed me of a treasure whose value thou canst never know? for her love was mine alone ere thou earnest between us, and by base arts and cruel force compelled her to be thine. Ha! wouldst thou avoid me? refuse to cross my sword! Draw, or I will proclaim thee coward in the face of the whole world!"

With a faint cry, Marie had thrown herself between them; but strength failed with the effort, and she would have fallen had not Morales upheld her with his left arm. But she had not fainted; every sense felt wrung into unnatural acuteness Except to support her, Morales had made no movement; his tall figure was raised to its fullest height, and his right arm calmly uplifted as his sole protection against Arthur. "Put up your sword," he said firmly, and fixing his large dark eyes upon his irritated adversary, with a gaze far more of sorrow than of anger, "I will not fight thee. Proclaim me what thou wilt. I fear neither thy sword nor thee. Go hence, unhappy boy; when this chafed mood is past, thou wilt repent this rashness, and perchance find it harder to forgive thyself than I shall to forgive thee. Go; thou art overwrought. We are not equals now."

Stanley involuntarily dropped the point of his sword. "I obey thee," he said, in that deep concentrated tone, which, betrays strong passion yet more than violent words; "obey thee, because I would not strike an undefended foe; but we shall meet again in a more fitting place and season. Till then, hear me, Don Ferdinand! We have hitherto been as companions in arms, and as friends, absent or together; from this moment the tie is broken, and for ever. I am thy foe! one who hath sworn to take thy life, or lose his own. I will compel thee to meet me! Ay, shouldst thou shun me, to the confines of the world I will track and find thee. Coward and spy! And yet men think thee noble!"

A bitter laugh of scorn concluded these fatal words. He returned his sword violently to its sheath; the tread of his armed heel was heard for a few seconds, and then all was silent.

Morales neither moved nor spoke, and Marie lifted her head to look on his face in terror. The angry words of Arthur had evidently fallen either wholly unheeded, or perhaps unheard. There was but one feeling expressed on those chiseled features, but one thought, but one conviction; a low, convulsive sob broke from her, and she fainted in his arms.

CHAPTER XIII.

"Why, when my life on that one hope, cast,
Why didst thou chain my future to her past?
Why not a breath to say she loved before?"

BULWER.

"Oh leave me not! or know
Before thou goest, the heart that wronged thee so
But wrongs no more."

BULWER.

In the first painful moments of awakening sense, Marie was only conscious of an undefined yet heavy weight on heart and brain; but as strength returned she started up with a faint cry, and looked wildly round her. The absence of Morales, the conviction that he had left her to the care of others, that for the first time he had deserted her couch of pain, lighted up as by an electric flash the marvellous links of memory, and the whole of that morning's anguish, every word spoken, every feeling endured, rushed back upon her with such overwhelming force as for the moment to deprive her of the little strength she had regained. Why could she not die? was the despairing thought that followed. What had she to live for, when it was her ill fate to wreck the happiness of all who loved her? and yet in that moment of agony she never seemed to have loved her husband more. It was of him she thought far more than of Arthur, whose angry words and fatal threat rung again and again in her ears.

"My Lord had only just left when you recovered consciousness, Senora," gently remarked her principal attendant, whose penetration had discovered the meaning of Marie's imploring look and passive silence, so far at least that it was Don Ferdinand she sought, and that his absence pained her. "He tarried till life seemed returning, and then reluctantly departed for the castle, where he had been summoned, he said, above an hour before."

"To the castle!" repeated Marie internally. "Ay, he will do his duty, though his heart be breaking. He will take his place and act his part, and men will report him calm, wise, collected, active as his wont, and little dream his wife, his treasured wife, has bowed his lofty spirit to the dust, and laid low his light of home. Tell me when he returns," she said aloud, "and bid all leave me but yourself."

Two hours passed, and Marie lay outwardly still and calm, neither speaking nor employed. But at the end of that time she started up hastily, resumed the robe which had been cast aside, and remained standing, as intently listening to some distant sound. Several minutes elapsed, and though she had sunk almost unconsciously on the seat Manuella proffered, it was not till full half an hour that she spoke.

"The Senor has returned," she said calmly; "bid Alberic hither."

The page came, and she quietly inquired if any strangers had entered with his master.

"No, Senora, he is alone."

"Has he long returned?"

"Almost half an hour, Senora. He went directly to his closet, desiring that he might not be disturbed."

Ten minutes more, and Marie was standing in her husband's presence, but unobserved. For the first time in his whole life had her light step approached him unheard. For two hours he had borne a degree of mental suffering which would either have crushed or roused any other man into wildest fury—borne it with such an unflinching spirit, that in neither look nor manner, nor even tone, had he departed from his usual self, or given the slightest occasion for remark. But the privacy of his closet obtained, the mighty will gave way, and the stormy waves rolled over him, deadening every sense and thought and feeling, save the one absorbing truth, that he had never been beloved. Father and child had deceived him; for now every little word, every trifling occurrence before his marriage in the Vale of Cedars rushed back on his mind, and Henriquez imploring entreaty under all circumstances to love and cherish her was explained.

"Ferdinand!" exclaimed a voice almost inarticulate from sobs; and starting, he beheld his wife kneeling by his side. "Oh! my husband, do not turn from me, do not hate me. I have none but thee."

He tried to withdraw his hand, but the words, the tone, unmanned him, and throwing his arm round her, he clasped her convulsively to his heart, and she felt his slow scalding tears fall one by one, as wrung from the heart's innermost depths, upon her cheek.

For several minutes there was silence. The strong man's emotion is as terrible to witness as terrible to feel. Marie was the first to regain voice; and in low beseeching accents she implored him to listen to her—to hear ere he condemned.

"Not thus," was his sole reply, as he tried to raise her from her kneeling posture to the cushion by his side.

"Yes, thus my husband. I will not rise till thou say'st thou canst forgive; wilt take the loving and the weak back to thy heart, if not to love as thou hast loved, to strengthen and forgive. I have not wronged thee. Were I false in word or thought I would not kneel to ask forgiveness, but crawl to thy feet and die! If thou couldst but know the many, many times I have longed to confess all; the agony to receive thy fond caress, thy trusting confidence, and know myself deceiving; the terror lest thou shouldst discover aught from other than myself; oh! were it not for thy deep woe, I could bless this moment, bidding me speak Truth once more!"

"And say thou hast never loved me? Wert true from duty, not from love? Marie, can I bear this?"

"Yes—for I do love thee. Oh! my husband, I turn to thee alone, under my God, for rest and peace. If I might not give thee the wild passions of my youth, when my heart was sought, and won ere I was myself conscious of the precipice I neared, I cling to thee now alone—I would be thine alone. Oh, take me to thy heart, and let me lie there. Ferdinand, Ferdinand! forgive me!—love—save me from myself!"

"Ay, now and ever! Come to my heart, beloved one!" answered her husband, rousing himself from all of personal suffering to comfort her; and he drew her to him till her head rested on his bosom. "Now tell me thy sorrowing tale, to me so wrapt in mystery. Fear not from me. It is enough thou clingest to me in such sweet guileless confidence still."

She obeyed him; and the heavy weight of suffering years seemed lightening as she spoke. From her first meeting Arthur, to that morning's harrowing interview, every feeling, every incident, every throb of reproach and dread were revealed with such touching and childlike truth, that even in his suffering, Morales unconsciously clasped his wife closer and closer to him, as if her very confidence and truth, rendered her yet dearer than before, and inexpressibly soothed at the very moment that they pained. Their interview was long, but fraught with mutual comfort. Morales had believed, when he entered his closet that day, that a dense cloud was folded round him, sapping the very elements of life; but though he still felt as if he had received some heavy physical blow, the darkness had fled from his spirit, and light dawned anew for both, beneath the heavenly rays of openness and Truth.

"And Arthur?" Marie said, as that long commune came to a close; and she looked up with the fearless gaze of integrity in her husband's face. "Thou wilt forgive him, Ferdinand? he knew not what he said."

"Trust me, beloved one. I pity and forgive him. He shall learn to love me, despite himself."

Great was the astonishment and terrible the disappointment of Don Luis Garcia at the visible failure of one portion of his nefarious schemes. Though seldom in Don Ferdinand's actual presence, he was perfectly aware that instead of diminishing, Morales' confidence in and love for his wife had both increased, and that Marie was happier and more quietly at rest than she had been since her marriage. But though baffled, Garcia was not foiled. The calm, haughty dignity which, whenever they did chance to meet, now characterized Don Ferdinand's manner towards him; the brief, stern reply, if words were actually needed; or complete silence, betraying as it did tire utter contempt and scorn with which his crafty design was regarded, heightened his every revengeful feeling, and hastened on his plans.

Two or three weeks passed: a calm security and peaceful happiness had taken the place of storm and dread in Marie's heart. She felt that it had been a secret consciousness of wrong towards her husband, the dread of discovery occasioning estrangement, the constant fear of encountering Stanley, which had weighed on her heart far more than former feelings; and now that the ordeal was past, that all was known, and she could meet her husband's eye without one thought concealed; now that despite of all he could love and cherish, aye, trust her still, she clung to him with love as pure and fond and true as ever wife might feel; and her only thought of Stanley was prayer that peace might also dawn for him. It was pain indeed to feel that the real reason of her wedding Ferdinand must for ever remain concealed. Could that have been spoken, one little sentence said, all would have been explained, and Stanley's bitter feelings soothed.

It was the custom of Ferdinand and Isabella to gather around them, about once a month, the wisest and the ablest of their realm—sometimes to hold council on public matters, at others merely in friendly discussion on various subjects connected with, politics, the church, or war. In these meetings merit constituted rank, and mind nobility. They commenced late, and continued several hours through the night. To one of these meetings Don Ferdinand Morales had received a summons as usual. As the day neared, he became conscious of a strange, indefinable sensation taking possession of heart and mind, as impossible to be explained as to be dismissed. It was as if some impassable and invisible, but closely-hovering evil were connected with the day, blinding him—as by a heavy pall—to all beyond. He succeeded in subduing the ascendency of the sensation, in some measure, till the day itself; when, as the hours waned, it became more and more overpowering. As he entered his wife's apartment, to bid her farewell ere he departed for the castle, it rose almost to suffocation in his throat, and he put his arm round her as she stood by the widely-opened casement, and remained by her side several minutes without speaking.

"Thou art not going to the castle yet, dearest?" she inquired. "Is it not much earlier than usual?"

"Yes, love; but I shall not ride to-night. I feel so strangely oppressed, that I think a quiet walk in the night air will recover me far more effectually than riding."

Marie looked up anxiously in his face. He was very pale, and his hair was damp with the moisture on his forehead. "Thou art unwell," she exclaimed; "do not go to-night, dearest Ferdinand,—stay with me. Thy presence is not so imperatively needed."

He shook his head with a faint smile. "I must go, love, for I have no excuse to stay away. I wish it were any other night, indeed, for I would so gladly remain with thee; but the very wish is folly. I never shrunk from the call of duty before, and cannot imagine what has come over me to-night; but I would sacrifice much for permission to stay within. Do not look so alarmed, love, the fresh air will remove this vague oppression, and give me back myself."

"Fresh air there is none," replied his young wife, "the stillness is actually awful—not a leaf moves, nor a breeze stirs. It seems too, more than twilight darkness; as if a heavy storm were brooding."

"It may be; oppression in the air is often the sole cause of oppression in the mind. I should be almost glad if it came, to explain this sensation."

"But if thou must go, thou wilt not loiter, Ferdinand."

"Why—fearest thou the storm will harm me, love? Nay, I have frightened thee into foreboding. Banish it, or I shall be still more loth to say farewell!"

He kissed her, as if to depart, but still he lingered though neither spoke; and then, as with an irresistible and passionate impulse, he clasped her convulsively to his heart, and murmuring hoarsely, "God for ever and ever bless thee, my own beloved!" released her, and was gone.

On quitting his mansion and entering the street, the dense weight of the atmosphere became more and more apparent. The heat was so oppressive that the streets were actually deserted—even the artisans had closed their stores; darkness had fallen suddenly, shrouding the beautiful twilight peculiar to Spain as with a pall. Morales unconsciously glanced towards the west, where, scarcely half-an-hour before, the sun had sunk gloriously to rest; and there all was not black. Resting on the edge of the hill, was a far-spreading crimson cloud, not the rosy glow of sunset, but the color of blood. So remarkable was its appearance, that Don Ferdinand paused in involuntary awe. The blackness closed gradually round it; but much decreased, and still decreasing in size, it floated onwards—preserving its blood-red hue, in appalling contrast with the murky sky. Slowly Morales turned in the direction of the castle, glancing up at times, and unable to suppress a thrill of supernatural horror, as he observed this remarkable appearance floating just before him wherever he turned. Denser and denser became the atmosphere, and blacker the sky, till he could not see a single yard before him; thunder growled in the distance, and a few vivid flashes of lightning momentarily illumined the gloom, but still the cloud remained. Its course became swifter; but it decreased in size, floating onwards, till, to Morales' strained gaze, it appeared to remain stationary over one particularly lonely part of the road, known by the name of the Calle Soledad, which he was compelled to pass; becoming smaller and smaller, till, as he reached the spot, it faded into utter darkness, and all around was black.

That same evening, about an hour before sunset, Arthur Stanley, overpowered by the heat, and exhausted with some fatiguing military duties, hastily unbuckled his sword, flung it carelessly from him, and, drinking off a large goblet of wine, which, as usual, stood ready for him on his table, threw himself on his couch, and sunk into a slumber so profound that he scarcely seemed to breathe. How he had passed the interval which had elapsed since his interview with Marie and her husband, he scarcely knew himself. His military duties were performed mechanically, a mission for the king to Toledo successfully accomplished; but he himself was conscious only of one engrossing thought, which no cooling and gentler temper had yet come to subdue. It was a relief to acquit Marie of intentional falsehood—a relief to have some imaginary object on which to vent bitterness and anger; and headstrong and violent without control or guide, when his passions were concerned, he encouraged every angry feeling against Morales, caring neither to define nor subdue them, till the longing to meet him in deadly combat, and the how to do so, became the sole and dangerous occupation of heart and mind.

Stanley's heavy and unnatural sleep had lasted some hours, when he was suddenly and painfully awakened by so loud and long a peal of thunder that the very house seemed to rock and shake with the vibration. He started up on his couch; but darkness was around him so dense that he could not distinguish a single object. This sleep had been unrefreshing, and so heavy an oppression rested on his chest, that he felt as if confined in a close cage of iron. He waved his arms to feel if he were indeed at liberty. He moved in free air, but the darkness seemed to suffocate him; and springing up, he groped his way to the window, and flung it open. Feverish and restless, the very excitement of the night seemed to urge him forth, thus to disperse the oppressive weight within. A flash of lightning playing on the polished sheath of his sword, he secured it to his side, and threw his mantle over his shoulders. As he did so his hand came in contact with the upper part of the sheath, from which the hilt should have projected; but, to his astonishment and alarm, no hilt was there—the sheath was empty.

In vain he racked his memory to ascertain whether he had left his sword in its scabbard, or had laid the naked blade, as was his custom, by him while he slept. The more he tried to think the more confused his thoughts became. His forehead felt circled with burning iron, his lips were dry and parched, his step faltering as if under the influence of some potent spell. He called for a light, but his voice sounded in his own ears thick and unnatural, and no one answered. His aged hosts had retired to rest an hour before, and though they had noticed and drew their own conclusions from his agitated movements, his call was unregarded. In five minutes more they heard him rush from the house; and anxious as she was to justify all the ways and doings of her handsome lodger, old Juanna was this night compelled to lean to her husband's ominously expressed belief, that no one would voluntarily go forth on such an awful night, save for deeds of evil.

His rapid pace and open path were illumined every alternate minute with, the vivid lightning, and the very excitement of the storm partially removed the incomprehensible sensations under which Stanley labored. He turned in the direction of the castle, perhaps with the unconfessed hope of meeting some of his companions in arms returning from the royal meeting, and in their society to shake off the spell which chained him. As he neared the Calle Soledad the ground suddenly became slippery, as with some thick fluid, of what nature the dense darkness prevented his discovering, his foot came in contact with some heavy substance lying right across his path. He stumbled and fell, and his dress and hands became literrally dyed with the same hue as the ground. He started up in terror; a long vivid flash lingering more than a minute in the air, disclosed the object against which he had fallen; and paralyzed with horror, pale, ghastly, as if suddenly turned to stone, he remained. He uttered no word nor cry; but flash after flash played around him, and still beheld him gazing in stupefied and motionless horror on the appalling sight before him.

CHAPTER XIV.

1st MONK.—The storm increases; hark! how dismally
    It sounds along the cloisters!

BERNARD.—As on I hastened, bearing thus my light,
    Across my path, not fifty paces off,
    I saw a murdered corse, stretched on its back,
    Smeared with new blood, as though but freshly slain.

JOANNA BAILLIE.

The apartment adjoining the council-room of the castle, and selected this night as the scene of King Ferdinand's banquet, was at the commencement of the storm filled with the expected guests. From forty to fifty were there assembled, chosen indiscriminately from the Castilians and Arragonese, the first statesmen and bravest warriors of the age. But the usual animated discussion, the easy converse, and eager council, had strangely, and almost unconsciously, sunk into a gloomy depression, so universal and profound, that every effort to break from it, and resume the general topics of interest, was fruitless. The King himself was grave almost to melancholy, though more than once he endeavored to shake it off, and speak as usual. Men found themselves whispering to each other as if they feared to speak aloud—as if some impalpable and invisible horror were hovering round them. It might have been that the raging storm without affected all within, with a species of awe, to which even the wisest and the bravest are liable when the Almighty utters His voice in the tempest, and the utter nothingness of men comes home to the proudest heart. But there was another cause. One was missing from the council and the board; the seat of Don Ferdinand Morales was vacant, and unuttered but absorbing anxiety occupied every mind. It was full two hours, rather more, from the given hour of meeting; the council itself had been delayed, and was at length held without him, but so unsatisfactory did it prove, that many subjects were postponed. They adjourned to the banquet-room; but the wine circled but slowly, and the King leant back on his chair, disinclined apparently for either food or drink.

"The storm increases fearfully," observed the aged Duke of Murcia, a kinsman of the King, as a flash of lightning blazed through the casements, of such extraordinary length and brilliance, that even the numerous lustres, with which the room was lighted, looked dark when it disappeared. It was followed by a peal of thunder, loud as if a hundred cannons had been discharged above their heads, and causing several glasses to be shivered on the board. "Unhappy those compelled to brave it."

"Nay, better out than in," observed another. "There is excitement in witnessing its fury, and gloom most depressing in listening to it thus."

"Perchance 'tis the shadow of the coming evil," rejoined Don Felix d'Estaban. "Old legends say, there is never a storm like this, without bringing some national evil on its wings."

"Ha! say they so?" demanded the King, suddenly, that his guests started. "And is there truth in it?"

"The lovers of such marvels would bring your Grace many proofs that, some calamity always followed such a tempest," replied Don Felix. "It may or may not be. For my own part, I credit not such things. We are ourselves the workers of evil—no fatality lurking in storms."

"Fated or casual, if evil has occurred to Don Ferdinand Morales, monarch and subject will alike have cause to associate this tempest with national calamity," answered the King, betraying at once the unspoken, but engrossing subject of his thoughts. "Who saw him last?"

Don Felix d'Estaban replied that he had seen him that day two hours before sunset.

"And where, my Lord—at home or abroad?"

"In his own mansion, which he said he had not quitted that day," was the rejoinder.

"And how seemed he? In health as usual?"

"Ay, my liege, save that he complained of a strange oppressiveness, disinclining him for all exertion."

"Did he allude to the council of to-night?"

"He did, my Lord, rejoicing that he should be compelled to rouse himself from his most unwonted mood of idleness."

"Then some evil has befallen him," rejoined the King; and the contraction of his brow denied the calmness, implied by his unmoved tone. "We have done wrong in losing all this time, Don Alonzo," he added, turning to the Senor of Aguilar, "give orders that a band of picked men scour every path leading hence to Morales' mansion: head them thyself, an thou wilt, we shall the more speedily receive tidings. Thine eyes have been more fixed on Don Ferdinand's vacant seat, than on the board this last hour; so hence, and speed thee, man. It may be he is ill: we have seen men stricken unto death from one hour to the other. If there be no trace of him in either path, hie thee to his mansion; but return not without news. Impalpable evil is ever worse than the tangible and real."

Don Alonzo scarcely waited the conclusion of the King's speech, so eager was he to depart; and the longing looks cast after him betrayed how many would have willingly joined him in his search.

"His wife?" repeated the King, in answer to some suggestions of his kinsman's. "Nay, man; hast thou yet to learn, that Morales' heart would break ere he would neglect his duty? No: physical incapacity would alone have sufficient power to keep him from us—no mental ill."

If the effort to continue indifferent conversation had been difficult before, it now became impossible. The very silence felt ominous. What evil could have befallen? was asked internally by each individual; but the vague dread, the undefined horror of something terrible impending, prevented all reply; and so nearly an hour passed, when, far removed as was the council-room from the main body of the castle, a confusion as of the entrance of many feet, and the tumultuary sound of eager voices, was distinguished, seeming to proceed from the great hall.

"It cannot be Don Alonzo so soon returned," remarked the Duke of Murcia; but even as he spoke, and before the King had time to make an impatient sign for silence, so intently was he listening, the Lord of Aguilar himself re-entered the apartment.

"Saints of heaven!" ejaculated the King, and his exclamation was echoed involuntarily by all around. The cheek of the warrior, never known to blanch before, was white as death; his eye haggard and wild; his step so faltering, that his whole frame reeled. He sunk on the nearest seat, and, with a shuddering groan, pressed both hands before his eyes.

"Wine! wine! give him wine!" cried Ferdinand impetuously, pushing a brimming goblet towards him. "Drink, man, and speak, in Heaven's name. What frightful object hast thou seen, to bid thee quail, who never quailed before? Where is Morales? Hast thou found him?"

"Ay," muttered Don Alonzo, evidently struggling to recall his energies, while the peculiar tone of the single monosyllable caused every heart to shudder.

"And where is he? Why came he not hither? Why neglect our royal summons?" continued the King, hurrying question after question with such an utter disregard of his usual calm, imperturbable cautiousness, that it betrayed far more than words how much he dreaded the Senor's reply. "Speak, man; what has detained him?"

"*Death!*" answered the warrior, his suppressed grief and horror breathing in his hollow voice; and rising, he approached the King's seat, and kneeling down, said in that low, concentrated tone, which reaches every ear, though scarce louder than a whisper, "Sire, he is murdered!"

"Murdered!" reiterated the King, as the word was echoed in all the various intonations of horror, grief, and indignation from all around; and he laid his hand heavily on Aguilar's shoulder—"Man, man, how can this be? Who would dare lift up the assassin's hand against him—him, the favorite of our subjects as of ourselves? Who had cause of enmity—of even rivalship with him? Thou art mistaken, man; it *cannot* be! Thou art scared with the sight of murder, and no marvel; but it cannot be Morales thou hast seen."

"Alas! my liege, I too believed it not; but the murdered corpse now lying in the hall will be too bloody witness of my truth."

The King released his hold, and without a word of rejoinder, strode from the apartment, and hastily traversing the long galleries, and many stairs, neither paused nor spoke, till, followed by all his nobles, he reached the hall. It was filled with soldiers, who, with loud and furious voices, mingled execrations deep and fearful on the murderer, with bitter lamentations on the victim. A sudden and respectful hush acknowledged the presence of the Sovereign; Ferdinand's brows were darkly knit, his lip compressed, his eyes flashing sternly over the dense crowd; but he asked no question, nor relaxed his hasty stride till he stood beside the litter on which, covered with a mantle, the murdered One was lying. For a single minute he evidently paused, and his countenance, usually so controlled as never to betray emotion, visibly worked with some strong feeling, which seemed to prevent the confirmation of his fears, by the trifling movement of lifting up the mantle. But at length, and with a hurried movement, it was cast aside; and there lay that noble form, cold, rigid in death! The King pushed the long, jetty hair, now clotted with gore, from the cheek on which it had fallen; and he recognized, too well, the high, thoughtful brow, now white, cold as marble; the large, dark eye, whose fixed and glassy stare had so horribly replaced the bright intelligence, the sparkling lustre so lately there. The clayey, sluggish white of death was already on his cheek; his lip, convulsively compressed, and the left hand tightly clenched, as if the soul had not been thus violently reft from the body, without a strong: pang of mortal agony. His right hand had stiffened round the hilt of his unsheathed sword, for the murderous blow had been dealt from behind, and with such fatal aim, that death must have been almost instantaneous, and the tight grasp of his sword the mere instinctive movement of expiring nature. Awe-struck, chilled to the heart, did the noble friends of the departed gather round him. On the first removal of the mantle, an irresistible yell of curses on the murderer burst forth from the soldiery, wrought into fury at thus beholding their almost idolized commander; but the stern woe on the Sovereign's face hushed them into silence; and the groan of grief and horror which escaped involuntarily from Ferdinand's lips, was heard throughout the hall.

"The murderer?" at length demanded many of the nobles at the same moment. "Who has dared do this awful deed? Don Alonzo, is there no clue to his person—no trace of his path?"

"There is trace and clue enough," was the brief and stern reply. "The murderer is secured!"

"Ha!" exclaimed the King, roused at once; "secured, sayest thou? In our bitter grief we had well-nigh forgotten justice. Bring forth the dastardly craven; we would demand the reason of this cowardly blow ere we condemn him to the death of torture which his crime demands. Let him confront his victim. Why do you pause, my Lord? Produce the murderer."

Still Don Alonzo stood irresolute, and a full minute passed ere he signed to the men who had accompanied him. A figure was instantly led forward, his arms strongly secured in his own mantle, and his hat so slouched over his face, that not a feature could be distinguished. Still there was something in his appearance that struck a cold chill of doubt to the heart of the King, and in a voice strangely expressive of emotion, he commanded—"Remove his hat and mantle: we should know that form."

He was obeyed, for there was no resistance on the part of the prisoner, whose inner dress was also stained with blood, as were his hands. His cheek was ashy pale; his eye bloodshot and pale; and his whole appearance denoting such excessive agitation, that it would have gone far to condemn him, even had there been no other proof.

"Stanley!" burst from the astonished King, as a wild cry ran round the hall, and "Death to the ungrateful foreigner!"—"Death to the base-born Englishman!"—"Tortures and death!" escaped, in every variety of intonation, from the fierce soldiery, who, regardless even of their Sovereign's presence, drew closer and closer round, clashing their weapons, and with difficulty restrained from tearing him to pieces where he stood.

"He was my foe," muttered the prisoner, almost unconscious of the import of his words, or how far they would confirm the suspicions against him. "He robbed me of happiness—he destined me to misery. I hated him; but I did not murder him. I swore to take his life or lose my own; but not thus—not thus. Great God! to see him lying there, and feel it might have been my hand. Men, men! would ye quench hatred, behold its object stricken before you by a dastard blow like this, and ye will feel its enormity and horror. I did not slay him; I would give my life to the murderer's dagger to call him back, and ask his forgiveness for the thoughts of blood I entertained against him; but I touched him not—my sword is stainless."

"Thou liest, false traitor!" exclaimed Don Felix, fiercely, and he held up the hilt and about four inches of a sword, the remainder of which was still in the body. "Behold the evidence to thy black lie! My liege, this fragment was found beside the body deluged in gore. We know the hilt too well to doubt, one moment, the name of its possessor; there is not another like it throughout Spain. It snapt in the blow, as if more honorable than its master, it could not survive so foul a stain. What arm should wield it save his own?"

A universal murmur of execration, acknowledged this convincing evidence; doubly confirmed, as it seemed to be by the fearful start and muttered exclamation, on the part of the prisoner the moment it was produced. The nobles thronged round the King, some entreating him to sentence the midnight assassin to instant execution; others, to retain him in severest imprisonment till the proofs of his guilt could be legally examined, and the whole European World hear of the crime, and its chastisement; lest they should say that as a foreigner, justice was refused to him. To this opinion the King leaned.

"Ye counsel well and wisely, my lords," he said. "It shall not be said, because the murdered was our subject, and the murderer an alien, that he was condemned without examination of proofs against him, or being heard in his own defence. Seven suns hence we will ourselves examine every evidence for or against him, which, your penetration, my lords, can collect. Till then, Don Felix, the prisoner is your charge, to be produced when summoned; and now away with the midnight assassin—he has polluted our presence too long. Away with the base ingrate, who has thus requited our trust and love; we would look on him no more."

With, a rapid movement the unfortunate young man broke from the guard, which, at Don Felix's sign, closed round and sought to drag him from the hall, and flung himself impetuously at Ferdinand's feet.

"I am no murderer!" he exclaimed, in a tone of such passionate agony, that to any less prejudiced than those around, it must at least have raised doubt as to his guilt. "I am not the base ingrate you would deem me. Condemn me to death an thou wilt, I kneel not to sue for life; for, dishonored and suspected, I would not accept it were it offered. Let them bring forward what they will, I am innocent. Here, before ye all, in presence of the murdered victim, by all held sacred in Heaven or on Earth, I swear I slew him not! If I am guilty I call upon the dead himself to rise, and blast me with his gaze!"

Involuntarily every eye turned towards the corpse; for, vague as such an appeal might seem now, the age was then but barely past, when the assistance of the murdered was often required in the discovery of the murderer. Many a brave heart grew chill, and brown cheeks blanched, in anticipation of the unearthly sign, so fully were they convinced of Stanley's guilt, but none came. The stagnated blood did not flow forth again—the eye did not glare with more consciousness than before—the cold hand did not move to point its finger at the prisoner; and Don Felix, fearing the effect of Stanley's appeal upon the King, signed to the guards, who rudely raised and bore him from the hall.

The tumults of these events had naturally spread far and wide over the castle, reaching the apartments of the Queen who, perceiving the awe and terror which the raging tempest had excited in her attendants, though incapable of aught like fear herself, had refrained from dismissing them as usual. The confusion below seeming to increase with every moment, naturally excited her surprise; and she commanded one of her attendants to learn its cause. Already terrified, none seemed inclined to obey, till a young girl, high spirited, and dauntless almost as Isabella herself, departed of her own free will, and in a few minutes returned, pale and trembling, with the dread intelligence, that Don Ferdinand Morales lay murdered in the hall, and that Arthur Stanley was his murderer.

Isabella paused not a moment, though the shock was so terrible that for the minute she became faint and sick, and hastily quitting her apartments, she entered the great hall at the moment the prisoner was being borne from it. Stupefied with contending feelings. Ferdinand did not perceive her entrance. The nobles, drawn together in little knots, were conversing in low eager tones, or endeavoring to reduce the tumultuary soldiery to more order; and the Queen moved on unperceived, till she stood beside the corpse. She neither shrunk from it, nor paled; but bending over him, murmured in a tone, that from its startling indication of her unexpected presence, readied the ear of all—"His poor, *poor* Marie!"

The effect was electric. Until that moment horror and indignation had been the predominant feeling; but with those words came the thought of his young, his beautiful, his treasured wife—the utter, utter desolation which that fearful death would bring to her; the contrast between her present position, and that in which they had so lately beheld her; and there was scarcely a manly spirit there, that did not feel unwonted moisture gather in his eyes, or his heart swell with an emotion never felt before.

"Now blessings on thy true woman's heart, my Isabel!" exclaimed the King, tenderly drawing her from the couch of the dead. "I dare vouch not one of us, mourning the noble dead, has, till now, cast a thought upon the living. And who shall breathe these fearful tidings? Who prepare the unfortunate Marie for the loss awaiting her, and yet tarry to behold and soothe her anguish?"

"That will I do," replied the Queen, instantly. "None else will prepare her so gently, so kindly; for none knew her husband's worth so well, or can mourn his loss more deeply. She shall come hither. And the murderer," she continued after a brief pause, and the change was almost startling from the

tender sympathy of the Woman to the indignant majesty of the Queen—
"Ferdinand, have they told me true as to his person—is he secured?"

"Ay," answered the King, briefly and bitterly: and from respect to his feelings, Isabella asked no more. Orders were issued for the body to be laid in one of the state apartments; a guard to be stationed at the entrance of the chamber, and measures taken to keep the events of that fatal night profoundly secret, lest confusion should be aroused in the easily excited populace, or her terrible loss too rudely reach the ears of the most painfully bereaved. These orders were punctually obeyed.

CHAPTER XV.

"Yet again methinks
Some unknown sorrow, ripe in Future's womb,
Is coming towards me; and my inward soul
With nothing trembles. At something it grieves
More than the parting with my lord."

SHAKSPEARE.

Long did Marie Morales linger where her husband had left her after his strangely passionate farewell. His tone, his look, his embrace haunted her almost to pain—all were so unlike his wonted calmness: her full heart so yearned towards him that she would have given worlds, if she had had them, to call him to her side once more—to conjure him again to forgive and assure her of his continued trust—to tell him she was happy, and asked no other love than his. Why had he left her so early? when she felt as if she had so much to say—so much to confide. And then her eye caught the same ominous cloud which had so strangely riveted Don Ferdinand's gaze, and a sensation of awe stole over her, retaining her by the casement as by some spell which she vainly strove to resist; until the forked lightnings began to illumine the murky gloom, and the thunder rolled awfully along. Determined not to give way to the heavy depression creeping over her, Marie summoned her attendants, and strenuously sought to keep up an animated conversation as they worked. Not expecting to see her husband till the ensuing morning, she retired to rest at the first partial lull of the storm, and slept calmly for many hours. A morning of transcendent loveliness followed the awful horrors of the night. The sun seemed higher in the heavens than usual, when Marie started from a profound sleep, with a vague sensation that something terrible had occurred; every pulse was throbbing, though, her heart felt stagnant within her. For some minutes she could not frame a distinct thought, and then her husband's fond farewell flashed back; but what had that to do with gloom? Ringing a little silver bell beside her, Manuella answered the summons, and Marie anxiously inquired for Don Ferdinand. Had he not yet returned? A sensation of sickness—the deadly sickness of indefinable dread—seemed to stupefy every faculty, as Manuella answered in the negative, adding, it was much beyond his usual hour.

"Send to the castle, and inquire if aught has detained him," she exclaimed; hastily rising as she spoke, and commencing a rapid toilet. She was scarcely attired before Alberic, with a pale cheek and voice of alarm, brought information that a messenger and litter from the palace were in the court, bringing the Queen's mandate for the instant attendance of Donna Marie.

"Oh! lady, dearest lady, let me go with thee," continued the boy, suddenly clasping her robe and bursting into tears. "My master—my good, noble master—something horrible has occurred, and they will not tell me what. Every face I see is full of horror—every voice seems suppressed—every—"

"Hush!" angrily interposed Manuella, as she beheld Marie's very lips lose their glowing tint, and her eyes gaze on vacancy. "For God's sake, still thine impudent tongue; thou'lt kill her with thy rashness."

"Kill! who is killed?" gasped Marie. "What did he say? Where is my husband?"

"Detained at the palace, dearest lady," readily answered Manuella. "This foolish boy is terrified at shadows. My lord is detained, and her Grace has sent a litter requiring thine attendance. We must haste, for she wills no delay. Carlotta, my lady's mantilla; quick, girl! Alberic, go if thou wilt: my Lord may be glad of thee! Ay, go," she continued some little time afterwards, as her rapid movements speedily placed her passive, almost senseless mistress, in the litter; and she caught hold of the page's hand with a sudden change of tone, "go; and return speedily, in mercy, Alberic. Some horror is impending; better know it than this terrible suspense."

How long an interval elapsed ere she stood in Isabella's presence, Marie knew not. The most incongruous thoughts floated, one after another, through her bewildered brain—most vivid amongst them all, hers and her husband's fatal secret: had it transpired? Was he sentenced, and she thus summoned to share his fate? And then, when partially relieved by the thought, that such a discovery had never taken place in Spanish annals—why should she dread an impossibility?—flashed back, clear, ringing, as if that moment spoken, Stanley's fatal threat; and the cold shuddering of every limb betrayed the aggravated agony of the thought. With her husband she could speak of Arthur calmly; to herself she would not even think his name: not merely lest he should unwittingly deceive again, but that the recollection of *his* suffering—and caused by her—ever created anew, thoughts and feelings which she had vowed unto herself to bury, and for ever.

Gloom was on every face she encountered in the castle. The very soldiers, as they saluted her as the wife of their general, appeared to gaze upon her with rude, yet earnest commiseration; but neither word nor rumor reached her ear. Several times she essayed to ask of her husband, but the words died in a soundless quiver on her lip. Yet if it were what she dreaded, that Stanley had fulfilled his threat, and they had fought, and one had fallen—why was she thus summoned? And had not Morales resolved to avoid him; for her sake not to avenge Arthur's insulting words? And again the thought of their fatal secret obtained ascendency. Five minutes more, and she stood alone in the presence of her Sovereign.

* * * * *

It was told; and with such deep sympathy, so gently, so cautiously, that all of rude and stunning shock was averted; but, alas! who could breathe of consolation at such a moment? Isabella did not attempt it; but permitted the burst of agony full vent. She had so completely merged all of dignity, all of the Sovereign into the woman and the friend, that Marie neither felt nor exercised restraint; and words mingled with her broken sobs and wild lament, utterly incomprehensible to the noble heart that heard. The awful nature of Don Ferdinand's death, Isabella had still in some measure concealed; but it seemed as if Marie had strangely connected it with violence and blood, and, in fearful and disjointed words, accused herself as its miserable cause.

"Why did not death come to me?" she reiterated; "why take him, my husband—my noble husband? Oh, Ferdinand, Ferdinand! to go now, when I have so learnt to love thee! now, when I looked to years of faithful devotion to prove how wholly the past was banished—how wholly I was thine alone! to atone for hours of suffering by years of love! Oh, how couldst thou leave me friendless—desolate?"

"Not friendless, not desolate, whilst Isabella lives," replied the Queen, painfully affected, and drawing Marie closer to her, till her throbbing brow rested on her bosom. "Weep, my poor girl, tears must flow for a loss like this; and long, long weeks must pass ere we may hope for resignation; but harrow not thyself by thoughts of more fearful ill than the reality, my child. Do not look on what might be, but what has been; on the comfort, the treasure, thou wert to the beloved one we have lost. How devotedly he loved thee, and thou—"

"And I so treasured, so loved. Oh, gracious Sovereign!" And Marie sunk down at her feet, clasping her robe in supplication. "Say but I may see him in life once more; that life still lingers, if it be but to tell me once more he forgives me. Oh, let me but hear his voice; but once, only once, and I will be calm—quite calm; I will try to bear this bitter agony. Only let me see him, hear him speak again. Thou knowest not, thou canst not know, how my heart yearns for this."

"See him thou shalt, my poor girl, if it will give thee aught of comfort; but hear him, alas! alas! my child, would that it might be! Would for Spain and her Sovereign's sake, then how much more for thine, that voice could be recalled; and life, if but for the briefest space, return! Alas! the blow was but too well aimed."

"The blow! what blow? How did he die? Who slew him?" gasped Marie; her look of wild and tearless agony terrifying Isabella, whose last words had escaped unintentionally. "Speak, speak, in mercy; let me know the truth?"

"Hast thou not thyself alluded to violence, and wrath, and hatred, Marie? Answer me, my child; didst thou know any one, regarding the generous Morales with such feelings? Could there be one to regard him as his foe?"

Crouching lower and lower at Isabella's feet, her face half buried in her robe, Marie's reply was scarcely audible; but the Queen's brow contracted.

"None?" she repeated almost sternly; "wouldst thou deceive at such a moment? contradict thyself? And yet I am wrong to be thus harsh. Poor sufferer!" she added, tenderly, as she vainly tried to raise Marie from the ground; "thou hast all enough to bear; and if, indeed, the base wretch who has dared thus to trample on the laws alike of God and man, and stain his own soul with the foul blot of midnight assassination, be him whom we have secured, thou couldst not know him as thy husband's foe. It is all mystery—thine own words not least; but his murder shall be avenged. Ay, had my own kinsman's been the hand to do the dastard deed."

"Murder! who was his murderer?" repeated Marie, the horror of such a fate apparently lost in other and more terrible emotion; "who could have raised his sword against my husband? Said I he had no foe? Had he not one, and I, oh, God! did not I create that enmity? But he would not have murdered him; oh, no—no: my liege, my gracious liege, tell me in mercy—my brain feels reeling—who was the murderer?"

"One thou hast known but little space, poor sufferer," replied the Queen, soothingly; "one whom of all others we could not suspect of such a deed. And even now, though appearances are strong against him, we can scarce believe it; that young foreign favorite of my royal husband, Arthur Stanley."

"STANLEY!" repeated Marie, in a tone so shrill, so piercing, that the wild shriek which it formed rung for many and many a day in the ears of the Queen. And as the word passed her lips she started to her feet, stood for a second erect, gazing madly on her royal mistress, and then, without one groan or struggle, dropped perfectly lifeless at her feet.

CHAPTER XVI.

List! hear ye, through the still and lonely night,
 The distant hymn of mournful voices roll
Solemn and low? It is the burial rite;
 How deep its sadness sinks into the soul,
 As slow the passing bell wakes its far ling'ring knoll.

CHARLES SWAIN.

Spain has often been regarded as an absolute monarchy; an opinion, no doubt, founded on the absolute measures of her later sovereigns. Ferdinand and Isabella certainly laid the foundation of the royal prerogative by the firmness and ability with which they decreased the power of the nobles, who, until their reign, had been like so many petty sovereigns, each with his independent state, and preserving his authority by the sword alone. When Ferdinand and Isabella, however, united their separate kingdoms under one denomination, neither Castile nor Arragon could be considered as an absolute monarchy. In Castile, the people, as representatives of the cities, had, from, early ages, obtained seats in the Cortes, and so in some measure balanced the power of the aristocracy. The Cortes, similar to our houses of parliament, could enact laws, impose taxes, and redress grievances, often making the condition of granting pecuniary aid to the Sovereign, his consent to the regulations they had laid down, and refusing the grant if he demurred. In addition to these privileges of the Cortes of Castile, the Junta of Arragon could coin money, declare war, and conclude peace; and what was still more remarkable, they could be neither prorogued nor dissolved by their Sovereign without their own consent. Alluding to the Castilians, a few years after the period of our tale, Robertson says—

> "The principles of liberty seem to have been better understood, by the Castilians than by any other people in Europe. They had acquired more liberal notions with respect to their own rights and privileges. They had formed more bold and generous sentiments concerning government, and discovered an extent of political knowledge to which the English themselves did not attain till nearly a century afterwards."

When we compare this state of things with the misery and anarchy pervading Castile before the accession of Isabella, we may have some idea of the influence of her vigorous measures, and personal character, on the happiness and freedom of her subjects. The laws indeed existed before, but they wanted the wisdom and moderation of an enlightened Sovereign, to give them force and power to act.

In the kingdom of Arragon, besides the Junta, or National Assemblage, there was always a Justizia, or supreme judge, whose power, in some respects, was even greater than the King's; his person was sacred; he could remove any of the royal ministers whom he deemed unworthy of the trust, and was himself responsible to none but the Cortes or Junta by whom he had been elected. The personal as well as the national rights of the Arragonese, were also more accurately defined than was usual in that age: no native of Arragon could be convicted, imprisoned, or tortured, without fair and legal evidence.[A]

[Footnote A: See History of Spain, by John Bigland.]

Such being the customs of the kingdom of Arragon, the power of the crown was more limited than Ferdinand's capacious mind and desire of dominion chose to endure: the Cortes, or nobles, there were pre-eminent; the people, as the Sovereign, ciphers, save that the rights of the former were more cared for than the authority of the latter. But Ferdinand was not merely ambitious; he had ability and energy, and so gradually were his plans achieved that he encountered neither rebellion nor dislike. The Cortes found that he frequently and boldly transacted business of importance without their interference; intrusted offices of state to men of inferior rank, but whose abilities were the proof of his discernment; took upon himself the office of Justizia, and, in conjunction with Isabella, re-established an institution which had fallen into disuse through the civil wars, but which was admirably suited for the internal security of their kingdom by the protection of the peasantry and lower classes: it was an association of all the cities of Castile and Arragon, known as the Sainta Hermandad, or Holy Brotherhood, to maintain a strong body of troops for the protection of travellers, and the seizure of criminals, who were brought before judges nominated by the confederated cities, and condemned according to their crime, without any regard to feudal laws. Against this institution the nobles of both kingdoms were most violently opposed, regarding it as the complete destroyer, which in reality it was, of all their feudal privileges, and taking from them the long possessed right of trying their own fiefs, and the mischievous facility of concealing their own criminals.

Thus much of history—a digression absolutely necessary for the clear elucidation of Ferdinand and Isabella's conduct with regard to the events just narrated. The trial of Arthur Stanley they had resolved should be conducted with all the formula of justice, the more especially that the fact of his being a foreigner had prejudiced many minds against him. Ferdinand himself intended to preside at the trial, with a select number of peers, to assist in the examination, and pronounce sentence, or confirm the royal mandate, as he should think fit. Nor was this an extraordinary resolution. Neither the victim, nor the supposed criminal, was of a rank which allowed a jury of an inferior grade. Morales had been fief to Isabella alone; and on Ferdinand, as Isabella's representative, fell the duty of his avenger. Arthur Stanley owned no feudal lord in Spain, save, as a matter of courtesy, the King, whose arms he bore. He was accountable, then, according to the feudal system, which was not yet entirely extinct, to Ferdinand alone for his actions, and before him must plead his innocence, or receive sentence for his crime. As his feudal lord, or suzerain, Ferdinand might at once have condemned him to death; but this summary proceeding was effectually prevented by the laws of Arragon and the office of the Holy Brotherhood; and therefore, in compliance with their mandates, royal orders were issued that every evidence for or against the prisoner should be carefully collected preparatory to the trial. More effectually to do this, the trial was postponed from seven to fourteen days after the discovery of the murder.

The excitement which this foul assassination excited in Segovia was so extreme, that the nobles were compelled to solicit Isabella's personal interference, in quieting the populace, and permitting the even course of justice: they had thronged in tumultuary masses round the prison where Stanley was confined, with wild shouts and imprecations, demanding his instant surrender to their rage, mingling groans and lamentations with yells and curses, in the most fearful medley. Old Pedro, who had been Arthur's host, unwittingly added fuel to the flame, by exulting in his prophecy that evil would come of Ferdinand's partiality for the white-faced foreigner; that he had seen it long, but guessed not how terribly his mutterings would end. By the Queen's permission, the chamber of state in which the body lay was thrown open to the eager citizens, who thronged in such crowds to behold the sole remains of one they had well nigh idolized, that the guards were compelled to permit the entrance of only a certain number every day. Here was neither state nor pomp to arrest the attention of the sight-loving populace: nought of royalty or gorgeous symbols. No; men came to pay the last tribute of admiring love and sorrow to one who had ever, noble as he was by birth, made himself one with them, cheering their sorrows, sharing their joys; treating age, however poor or lowly, with the reverence springing from the heart, inspiring youth to deeds of worth and honor, and by his own example, far more eloquently than by his words, teaching all and every age the duties demanded by their country and their homes, to their families and themselves. And this man was snatched from them, not alone by the ruthless hand of death, but by midnight murder. Was it marvel, the very grief his loss occasioned should rouse to wildest fury men's passions against his murderer?

It was the evening of the fifth day after the murder, that with a degree of splendor and of universal mourning, unrivalled before in the interment of any subject, the body of Ferdinand Morales was committed to the tomb. The King himself, divested of all insignia of royalty, bareheaded, and in a long mourning cloak, headed the train of chief mourners, which, though they counted no immediate kindred, numbered twenty or thirty of the highest nobles, both of Arragon and Castile. The gentlemen, squires, and pages of Morales' own household followed: and then came on horse and on foot, with arms reversed, and lowered heads, the gallant troops who had so often followed Morales to victory, and under him had so ably aided in placing Isabella on her throne; an immense body of citizens, all in mourning, closed the procession. Every shop had been closed, every flag half-masted; and every balcony, by which the body passed, hung with black. The cathedral church was thronged, and holy and thrilling the service which consigned dust to dust, and hid for ever from the eyes of his fellow men, the last decaying remains of one so universally beloved. The coffin of ebony and silver, partly open, so as to disclose the face of the corpse, as was customary with Catholic burials of those of high or priestly rank, and the lower part covered with a superb velvet pall, rested before the high altar during the chanted service; at the conclusion of which the coffin was closed, the lid screwed down, and lowered with slow solemnity into the vault beneath. A requiem, chanted by above a hundred of the sweetest and richest voices, sounding in thrilling unison with the deep bass and swelling notes of the organ, had concluded the solemn rites, and the procession departed as it came; but for some days the gloom in the city continued; the realization of the public loss seemed only beginning to be fully felt, as excitement subsided.

Masses for the soul of the Catholic warrior, were of course sung for many succeeding days. It was at midnight, a very short time after this public interment, that a strange group were assembled within the cathedral vaults, at the very hour that mass for the departed was being chanted in the church above their heads; it consisted of monks and travelling friars, accompanied by five or six of the highest nobility; their persons concealed in coarse mantles and shrouding hoods; they had borne with them, through the subterranean passages of the crypt, leading to the vaults, a coffin so exactly similar in workmanship and inscription to that which contained the remains of their late companion, that to distinguish the one from the other was impossible. The real one, moved with awe and solemnity, was conveyed to a secret recess close to the entrance of the crypt, and replaced in the vault by the one they had brought with them. As silently, as voicelessly as they had entered and done their work, so they departed. The following night, at the same hour, the coffin of Morales, over which had been nailed a thick black pall, so that neither name, inscription, nor ornament could be perceived, was conveyed from Segovia in a covered cart, belonging, it appeared, to the monastery of St. Francis, situated some leagues southward, and attended by one or two monks and friars of the same order. The party proceeded leisurely, travelling more by night than by day, diminishing gradually in number till, at the entrance of a broad and desolate plain, only four remained with the cart. Over this plain they hastened, then wound through a circuitous path concealed in prickly brushwood, and paused before a huge, misshapen crag, seemingly half buried in the earth: in this a door, formed of one solid stone, flew back at their touch; the coffin, taken with reverence from the cart, was borne on their shoulders through the dark and narrow passage, and down the winding stair, till they stood in safety in the vale; in the secret entrance by which they entered, the lock closed as they passed, and was apparently lost in the solid wall. Three or four awaited them—nobles, who had craved leave of absence for a brief interval from the court, and who had come by different paths to the secret retreat (no doubt already recognized by our readers as the Vale of Cedars), to lay Morales with his fathers, with the simple form, yet solemn service peculiar to the burials of their darkly hidden race. The grave was already dug beside that of Manuel Henriquez; the coffin, resting during the continuance of a brief prayer and psalm in the little temple, was then borne to the ground marked out, which, concealed by a thick hedge of cypress and cedar, lay some little distance from the temple; for, in their secret race, it was not permitted for the house destined to the worship of the Most High, to be surrounded by the homes of the dead. A slow and solemn hymn accompanied the lowering of the coffin; a prayer in the same unknown language; a brief address, and the grave was filled up; the noble dead left with his kindred, kindred alike in blood as faith; and ere the morning rose, the living had all departed, save the few retainers of the house of Henriquez and Morales, to whose faithful charge the retreat had been intrusted. No proud effigy marked those simple graves; the monuments of the dead were in the hearts of the living. But in the cathedral of Segovia a lordly monument arose to the memory of Ferdinand Morales, erected, not indeed for idle pomp, but as a tribute from the gratitude of a Sovereign—and a nation's love.

CHAPTER XVII.

ANGELO. We must not make a scarecrow of the law,
Setting it up to fear the birds of prey;
And let it keep one shape, till custom make it
Their perch, and not their terror.

ESCALUS. Ay, but yet
Let us be keen, and rather cut a little,
Than fall and bruise to death.

SHAKSPEARE.

On the evening preceding the day appointed for the trial, Isabella, unattended and unannounced, sought her husband's private closet; she found him poring so intently over maps and plans, which strewed the tables before him, that she spoke before he perceived her.

"Just come when most wished for, dear wife, and royal liege," was his courteous address, as he rose and gracefully led her to a seat beside his own. "See how my plans for the reduction of these heathen Moors are quietly working; they are divided within themselves, quarrelling more and more fiercely. Pedro Pas brings me information that the road to Alhama is well nigh defenceless, and therefore the war should commence in that quarter. But how is this, love?" he added, after speaking of his intended measures at some length, and perceiving that they failed to elicit Isabella's interest as usual. "Thy thoughts are not with me this evening."

"With thee, my husband, but not with the Moors," replied the Queen, faintly smiling. "I confess to a pre-occupied mind; but just now my heart is so filled with sorrowing sympathy, that I can think but of individuals, not of nations. In the last council, in which the question of this Moorish war was agitated, our faithful Morales was the most eloquent. His impassioned oratory so haunted me, as your Grace spoke, that I can scarcely now believe it hushed for ever, save for the too painful witness of its truth."

"His lovely wife thou meanest, Isabel? Poor girl! How fares she?"

"As she has been since that long faint, which even I believed was death; pale, tearless, silent. Even the seeing of her husband's body, which I permitted, hoping the sight would break that marble calm, has had no effect, save to increase, if possible, the rigidity of suffering. It is for her my present errand."

"For her!" replied the King, surprised. "What can I do for her, apart from thee?"

"I will answer the question by another, Ferdinand. Is it true that she must appear as evidence against the murderer in to-morrow's trial?"

"Isabella, this must be," answered the King, earnestly. "There seems to me no alternative; and yet surely this cannot be so repugnant to her feelings. Would it not be more injustice, both to her, and to the dead, to withhold any evidence likely to assist in the discovery of the murderer?"

"But why lay so much stress on her appearance? Is there not sufficient evidence without her?"

"Not to satisfy me as to Stanley's guilt," replied the King. "I have heard indeed from Don Luis Garcia quite enough, *if it be true evidence*, to condemn him. But I like not this Garcia; it is useless now to examine wherefore. I doubt him so much, that I would not, if possible, lay any stress upon his words. He has declared on oath that he saw Stanley draw his sword upon Morales, proclaim aloud his undying hatred, and swear that he would take his life or lose his own; but that, if I were not satisfied with this assurance, Donna Marie herself had been present, had seen and heard all, and could no doubt give a very efficient reason, in her own beautiful person, for Stanley's hatred to her husband, as such matters were but too common in Spain. I checked him with a stern rebuke; for if ever there were a double-meaning hypocrite, this Don Luis is one. Besides, I cannot penetrate how he came to be present at this stormy interview. He has evaded, he thinks successfully, my questions on this head; but if, as I believe, it was dishonorably obtained, I am the less inclined to trust either him or his intelligence. If Marie were indeed present, which he insists she was, her testimony is the most important of any. If she confirm Don Luis's statement, give the same account of the interview between her husband and Stanley, and a reason for this suddenly proclaimed enmity; if she swear that he did utter such threatening words, I will neither hope nor try to save him; he is guilty, and must die. But if she deny that he thus spoke; if she declares on oath that she knew of no cause for, nor of the existence of any enmity, I care not for other proofs, glaring though they be. Accident or some atrocious design against him, as an envied foreigner, may have thrown them together. Let Marie swear that this Garcia has spoken falsely, and Stanley shall live, were my whole kingdom to implore his death. In Donna Marie's evidence there can be no deceit; she can have no wish that Stanley should be saved; as her husband's supposed murderer, he must be an object of horror and loathing. Still silent Isabel? Is not her evidence required?"

"It is indeed. And yet I feel that, to demand it, will but increase the trial already hers."

"As how?" inquired the King, somewhat astonished. "Surely thou canst not mean—"

"I mean nothing; I know nothing," interrupted Isabella hastily. "I can give your Grace no reason, save my own feelings. Is there no way to prevent this public exposure, and yet serve the purpose equally?"

Ferdinand mused. "I can think of none," he said. "Does Marie know of this summons? and has her anguish sent thee hither? Or is it merely the pleadings of thine own heart, my Isabel?"

"She does not know it. The summons appeared to me so strange and needless, I would not let her be informed till I had sought thee."

"But thou seest it is not needless!" answered the King anxiously, for in the most trifling matter he ever sought her acquiescence.

"Needless it is not, my liege. The life of the young foreigner, who has thrown himself so confidingly on our protection and friendship, must not be sacrificed without most convincing proofs of his guilt. Marie's evidence is indeed important; but would not your Grace's purpose be equally attained, if that evidence be given to me, her native Sovereign, in private, without the dread formula which, if summoned before a court of justice, may have fatal effects on a mind and frame already so severely tried? In my presence alone the necessary evidence may be given with equal solemnity, and with less pain to the poor sufferer herself."

King Ferdinand again paused in thought. "But her words must be on oath, Isabel. Who will administer that oath?"

"Father Francis, if required. But it will surely be enough if she swear the truth to me. She cannot deceive me, even if she were so inclined. I can mark a quivering lip or changing color, which others might pass unnoticed."

"But how will this secret examination satisfy the friends of the murdered?" again urged the cautious King. "How will they be satisfied, if I acquit Stanley from Donna Marie's evidence, and that evidence be kept from them?"

"Is not the word of their Sovereign enough? If Isabella say so it is, what noble of Castile would disgrace himself or her by a doubt as to its truth?" replied the Queen proudly. "Let me clearly understand all your Grace requires, and leave the rest to me. If Marie corroborates Garcia's words, why, on his evidence sentence may be pronounced without her appearance in it at all; but if she deny in the smallest tittle his report, in my presence they shall confront each other, and fear not the truth shall be elicited, and, if possible, Stanley saved. I may be deceived, and Marie not refuse to appear as witness against him; if so, there needs not my interference. I would but spare her increase of pain, and bid her desolate heart cling to me as her mother and her friend. When my subjects look upon me thus, my husband, then, and then only is Isabella what she would be."

"And do they not already thus regard thee, my own Isabel?" replied the King, gazing with actual reverence upon her; "and as such, will future ages reverence thy name. Be it as thou wilt. Let Marie's own feelings decide the question. She *must* take part in this trial, either in public or private; she *must* speak on oath, for life and death hang on her words, and her decision must be speedy. It is sunset now, and ere to-morrow's noon she must have spoken, or be prepared to appear."

Ere Queen Isabella reached her own apartments her plan was formed. Don Luis's tale had confirmed her suspicions as to the double cause of Marie's wretchedness; she had herself administered to her while in that dead faint— herself bent over her, lest the first words of returning consciousness should betray aught which the sufferer might wish concealed; but her care had been needless: no word passed those parched and ashy lips. The frame, indeed, for some days was powerless, and she acceded eagerly to Isabella's earnest proffer (for it was not command) to send for her attendants, and occupy a suite of rooms in the castle, close to her royal mistress, in preference to returning to her own home; from which, in its desolate grandeur, she shrunk almost in loathing.

For seven days after her loss she had not quitted her apartment, seen only by the Queen and her own woman; but after that interval, at Isabella's gently expressed wish, she joined her, in her private hours, amongst her most favored attendants; called upon indeed for nothing save her presence! And little did her pre-occupied mind imagine how tenderly she was watched, and with what kindly sympathy her unexpressed thoughts were read.

On the evening in question, Isabella was seated, as was her frequent custom, in a spacious chamber, surrounded by her female attendants, with whom she was familiarly conversing, making them friends as well as subjects, yet so uniting dignity with kindness, that her favor was far more valued and eagerly sought than had there been no superiority; yet, still it was more for her perfect womanhood than her rank that she was so reverenced, so loved. At the farther end of the spacious chamber were several young girls, daughters of the nobles of Castile and Arragon, whom Isabella's maternal care for her subjects had collected around her, that their education might be carried on under her own eye, and so create for the future nobles of her country, wives and mothers after her own exalted stamp. They were always encouraged to converse freely and gayly amongst each other; for thus she learned their several characters, and guided them accordingly. There was neither restraint nor heaviness in her presence; for by a word, a smile, she could prove her interest in their simple pleasures, her sympathy in their eager youth.

Apart from all, but nearest Isabella, silent and pale, shrouded in the sable robes of widowhood—that painful garb which, in its voiceless eloquence of desolation, ever calls for tears, more especially when it shrouds the young; her beautiful hair, save two thick braids, concealed under the linen coif—sat Marie, lovely indeed still, but looking like one

> "Whose heart was born to break—
> A face on which to gaze, made every feeling ache."

An embroidery frame was before her, "but the flowers grew but slowly beneath her hand. About an hour after Isabella had joined her attendants, a light signal was heard at the tapestried door of the apartment. The Queen was then sitting in a posture of deep meditation; but she looked up, as a young girl answered the summons, and then turned towards her Sovereign.

"Well, Catherine?"

"Royal madam, a page, from his Grace the King, craves speech of Donna Marie."

"Admit him then."

The boy entered, and with a low reverence advanced towards Marie. She looked up in his face bewildered—a bewilderment which Isabella perceived changed to a strong expression of mental torture, ere he ceased to speak.

"Ferdinand, King of Arragon and Castile," he said, "sends, with all courtesy, his royal greeting to Donna Marie Henriquez Morales, and forthwith commands her attendance at the solemn trial which is held to-morrow's noon; by her evidence to confirm or refute the charge brought against the person of Arthur Stanley, as being and having been the acknowledged enemy of the deceased Don Ferdinand Morales (God assoilize his soul!) and as having uttered words of murderous import in her hearing. Resolved, to the utmost of his power, to do justice to the living as to avenge the dead, his royal highness is compelled thus to demand the testimony of Donna Marie, as she alone can confirm or refute this heavy and most solemn charge."

There was no answer; but it seemed as if the messenger required none—imagining the royal command all sufficient for obedience—for he bowed respectfully as he concluded, and withdrew. Marie gazed after him, and her lip quivered as if she would have spoken—would have recalled him; but no word came, and she drooped her head on her hands, pressing her slender fingers strongly on her brow, as thus to bring back connected thought once more. What had he said? She must appear against Stanley—she must speak his doom? Why did those fatal words which must condemn him, ring in her ears, as only that moment spoken? Her embroidery fell from her lap, and there was no movement to replace it. How long she thus sat she knew not; but, roused by the Queen's voice uttering her name, she started, and looked round her. She was alone with Isabella; who was gazing on her with such unfeigned commiseration, that, unable to resist the impulse, she darted forwards, and sinking at her feet, implored—

"Oh, madam—gracious madam! in mercy spare me this!"

The Queen drew her tenderly to her, and said, with evident emotion—

"What am I to spare thee, my poor child? Surely thou wouldst not withhold aught that can convict thy husband's murderer? Thou wouldst not in mistaken mercy elude for him the justice of the law?"

"No—no," murmured Marie; "let the murderer die; but not Stanley! Oh, no—no; he would not lift his hand against my husband. Who says he slew him? Why do they attach so foul a crime to his unshadowed name? Let the murderer die; but it is not Arthur: I know it is not. Oh, do not slay him too!"

Marie knew not the wild entreaty breathing in her words: but the almost severely penetrating gaze which Isabella had fixed upon her, recalled her to herself; a crimson flush mounted to cheek and brow, and, burying her face in the Queen's robe, she continued less wildly—

"Oh, madam, bear with me; I know not what I say. Think I am mad; but oh, in mercy, ask me no question. Am I not mad, to ask thee to spare—spare—him they call my husband's murderer? Let him die," and the wild tone returned, "if he indeed could strike the blow; but oh, let not my lips pronounce his death-doom! Gracious Sovereign, do not look upon me thus—I cannot bear that gaze."

"Fear me not, poor sufferer," replied Isabella, mildly; "I will ask no question—demand nought that will give thee pain to answer—save that which justice compels me to require. That there is a double cause for all this wretchedness, I cannot but perceive, and that I suspect its cause I may not deny; but guilty I will not believe thee, till thine own words or deeds proclaim it. Look up then, my poor child, unshrinkingly; I am no dread Sovereign to thee, painful as is the trial to which I fear I must subject thee. There are charges brought against young Stanley so startling in their nature, that, much as we distrust his accuser, justice forbids our passing them unnoticed. On thy true testimony his Grace the King relies to confirm or refute them. Thy evidence must convict or save him."

"My evidence!" repeated Marie. "What can they ask of me of such weight? Save him." she added, a sudden gleam of hope irradiating her pallid face, like a sunbeam upon snow? "Did your Grace say *I* could save him? Oh, speak, in mercy!"

"Calm this emotion then, Marie, and thou shalt know all. It was for this I called thee hither. Sit thee on the settle at my feet, and listen to me patiently, if thou canst. 'Tis a harsh word to use to grief such as thine, my child," she added, caressingly, as she laid her hand on Marie's drooping head; "and I fear will only nerve thee for a still harsher trial. Believe me, I would have spared thee if I could; but all I can do is to bid thee choose the lesser of the two evils. Mark me well: for the Sovereign of the murdered, the judge of the murderer, alike speak through me." And clearly and forcibly she narrated all, with which our readers are already acquainted, through her interview with the King. She spoke very slowly, as if to give Marie time to weigh well each sentence. She could not see her countenance; nay, she purposely refrained from looking at her, lest she should increase the suffering she was so unwillingly inflicting. For some minutes she paused as she concluded; then, as neither word nor sound escaped from Marie, she said, with emphatic earnestness—"If it will be a lesser trial to give thine evidence on oath to thy Queen alone, we are here to receive it. Our royal husband—our loyal subjects—will be satisfied with Isabella's report. Thy words will be as sacred—thy oath as valid—as if thy testimony were received in public, thy oath administered by one of the holy fathers, with all the dread formula of the church. We have repeated all to which thy answers will be demanded; it remains for thee to decide whether thou wilt speak before his Grace the King and his assembled junta, or here and now before thy native Sovereign. Pause ere thou dost answer—there is time enough."

For a brief interval there was silence. The kind heart of the Queen throbbed painfully, so completely had her sympathy identified her with the beautiful being, who had so irresistibly claimed her cherishing love. But ere she had had time to satisfy herself as to the issue of the struggle so silently, yet so fearfully at work in her companion, Marie had arisen, and with dignity and fearlessness, strangely at variance with the wild agony of her words and manner before, stood erect before her Sovereign; and when she spoke, her voice was calm and firm.

"Queen of Spain!" she said. "My kind, gracious Sovereign! Would that words could speak one-half the love, the devotion, all thy goodness has inspired; but they seem frozen, all frozen now, and it may be that I may never even prove them—that it will be my desolate fate, to seem less and less worthy of an affection I value more than life. Royal madam! I will appear at to-morrow's trial! Your Grace is startled; deeming it a resolve as strange as contradictory. Ask not the wherefore, gracious Sovereign: it is fixed unalterably. I will obey his Grace's summons. Its unexpected suddenness startled me at first; but it is over. Oh, madam," she continued—tone, look, and manner becoming again those of the agitated suppliant, and she sunk once more at Isabella's feet: "In my wild agony I have forgotten the respect and deference due from a subject to her Sovereign; I have poured forth my misery, seemingly as regardless of kindness, as insensible to the wide distance between us. Oh, forgive me, my gracious Sovereign; and in token of thy pardon, grant me but one boon!"

"Nought have I to forgive, my suffering child," replied the Queen, powerfully affected, and passing her arm caressingly round her kneeling favorite; "what is rank—sovereignty itself—in hours of sorrow? If I were so tenacious of dignity as thou fearest, I should have shrunk from that awful presence—affliction from a Father's hand—in which his children are all equals, Marie. And as for thy boon: be it what it may, I grant it."

"Thou sayest so now, my liege; but when the hour to grant it comes, every feeling will revolt against it; even thine, my Sovereign, kind, generous, as thou art. Oh, Madam, thou wilt hear a strange tale to-morrow—one so fraught with mystery and marvel, thou wilt refuse to believe; but when the trial of to-morrow is past, then think on what I say now: what thou nearest will be TRUE—true as there is a heaven above us; I swear it! Do not look upon me thus, my Sovereign; I am not mad—oh, would that I were! Dark, meaningless as my words seem now, to-morrow they will be distinct and clear enough. And then—then, if thou hast ever loved me, oh, grant the boon I implore thee now: whatever thou mayest hear, do not condemn me—do not cast me wholly from thee. More than ever shall I need thy protecting care. Oh, my Sovereign—thou who hast taught me so to love thee, in pity love me still!"

"Strange wayward being," said Isabella, gazing doubtingly on the imploring face upturned to hers; "towards other than thyself such mystery would banish love for ever; but I will not doubt thee. Darkly as thou speakest, still I grant the boon. What can I hear of thee, to cast thee from me?"

"Thou wilt hear of deceit, my liege," replied Marie, very slowly, and her eyes fell beneath the Queen's gaze; "thou wilt hear of long years of deceit and fraud, and many—many tongues will speak their scorn and condemnation. Then wilt thou grant it—then?"

"Even then," replied Isabella fearlessly; "an thou speakest truth at last, deceit itself I will forgive. But thou art overwrought and anxious, and so layest more stress on some trivial fault than even I would demand. Go to thy own chamber now, and in prayer and meditation gain strength for to-morrow's trial. Whatever I may hear, so it be not meditated and unrepented guilt, (which I know it cannot be,) I will forgive, and love thee still. The holy saints bless and keep thee, my fair child!"

And as Marie bent to salute the kind hand extended to her, Isabella drew her towards her, and fondly kissed her cheek. The unexpected caress, or some other secret feeling, subdued the overwrought energy at once; and for the first time since her husband's death, Marie burst into natural tears. But her purpose changed not; though Isabella's gentle and affectionate soothing rendered it tenfold more painful to accomplish.

CHAPTER XVIII.

LEONTES.—These sessions, to our great grief, we pronounce
Even pushes 'gainst our heart.
  Let us be cleared
Of being tyrannous, since we openly
Proceed in justice—which shall have due course,
Even to the guilt, or the purgation.
Produce the prisoner!—SHAKSPEARE.

The day of trial dawned, bright, sunny, cloudless, as was usual in beautiful Spain—a joyous elasticity was in the atmosphere, a brilliance in the heavens, which thence reflected on the earth, so painfully contrasted with misery and death, that the bright sky seemed to strike a double chill on the hearts of those most deeply interested.

Never had the solemn proceedings of justice created so great an excitement; not only in Segovia itself, but the towns and villages, many miles round, sent eager citizens and rustic countrymen to learn the issue, and report it speedily to those compelled to stay at home. The universal mourning for Morales was one cause of the popular excitement; and the supposition of the young foreigner being his murderer another.

The hall of the castle was crowded at a very early hour, Isabella having signified not only permission, but her wish that as many of her citizen subjects as space would admit should be present, to witness the faithful course of justice. Nearest to the seat destined for the King, at the upper end of the hall, were ranged several fathers from an adjoining convent of Franciscans, by whom a special service had been impressively performed that morning in the cathedral, in which all who had been summoned to preside at the trial had solemnly joined.

The Monks of St. Francis were celebrated alike for their sterling piety, great learning, and general benevolence. Their fault, if such it could be termed in a holy Catholic community, was their rigid exclusiveness regarding religion; their uncompromising and strict love for, and adherence to, their own creed; and stern abhorrence towards, and violent persecution of, all who in the slightest degree departed from it, or failed to pay it the respect and obedience which they believed it demanded. At their head was their Sub-Prior, a character whose influence on the after position of Spain was so great, that we may not pass it by, without more notice than our tale itself perhaps would demand. To the world, as to his brethren and superiors, in the monastery, a stern unbending spirit, a rigid austerity, and unchanging severity of mental and physical discipline, characterized his whole bearing and daily conduct. Yet, his severity proceeded not from the superstition and bigotry of a weak mind or misanthropic feeling. Though his whole time and thoughts appeared devoted to the interest of his monastery, and thence to relieving and guiding the poor, and curbing and decreasing the intemperate follies and licentious conduct of the laymen, in its immediate neighborhood; yet his extraordinary knowledge, not merely of human nature, but of the world at large—his profound and extensive genius, which, in after years was displayed, in the prosecution of such vast schemes for Spain's advancement, that they riveted the attention of all Europe upon him—naturally won him the respect and consideration of Ferdinand and Isabella, whose acute penetration easily traced the natural man, even through the thick veil of monkish austerity. They cherished and honored him, little thinking that, had it not been for him, Spain would have sunk at their death, into the same abyss of anarchy and misery, from which their vigorous measures had so lately roused, and, as they hoped, So effectually guarded her.

When Torquemada, Isabella's confessor, was absent from court, which not unfrequently happened, for his capacious mind was never at peace unless actively employed—Father Francis, though but the Sub-Prior of a Franciscan monastery, always took his place, and frequently were both sovereigns guided by his privately asked and frankly given opinions, not only on secular affairs, but on matters of state, and even of war. With such a character for his Sub-Prior, the lordly Abbot of the Franciscans was indeed but a nominal dignitary, quite contented to enjoy all the indulgences and corporeal luxuries, permitted, or perhaps winked at, from his superior rank, and leaving to Father Francis every active duty; gladly, therefore, he deputed on him the office of heading the Monks that day summoned to attend King Ferdinand.

Not any sign of the benevolence and goodness—in reality the characteristics of this extraordinary man—was visible on his countenance as he sat. The very boldest and haughtiest of the aristocracy, involuntarily perhaps, yet irresistibly, acknowledged his superiority. Reverence and awe were the emotions first excited towards his person: but already was that reverence largely mingled with the love which some three years afterwards gave him such powerful influence over the whole sovereignty of Spain. Next to the holy fathers, and ranged according to rank and seniority, were the nobles who had been selected to attend, the greater number of whom, were Castilians, as countrymen of the deceased. Next to them were the Santa Hermandad, or Brethren of the Associated Cities, without whose presence and aid, no forms of justice, even though ruled and guided by royalty itself, were considered valid or complete. A semicircle was thus formed, the centre of which was the King's seat; and opposite to him, in the hollow, as it were of the crescent, a space left for the prisoner, accusers, and witnesses. Soldiers lined the hall; a treble guard being drawn up at the base of the semicircle, and extending in a wide line right and left, behind the spot destined for the prisoner. There was still a large space left, and this was so thronged with citizens, that it presented the appearance of a dense mass of human heads, every face turned in one direction, and expressive in various ways of but one excitement, one emotion.

There was not a smile on either of the stern countenances within the hall. As the shock and horror of Don Ferdinand's fate in some measure subsided, not only the nobles, but the soldiers themselves, began to recall the supposed murderer in the many fields of honorable warfare, the many positions of mighty and chivalric bearing in which they had hitherto seen the young Englishman play so distinguished a part; and doubts began to arise as to the possibility of so great a change, and in so short a time. To meet even a supposed enemy in fair field, and with an equality of weapons, was the custom of the day; such, therefore, between Stanley and Morales, might have excited marvel as to the *cause*, but not as to the *act*. But murder! it was so wholly incompatible with even the very lowest principles of chivalry (except when the unfortunate victim was of too low a rank to be removed by any other means), that when they recalled the gallantry, the frankness of speech and deed, the careless buoyancy, the quickly subdued passion, and easily accorded forgiveness of injury, which had ever before characterized young Stanley, they could not believe his guilt: but then came the recollection of the startling proofs against him, and such belief was almost involuntarily suspended. There was not a movement in that immense concourse of human beings, not a word spoken one to the other, not a murmur even of impatience for the appearance of the King. All was so still, so mute, that, had it not been for the varied play of countenances, any stranger suddenly placed within the circle might have imagined himself in an assemblage of statues.

Precisely at noon, the folding-doors at the upper end of the hall were thrown widely but noiselessly back, and King Ferdinand, attended by a few pages and gentlemen, slowly entered, and taking his seat, gazed a full minute, inquiringly and penetratingly around him, and then resting his head on his hand, remained plunged in earnest meditation some moments before he spoke.

It was a strange sight—the noiseless, yet universal rising of the assemblage in honor to their Sovereign, changing their position as by one simultaneous movement. Many an eye turned towards him to read on his countenance the prisoner's doom; but its calm, almost stern expression, baffled the most penetrating gaze. Some minutes passed ere Ferdinand, rousing himself from his abstraction, waved his hand, and every seat was instantaneously resumed, and so profound was the silence, that every syllable the Monarch spoke, though his voice was not raised one note above his usual pitch, was heard by every member of those immense crowds, as individually addressing each.

"My Lords and holy Fathers, and ye Associated Brethren," he said, "the cause of your present assemblage needs no repetition. Had the murdered and the supposed murderer been other than they are, we should have left the course of justice in the hands of those appointed to administer it, and interfered not ourselves save to confirm or annul the sentence they should pronounce. As the case stands, we are deputed by our illustrious Consort and sister Sovereign, Isabella of Castile, to represent her as Suzerain of the deceased (whom the saints assoilize), and so ourselves guide the proceedings of justice on his murderer. Our prerogative as Suzerain and Liege would permit us to condemn to death at once; but in this instance, my Lords and holy Fathers, we confess ourselves unwilling and incapable of pronouncing judgment solely on our own responsibility. The accused is a friendless foreigner, to whom we have been enabled to show some kindness, and therefore one towards whom we cannot feel indifference: he has, moreover, done us such good service both in Spain and Sicily, that even the grave charge brought against him now, cannot blot out the memories of the past. We find it difficult to believe that a young, high-spirited, honorable warrior, in whose heart every chivalric feeling appeared to beat, could become, under any temptation, under any impulse, that base and loathsome coward—a midnight murderer! On your counsels, then, we implicitly depend: examine, impartially and deliberately, the proofs for and against, which will be laid before you. But let one truth be ever present, lest justice herself be but a cover for prejudice and hate. Let not Europe have cause to say, that he who, flying from the enemies and tyrants of his own land, took refuge on the hearths of our people, secure there of kindness and protection, has found them not. Were it a countryman we were about to judge, this charge were needless; justice and mercy would, if it were possible, go hand in hand. The foreigner, who has voluntarily assumed the name and service of a son of Spain, demands yet more at our hands. My Lords and holy Fathers, and ye Associated Brethren, remember this important truth, and act accordingly: but if, on a strict, unprejudiced examination of the evidence against the prisoner, ye pronounce him guilty, be it so: the scripture saith, 'blood must flow for blood!'"

A universal murmur of assent filled the hall as the King ceased: his words had thrilled reprovingly on many there present, particularly amongst the populace, who felt, even as the Monarch spoke, the real cause of their violent wrath against the murderer. Ere, however, they had time to analyze why the violent abhorrence of Stanley should be so calmed merely at the King's words, the command, "Bring forth the prisoner!" occasioned an intensity of interest and eager movement of the numerous heads towards the base of the hall, banishing every calmer thought. The treble line of soldiers, forming the base of the crescent, divided in the centre, and wheeling backwards, formed two files of dense thickness, leaving a lane between them through which the prisoner and his guards were discerned advancing to the place assigned. He was still heavily fettered, and his dress, which he had not been permitted to change, covered with dark, lurid stains, hung so loosely upon him, that his attenuated form bore witness, even as the white cheek and haggard eye, to the intense mental torture of the last fortnight. His fair hair lay damp and matted on his pale forehead; but still there was that in his whole bearing which, while it breathed of suffering, contradicted every thought of guilt. He looked round him steadily and calmly, lowered his head a moment in respectful deference to the King, and instantly resumed the lofty carriage which suffering itself seemed inadequate to bend. King Ferdinand fixed his eyes upon him with an expression before which the hardiest guilt must for the moment have quailed; but not a muscle of the prisoner's countenance moved, and Ferdinand proceeded to address him gravely, yet feelingly.

"Arthur Stanley," he said, "we have heard from Don Felix d'Estaban that you have refused our proffered privilege of seeking and employing some friends, subtle in judgment, and learned in all the technicalities of such proceedings, as to-day will witness, to undertake your cause. Why is this? Is your honor of such small amount, that you refuse even to accept the privilege of defence? Are you so well prepared yourself to refute the evidence which has been collected against you, that you need no more? Or have we indeed heard aright, that you have resolved to let the course of justice proceed, without one effort on your part to avert an inevitable doom? This would seem a tacit avowal of guilt; else, wherefore call your doom inevitable? If conscious of innocence, have you no hope, no belief in the Divine Justice, which can as easily make manifest innocence as punish crime? Ere we depute to others the solemn task of examination, and pronouncing sentence, we bid you speak, and answer as to the wherefore of this rash and contradictory determination—persisting in words that you are guiltless, yet refusing the privilege of defence. Is life so valueless, that you cast it degraded from you? As Sovereign and Judge, we command you answer, lest by your own rash act the course of justice be impeded, and the sentence of the guilty awarded to the innocent. As man to man, I charge thee speak; bring forward some proof of innocence. Let me not condemn to death as a coward and a murderer, one whom I have loved and trusted as a friend! Answer—wherefore this strange callousness to life—this utter disregard of thine honor and thy name?"

For a moment, while the King addressed him as man to man, the pallid cheek and brow of the prisoner flushed with painful emotion, and there was a scarcely audible tremulousness in his voice as he replied:

"And how will defence avail me? How may mere assertion deny proof, and so preserve life and redeem honor? My liege, I had resolved to attempt no defence, because I would not unnecessarily prolong the torture of degradation. Had I one proof, the slightest proof to produce, which might in the faintest degree avail me, I would not withhold it; justice to my father's name would be of itself sufficient to command defence. But I have none! I cannot so perjure myself as to deny one word of the charges brought against me, save that of murder! Of thoughts of hate and wrath, ay, and blood, but such blood as honorable men would shed, I am guilty, I now feel, unredeemably guilty, but not of murder! I am not silent because conscious of enacted guilt. I will not go down to the dishonored grave, now yawning for me, permitting, by silence, your Highness, and these your subjects, to believe me the monster of ingratitude, the treacherous coward which appearances pronounce me. No!" he continued, raising his right hand as high as his fetters would permit, and speaking in a tone which fell with the eloquence of truth, on every heart—"No: here, as on the scaffold—now, as with my dying breath, I will proclaim aloud my innocence; I call on the Almighty Judge himself, as on every Saint in heaven, to attest it—ay, and I believe it WILL be attested, when nought but my memory is left to be cleared from shame— I am not the murderer of Don Ferdinand Morales! Had he been in every deed my foe—had he given me cause for the indulgence of those ungovernable passions which I now feel were roused against him so causelessly and sinfully, I might have sought their gratification by honorable combat, but not by midnight murder! I speak not, I repeat, to save my life: it is justly forfeited for thoughts of crime! I speak that, when in after years my innocence will be made evident by the discovery of the real assassin, you will all remember what I now say—that I have not so basely requited the King and Country who so generously and trustingly befriended me—that I am no murderer!"

"Then, if so convinced of innocence, young man, wherefore not attempt defence?" demanded the Sub-Prior of St. Francis. "Knowest thou not that wilfully to throw away the life intrusted to you, for some wise purpose, is amenable before the throne of the Most High as self-committed murder? Proofs of this strongly asserted innocence, thou must have."

"I have none," calmly answered the prisoner, "I have but words, and who will believe them? Who, here present, will credit the strange tale, that, tortured and restless from mental suffering, I courted the fury of the elements, and rushed from my quarters on the night of the murder *without* my sword?—that, in securing the belt, I missed the weapon, but still sought not for it as I ought?—who will believe that it was accident, not design, which took me to the Calle Soledad? and that it was a fall over the murdered body of Don Ferdinand which deluged my hands and dress with the blood that dyed the ground? Who will credit that it was seeing him thus which chained me, paralyzed, horror-stricken, to the spot? In the wild fury of my passions I had believed him my enemy, and sworn his death; then was it marvel that thus beholding him turned me well-nigh to stone, and that, in my horror, I had no power to call for aid, or raise the shout after the murderer, for my own thoughts arose as fiends, to whisper, such might have been nay work— that I had wished his death? Great God! the awful wakening from the delusion of weeks—the dread recognition in that murdered corse of my own thoughts of sin!" He paused involuntarily, for his strong agitation completely choked his voice, and shook his whole frame. After a brief silence, which none in the hall had heart to break, he continued calmly, "Let the trial proceed, gracious Sovereign. Your Highness's generous interest in one accused of a crime so awful, comprising the death, not of a subject only, but of a friend, does but add to the heavy weight of obligation already mine, and would of itself excite the wish to live, to prove that I am not so utterly unworthy; but I feel that not to such as I, may the Divine mercy be so shown, as to bring forward the real murderer. The misery of the last fortnight has shown me how deeply I have sinned in thought, though not in deed; and how dare I, then, indulge the wild dream that my innocence will be proved, until too late, save for mine honor? My liege, I have trespassed too long on the time of this assemblage; let the trial proceed."

So powerful was the effect of his tone and words, that the impulse was strong in every heart to strike off his fetters, and give him life and freedom. The countenance of the Sub-Prior of St. Francis alone retained its unmoved calmness, and its tone, its imperturbable gravity, as he commanded Don Felix d'Estaban to produce the witnesses; and on their appearance, desired one of the fathers to administer the oath.

CHAPTER XIX.

"His unaltering-cheek
Still vividly doth hold its natural hue,
And his eye quails not. Is this innocence?"

MRS. HEMANS.

During the examination of Don Alonzo of Aguilar, and of old Pedro and Juana, the prisoner remained with his arms calmly folded and head erect, without the smallest variation of feature or position denoting either anxiety or agitation. Don Alonzo's statement was very simple. He described the exact spot where he had found the body, and the position in which it lay; the intense agitation of Stanley, the bloody appearance of his clothes, hands, and face, urging them to secure his person even before they discovered the broken fragment of his sword lying beside the corse. His account was corroborated, in the very minutest points, by the men who had accompanied him, even though cross-questioned with unusual particularity by Father Francis. Old Pedro's statement, though less circumstantial, was, to the soldiers and citizens especially, quite as convincing. He gave a wordy narrative of Senor Stanley's unnatural state of excitement from the very evening he had become his lodger—that he had frequently heard him muttering to himself such words as "blood" and "vengeance." He constantly appeared longing for something; never eat half the meals provided for him— a sure proof, in old Pedro's imagination, of a disordered mind, and that the night of the murder he had heard him leave the house, with every symptom of agitation. Old Juana, with very evident reluctance, confirmed this account; but Father Francis was evidently not satisfied. "Amongst these incoherent ravings of the prisoner, did you ever distinguish the word 'murder?'" he demanded—a question which would be strange, indeed, in the court of justice of the present day, but of importance in an age when such words as blood and vengeance, amongst warriors, simply signified a determination to fight out their quarrel in (so-called) honorable combat. The answer, after some hesitation, was in the negative. "Did you ever distinguish any name, as the object of Senor Stanley's desired vengeance?"

Pedro immediately answered "No;" but there was a simper of hesitation in old Juana, that caused the Sub-Prior to appeal to her. "Please your Reverence, I only chanced to hear the poor young man say, 'Oh, Marie! Marie!' one day when I brought him his dinner, which he put away untouched, though I put my best cooking in it."

A slight, scarcely perceptible flush passed over the prisoner's cheek and brow. The King muttered an exclamation; Father Francis's brow contracted, and several of the nobles looked uneasily from one to the other.

"At what time did the prisoner leave his apartments the night of the murder?" continued the Sub-Prior.

"Exactly as the great bell of the cathedral chimed eleven," was the ready reply from Pedro and Juana at the same moment.

"Did you hear nothing but his hasty movements, as you describe? Did he not call for attendance, or a light? Remember, you are on oath," he continued sternly, as he observed the hesitation with which old Pedro muttered "No;" and that Juana was silent. "The church punishes false swearers. Did he speak or not?"

"He called for a light, please your Reverence, but—"

"But you did not choose to obey at an hour so late!" sternly responded Father Francis; "and by such neglect may be guilty of accelerating the death of the innocent, and concealing the real murderer! You allege that Senor Stanley returned from some military duty at sunset, and slept from then till just before eleven, so soundly that you could not rouse him even for his evening meal. This was strange for a man with murder in his thoughts! Again, that he called for a light, which, you neglected to bring; and Senor Stanley asserts that he missed his sword, but rushed from the house without it. Your culpable neglect, then, prevents our discovering the truth of this assertion; yet you acknowledge he called loudly for light; this appears too unlikely to have been the case, had the prisoner quitted the house with the intention to do murder."

"Intention at that moment he might not have had, Reverend Father," interposed the head of the Associated Brethren, who had taken an active part in the examination. "Were there no evidence as to premeditated desire of vengeance, premeditated insult, and long-entertained enmity, these conclusions might have foundation. As the case stands, they weigh but little. Where evil passions have been excited, opportunity for their indulgence is not likely to pass unused."

"But evidence of that long-entertained enmity and premeditated vengeance we have not yet examined," replied the Sub-Prior. "If it only rest on the suppositions of this old couple, in one of whom it is pretty evident, prejudice is stronger than clearly defined truth, methinks that, despite this circumstantial evidence, there is still hope of the prisoner's innocence, more especially as we have one other important fact to bring forward. You are certain," he continued, addressing old Pedro, "that the bell chimed eleven when Senor Stanley quitted your dwelling?" The man answered firmly in the affirmative. "And you will swear that the Senor slept from sunset till that hour?"

"I dare not swear to it, your Reverence, for Juana and I were at a neighbor's for part of that time; but on our return, Juana took up his supper again, and found him so exactly in the same position as we had left him, that we could not believe he had even moved."

"Was he alone in the house during this interval?"

"No; the maid Beta was at her work in the room below Senor Stanley's."

"Let her be brought here."

The order was so rapidly obeyed, that it was very evident she was close at hand; but so terribly alarmed at the presence in which she stood, as to compel the Sub-Prior to adopt the gentlest possible tone, to get any answer at all. He merely inquired if, during the absence of her master and mistress, she had heard any movement in the prisoner's room. She said that she thought she had—a quiet, stealthy step, and also a sound as if a door in the back of the house closed; but the sounds were so very indistinct, she had felt them at the time more like a dream than reality; and the commencement of the storm had so terrified her, that she did not dare move from her seat.

"And what hour was this?"

It might have been about nine; but she could not say exactly. And from the assertion that she did hear a slight sound, though puzzlingly cross-questioned, she never wavered. The King and the Sub-Prior both looked disappointed. The chief of the Santa Hermandad expressed himself confirmed in his previous supposition.

The prisoner retained his calmness; but a gleam of intelligence seemed to flit across his features.

"You would speak, Senor Stanley," interposed the King, as the girl was dismissed. "We would gladly hear you."

"I would simply say, your Highness," replied Stanley, gratefully, "that it is not unlikely Beta may have heard such sounds. I am convinced my evening draught was drugged; and the same secret enemy who did this, to give him opportunity undiscovered to purloin my sword—may, nay, *must* have entered my chamber during that deathlike sleep, and committed the theft which was to burden an innocent man with his deed of guilt. The deep stillness in the house might have permitted her ear to catch the step, though my sleep was too profound. I could hardly have had time to waken, rise, commit the deed of death, and return to such a completely deceiving semblance of sleep, in the short hour of Pedro and Juana's absence; and if I had, what madness would have led me there again, and so appalled me, as to prevent all effort of escape?"

"Conscience," replied the chief of the Santa Hermandad, sternly. "The impelling of the Divine Spirit, whom you had profaned, and who in justice so distracted you, as to lead you blindly to your own destruction—no marvel the darkness oppressed, and the storm appalled you; or that heaven in its wrath should ordain the events you yourself have described—the fall over your own victim, and the horror thence proceeding. We have heard that your early years have been honorable, Senor Stanley, and to such, guilt is appalling even in its accomplishment. Methinks, Father Francis, we need now but the evidence of the premeditation."

"Your pardon, brother; but such, conclusions are somewhat over-hasty. It is scarcely probable, had Senor Stanley returned after the committal of such a deed, that his reentrance should not have been heard as well as his departure; whereas the witness expressly declares, that though her attention was awakened by the previous faint sound, and she listened frequently, she never heard another movement, till her master and mistress's return; and as they went into the Senor's room directly, and found him without the very least appearance of having moved, justice compels us to incline to the belief in Senor Stanley's suggestion—that he could scarcely have had sufficient time to rouse, depart, do murder, and feign sleep during Pedro Benito's brief interval of absence."

"We will grant that so it may be, Reverend Father, but what proof have we that the murder had not been just committed when the body and the assassin were discovered?"

Father Francis replied, by commanding the appearance of Don Ferdinand's steward, and after the customary formula, inquired what hour his late lamented master had quitted his mansion the night of the murder. The man replied, without hesitation, "Exactly as the chimes played the quarter before nine."

"But was not that unusually early? The hour of meeting at the castle was ten, and the distance from Don Ferdinand's mansion not twenty minutes' ride, and scarce forty minutes' walk. Are you perfectly certain as to the hour?"

"I can take my oath upon it, your Reverence, and Lopez will say the same. Our sainted master (Jesu rest his soul!) called to him a few minutes before he entered my lady's room, and told him not to get his horse ready, as he should walk to the castle. Lopez asked as to who should attend him, and his reply was he would go alone. He had done so before, and so we were not surprised; but we were grieved at his look, for it seemed of suffering, unlike himself, and were noticing it to each other as he passed us, after quitting my lady, and so quickly and so absorbed, that he did not return our salutation, which he never in all his life neglected to do before. My poor, poor master! little did we think we should never see him again!" And the man's unconstrained burst of grief excited anew the indignation of the spectators against the crime, till then almost forgotten, in the intense interest as to the fate of the accused. Lopez was called, and corroborated the steward's account exactly.

"If he left his house at a quarter before nine, at what hour, think you, he would reach the Calle Soledad?"

From ten to fifteen minutes past the hour, your Reverence, unless detained by calling elsewhere on his way."

"Did he mention any intention of so doing?" The answer was in the negative. "According to this account, then, the murder must have taken place between nine and ten; and Senor Stanley was not heard to quit his apartment till eleven. This would corroborate his own assertion, that the deed was committed ere he reached the spot."

"But what proof have we that Don Ferdinand was not detained on his way?" replied the chief of the Santa Hermandad. "His domestics assert no more than the hour of his quitting the house."

"The hour of the royal meeting was ten," rejoined the Sub-Prior; "he was noted for regularity, and was not likely to have voluntarily lingered so long, as not even to reach the Calle till one hour afterwards."

"Not voluntarily; but we have heard that he appeared more suffering than he was ever seen to do. His illness might have increased, and so cause detention; and yet, on even partial recovery, we know him well enough to believe he would still have endeavored to join his Highness."

"He would; but there is evidence that when brought to the castle, he had been dead at the very least three hours. Let Curador Benedicto come forward."

A respectable man, dressed in black, and recognized at once as the leech or doctor of the royal household, obeyed the summons, and on being questioned, stated that he had examined the body the very moment it had been conveyed to the castle, in the hope of discovering some signs of animation, however faint. But life was totally extinct, and, according to his judgment, had been so at the very least three hours."

"And what hour was this?"

"Just half-an-hour after midnight."

A brief silence followed the leech's dismissal; Ferdinand still seemed perplexed and uneasy, and not one countenance, either of the nobles or Associated Brethren, evinced satisfaction.

"Our task, instead of decreasing in difficulty, becomes more and more complicated, my lords and brethren," observed the Sub-Prior, after waiting for the chief of the Santa Hermandad to speak. "Had we any positive proof, that Senor Stanley really slept from the hour of sunset till eleven the same evening, and never quitted his quarters until then, we might hope that the sentence of Curador Benedicto, as to the length of time life had been extinct in his supposed victim, might weigh strongly against the circumstantial chain of evidence brought against him. Believing that the prisoner having slept from the hour of sunset to eleven was a proven and witnessed fact, I undertook the defensive and argued in his favor. The sounds heard by the girl Beta may or may not have proceeded from the stealthy movements of the accused, and yet justice forbids our passing them by unnoticed. The time of this movement being heard, and that of the murder, according to the leech's evidence, tally so exactly that we cannot doubt but the one had to do with the other; but whether it were indeed the prisoner's step, or that of the base purloiner of his sword, your united judgment must decide. Individual supposition, in a matter of life or death, can be of no avail. My belief, as you may have discovered, inclines to the prisoner's innocence. My brother, the chief Hermano, as strongly believes in his guilt. And it would appear as if the evidence itself, supports the one judgment equally with the other; contradictory and complicated, it has yet been truthfully brought forward and strictly examined. Your united judgment, Senors and Hermanos, must therefore decide the prisoner's fate."

"But under your favor, Reverend Father, all the evidence has not been brought forward," rejoined the chief Hermano. "And methinks that which is still to come is the most important of the whole. That the business is complicated, and judgment most difficult, I acknowledge, and therefore gladly avail myself of any remaining point on which the scale may turn. Sworn as I am to administer impartial justice, prejudice against the prisoner I can have none; but the point we have until now overlooked, appears sufficient to decide not only individual but general opinion. I mean the *premeditated vengeance* sworn by the prisoner against the deceased—long indulged and proclaimed enmity, and premeditated determination to take his life or lose his own. Don Ferdinand Morales—be his soul assoilized!—was so universally beloved, so truly the friend of all ranks and conditions of men, that to believe in the existence of any other enmity towards his person is almost impossible. We have evidence that the prisoner was at feud with him—was harboring some design against him for weeks. It may be he was even refused by Don Ferdinand the meeting he desired, and so sought vengeance by the midnight dagger. Let the evidence of this enmity be examined, and according or not as premeditated malice is elicited, so let your judgment be pronounced."

"Ay, so let it be," muttered the King as a loud murmur of assent ran through the hall. "We have two witnesses for this; and, by heaven, if the one differ from the other in the smallest point, the prisoner may still be reprieved!"

Whether the royal observation was heard or not, there was no rejoinder, for at the summoning of the chief Hermano, Don Luis Garcia stood before the assemblage. His appearance excited surprise in many present, and in none more than the prisoner himself. He raised his head, which had been resting on his hand during the address of the Sub-Prior, and the reply of the Hermano, and looked at the new witness with bewildered astonishment. As Don Luis continued his relation of the stormy interview between the deceased and the accused, and the words of threatening used by the latter, astonishment itself, changed into an indignation and loathing impossible to be restrained.

"Thou base dishonored villain!" he exclaimed, so suddenly and wrathfully that it startled more by its strange contrast with his former calmness than by its irreverent interruption to the formula of the examination; "where wert thou during this interview? Hearing so well, and so invisibly concealed, none but the voluntary spy could have heard all this; so skilfully detailed that thou wouldst seem in very truth *witness* as well as hearer. What *accident* could have led thee to the most retired part of Don Ferdinand's garden, and, being there, detained thee? Thou treacherous villain! and on thy evidence—evidence so honorably, so truthfully obtained, my life or death depends! Well, be it so."

"But so it shall not be," interposed the King himself, ere either Sub-Prior or the Hermano could reply; "even as the prisoner, we ourselves hold evidence dishonestly obtained of little moment—nay, of no weight whatever. Be pleased, Don Luis Garcia, to explain the casualty which led you, at such an important moment, to Don Ferdinand's grounds; or name some other witness. The voluntary listener is, in our mind, dishonorable as the liar, and demanding no more account."

With a mien and voice of the deepest humility, Don Luis replied; grieving that his earnest love of justice should expose him to the royal displeasure; submitting meekly to unjust suspicion as concerned himself, but still upholding the truth and correctness of his statement. The other witness to the same, he added mysteriously, he had already named to his Royal Highness.

"And she waits our pleasure," replied the King; "Don Felix d'Estaban, be pleased to conduct the last witness to our presence."

CHAPTER XX.

But love is strong. There came
Strength upon Woman's fragile heart and frame;
There came swift courage.

MRS. HEMANS.

Death has no pang
More keen than this. Oh, wherefore art thou here?

MRS. HEMANS.

A profound silence followed Don Felix's departure. Don Luis had so evidently evaded the King's demand, as to how he had witnessed this important interview, that even those most prejudiced in his favor, on account of his extreme sanctity, found themselves doubting his honor; and those who had involuntarily been prejudiced against him, by the indefinable something pervading his countenance and voice, doubly rejoiced that their unspoken antipathy had some foundation. In modern courts of justice, to refuse the validity of evidence merely because the manner of obtaining it was supposed dishonorable, would be pronounced the acme of folly and romance. In the age of which we write, and in Spain especially, the sense of honor was so exquisitely refined, that the King's rebuke, and determination not to allow the validity of Don Luis's evidence, unless confirmed by an honorable witness, excited no surprise whatever; every noble, nay, every one of the Associated Brethren, there present, would have said the same; and the eager wonder, as to the person of the witness on whom so much stress was laid, became absolutely intense. The prisoner was very evidently agitated; his cheek flushed and paled in rapid alternation, and a suppressed but painful exclamation escaped from him as Don Felix re-entered, leading with him a female form; but the faint sound was unheard, save by the King and the Sub-Prior, who had been conversing apart during d'Estaban's absence—lost in the irrepressible burst of wonder and sympathy, which broke from all within the hall, as in the new witness, despite the change of garb, and look, from the dazzling beauty of health and peace, to the attenuated form of anxiety and sorrow, they recognized at once the widow of the murdered, Donna Marie. Nor was this universal sympathy lessened, when, on partially removing her veil, to permit a clear view of the scene around her, her sweet face was disclosed to all—profoundly, almost unnaturally, calm, indeed—but the cheek and lips were perfectly colorless; the ashy whiteness of the former rendered them more striking from the long black lash resting upon it, unwetted by a single tear: and from the peculiarly dark eye appearing the larger, from the attenuation of the other features. One steady and inquiring glance she was seen to fix upon the prisoner, and then she bent in homage to the Sovereign; and emotion, if there were any, passed unseen.

"Sit, lady," said the King, with ready courtesy, touched more than he could have imagined possible, by the change fourteen short days had wrought. "We would feign render this compelled summons as brief and little fatiguing as may be: none can grieve more than ourselves at this harsh intrusion on thy hours of sorrow; but in a great measure the doom of life or death rests with thee, and justice forbids our neglecting evidence so important. Yet sit, lady; we command it."

"It needs not, gracious Sovereign; my strength will not fail me," replied Marie, her sweet voice falling distinctly on every ear, while Stanley started at its calmness; and she gracefully refused the seat Don Felix proffered. "Give no more thought to me than to any other witness; it is not a subject's place to sit in presence of her Sovereign."

But Ferdinand's kindliest feelings were excited, and instead of permitting the Sub-Prior to give the necessary details, he himself, with characteristic brevity, but clearly and kindly, narrated the progress of the evidence for and against the prisoner, and how great the weight laid on the proofs, if there were any, of acknowledged enmity, and premeditated injury, on the part of the accused towards the deceased. The questions to which he was compelled to request her reply were simply, "Was she aware of any cause of hatred existing between the accused and the deceased?" "Had she ever heard opprobrious and insulting epithets used by the former or the latter?" "or any threat, implying that the death of Don Ferdinand Morales was desired by the prisoner?" "Had she ever seen the prisoner draw his sword upon the deceased?—and had she any reason to believe that Don Ferdinand had ever refused, or intended to refuse to meet the prisoner in honorable combat, and so urged the gratification of vengeance by a deed of murder? Reverend Father," continued the King, "be pleased yourself to administer the customary oath."

Father Francis instantly rose from his seat, and taking the large and richly embossed silver crucifix from the Monk, who had administered the oath to all the other witnesses, himself approached Marie. "Marie Henriquez Morales," he said, as he reverentially held the solemn symbol of his religion before her, "art thou well advised of the solemnity of the words thou art called upon to speak? If so, swear to speak the truth, the whole truth, and nothing but the truth. Swear by the Holy Symbol which I support; by the unpronounceable name of the Father, by the flesh and blood, the resurrection and the life of our Lord and Saviour Christ Jesu; by the Holy Spirit; by the saving and glorious Trinity; by the goodly army of Saints and

Martyrs; daughter, swear, and the blessing or the curse be with you as you swear true or falsely."

The fine countenance of the Sub-Prior glowed with the holy enthusiasm of his appeal; his form, as he stood, one hand clasping the crucifix, the other emphatically raised, seemed dilated to unusual height and majesty, and the deep solemnity of his accents so enhanced the awful responsibility of the oath, that it thrilled throughout the multitude as it had never done before. So deep was the stillness which followed, that not one of those vast crowds seemed to breathe. To the prisoner it was a moment of intense emotion: for if, indeed, Marie had once told him truth, that oath, to her, even in its solemnity, was as nought; but ere he could even think as to the wording of her answer, that answer came, and so distinct, so unfalteringly spoken, that there was not one person present who even strained his ear to catch the words.

"Reverend Father," she said, "I am grateful for thy counsel; and, believe me, am well advised of the truth and solemnity of the words I speak. But I cannot aid his Grace, and these his subjects, in their decision as to the prisoner's sentence. My evidence is valueless. I belong to that race whose word is never taken as witness, for or against, in a court of justice. I cannot take the oath required, for I deny the faith in which it is administered. I am a JEWESS!"

A wild cry, in every variety of intonation—astonishment, horror, wrath, and perhaps terror, ran through the hall—from Sovereign, Noble, Monk, and Citizen, simultaneously. Father Francis staggered back several paces, as if there were contamination in remaining by her side, and then stood as rooted to the ground, his hand convulsively grasping the crucifix which had nearly fallen from his hold; his lips apart, his nostrils slightly distended, and his eyes almost starting from their sockets, in the horrified and astonished gaze he fixed upon the pale and fragile being who had dared speak such impious words. The attendant fathers rose simultaneously, and formed a semicircle round their superior, ready, at his slightest signal, to hurl down on her the anathema of the church; reverence to the Sub-Prior alone preventing the curse from instantly bursting forth. The nobles, the Associated Brethren, Ferdinand himself, started almost unconsciously to their feet, and an eager rush brought many of the citizens still nearer to the scene of action. The prisoner, with an irresistible impulse, darted forwards, and ere any one had recovered from his trance of bewilderment, had flung himself at Marie's feet.

"Marie! Marie!" he exclaimed, in a voice so hoarse and choked, its words were heard by her alone. "Oh! why hast thou done this? Why not take the required oath, and condemn me at once? Marie, I am unworthy of such self-sacrifice!"

"Ha! didst thou slay him then? Have I judged thee too kindly, Arthur," she answered; and the hand she laid heavily on his shoulder trembled so violently, it was evident she had thus placed it only to save her from sinking to the ground, for the unnatural strength had gone.

"No!" he exclaimed, in a tone and with a look that satisfied her at once, and there was no time for more. The King had perceived that the Sub-Prior was recovering composure, and with it energy of action; though himself a zealous Catholic, he felt compelled to save Marie. "Hold! hold!" he said hastily, as Father Francis was about to speak. "Reverend Father, we pray thee, be not over hasty in this matter; these are strange and terrible words; but they are meaningless; they must be. Her misery has turned her brain; she is mad; heed her not; be silent all of ye! See how she glares upon the prisoner! Is that the look of sanity? By St. Francis, we have done wrong to call her hither! Stand back, good fathers. Remove the prisoner; and let Donna Marie be conducted from the hall. Our Consort should have warned us of this!"

"Forbear, my liege!" replied the Sub-Prior sternly. "The blaspheming words were all too calmly and collectively spoken for the ravings of madness. Let not the false unbeliever pass hence till at least she has done reverence to the sacred symbol, she has, by daring denial, insulted. As thou wouldst save thine own soul from hell-fire, my liege, interfere not in this!"

As he spoke, several soldiers had endeavored rudely to drag Arthur from Marie: he strove fiercely for freedom, for but one hour's power to protect her, but in vain. And the look she fixed upon him, as he was torn from her, from its contrast with her previous profound calm, did indeed seem almost of madness. The excitement which had enabled her to make this dread avowal—an avowal comprising such variety, and terrible danger, that the magnitude of the sacrifice comprised in the confession can now scarcely be understood; danger, not merely from the vengeance of the church for long years of fraud, nor from the secret and awful tribunal of whose existence she was conscious (though not of its close vicinity); not merely these, but danger from the wrath, and terrors of the secret members of her own faith, who might naturally imagine their own safety endangered in the suspicion, engendered by her rash confession. Of all this she had thought; had believed herself strengthened to brave and bear every possible suffering, rather than breathe those words which must seal Stanley's fate; but now that she had spoken, though she would not have recalled them if she could—such an overpowering, crushing sense of all she had drawn upon herself, such fearful, spectral shapes of indefinable horror came upon her, that, as the Sub-Prior stood again before her with the uplifted cross, bidding her kneel and acknowledge him whose fate it imaged—she burst into a wild hysteric laugh, and fell prone upon the floor.

"Said I not she was mad? And what need was there for this unmanly violence?" angrily exclaimed the Monarch; and, starting from his seat, he authoritatively waved back the denouncing monks, and himself bent over Marie. The Duke of Murcia, Don Felix d'Estaban, the Lord of Aguilar, and several other nobles following the Sovereign's example, hastened to her assistance. But to restore animation was not in their power, and on the King's whispered commands, Don Felix gently, even tenderly raised her, and bore her in his arms from the hall. Even in that moment of excitement Ferdinand could not forbear glancing at the prisoner, whose passionate struggles to escape from the guard, when Marie fell, had been noticed by all, and unhappily, combined with, his previous irritation, but confirmed the unspoken suspicions of many as to the real cause of his enmity against Don Ferdinand. The expression of his countenance was of such contending, terrible suffering, that the King hastily withdrew his gaze, vainly endeavoring to disbelieve, as he had done, the truth of Garcia's charge.

Order was at length universally restored, and after a brief silence, the chief of the Santa Hermandad demanded of the prisoner if he had aught to say in his defence, or reply himself to Don Luis Garcia's charge. The reply was a stern, determined negative; and, deputed so to do by the Sub-Prior, who seemed so absorbed in the horror of Marie's daring avowal, as to be incapable of further interference, the Hermano proceeded to sum up the evidence. As the widow of the deceased had so strangely, yet effectually deprived them of her evidence, he said, he thought some slight regard ought to be paid to Don Luis Garcia's words; but even without doing so, the circumstantial evidence, though contradictory and complicated, was enough in his opinion to convict the prisoner; but he referred to his associates and to the peers then present, to pronounce sentence. His task was but to sum up the evidence, which he trusted he had done distinctly; his opinion was that of but one individual; there were at least fifty or sixty voices, to confirm or to oppose it.

Deep and sustained as had been the interest throughout the trial, it was never more intense than during the awful pause which heralded the prisoner's doom. It was spoken at length; the majority alike of the nobles and of the Santa Hermandad, believed and pronounced him guilty, and sentence of death was accordingly passed; but the Duke of Murcia then stepped forward, and urged the following, not only in the name of his brother peers, but in the name of his native sovereign, Isabella; that in consideration of the complicated and contradictory evidence, of the prisoner's previous high character, and of his strongly protested innocence, a respite of one month should be granted between sentence and execution, to permit prayers to be offered up throughout Spain for the discovery of the real murderer, or at least allow time for some proof of innocence to appear; during which time the prisoner should be removed from the hateful dungeon he had till that morning occupied, and confined under strict ward, in one of the turrets of the castle; and that, if at the end of the granted month affairs remained as they were then, that no proof of innocence appeared, a scaffold was to be erected in the Calle Soledad, on the exact spot where the murder was committed; there the prisoner, publicly degraded from the honors and privileges of chivalry, his sword broken before him, his spurs ignominiously struck from his heels, would then receive the award of the law, death from hanging, the usual fate of the vilest and commonest malefactors.

Ferdinand and the Sub-Prior regarded him attentively while this sentence was pronounced, but not a muscle in his countenance moved; what it expressed it would have been difficult to define; but it seemed as if his thoughts were on other than himself. The King courteously thanked the assemblage for their aid in a matter so momentous, and at once ratified their suggestion. The Associated Brethren were satisfied that it was Isabella's will; confident also in their own power to prevent the evasion, and bring about the execution of the sentence, if still required, at the termination of the given time; and with a brief but impressive address from the Sub-Prior to the prisoner, the assemblage dispersed.

But the excitement of the city ceased not with the conclusion of the trial: not alone the populace, but the nobles themselves, even the Holy Fathers and Associated Brethren were seen, forming in various groups, conversing eagerly and mysteriously. The interest in the prisoner had in some measure given way to a new excitement. Question followed question, conjecture followed conjecture, but nothing could solve the mystery of Donna Marie's terrible avowal, or decrease the bewilderment and perplexity which, from various causes, it created in every mind. One alone, amongst the vast crowds which had thronged the trial, shunned his fellows. Not a change in the calm, cold, sneering expression of Don Luis Garcia's countenance had betrayed either surprise at, or sympathy with, any one of the various emotions stirring that vast multitude of human hearts; he had scarcely even moved his position during the continuance of the trial, casting indeed many a glance on the immediate scene of action, from beneath his thick and shadowy eyebrows, which concealed the sinister gaze from observation. He shunned the face of day; but in his own dark haunts, and with his hellish colleagues, plans were formed and acted on, with a rapidity which, to minds less matured in iniquity, would have seemed incredible.

CHAPTER XXI.

The quality of mercy is not strain'd,
It droppeth as the gentle rain from Heaven
Upon the place beneath. It is twice blessed,
It blesseth him that gives, and him that takes;
'Tis mightiest in the mightiest; it becomes
The throned monarch better than his crown.

SHAKSPEARE.

The interest attending a trial, in which royalty had evinced such powerful sympathy, naturally extended to every member of Isabella's female train: her anxiety as to the issue had been very visible, notwithstanding her calm and quiet demeanor. The Infanta Isabella and the Infant Don Juan were with her during the morning as usual; but even their infantile caresses, dearer to her true woman's heart than all her vast possessions, had failed to disperse the anxiety of thought. Few can peruse the interesting life of Isabella of Castile without being struck by the fact, that even as her public career was one of unmixed prosperity for her country and herself, her private sorrows and domestic trials vied, in their bitterness, with those of the poorest and humblest of her subjects. Her first-born, the Infanta Isabella, who united all the brilliant and endearing qualities of her mother, with great beauty, both of face and form, became a loving bride only to become a widow—a mother, only to gaze upon her babe, and die; and her orphan quickly followed. Don Juan, the delight and pride and hope of his parents, as of the enthusiasm and almost idolatry of their subjects, died in his twentieth year. The hapless Catherine of Arragon, with whose life of sorrow and neglect every reader of English history is acquainted, though they sometimes forget her illustrious parentage; her sorrows indeed Isabella was spared, as she died before Henry the Eighth ascended the English throne. But it was Juana, the wife of Philip, and mother of Charles V., whose intellects, always feeble, and destroyed by the neglect and unkindness of the husband she idolized, struck the last and fatal blow. And she, whom all Europe regarded with unfeigned veneration— she whom her own subjects so idolized, they would gladly have laid down a thousand lives for hers—she fell a victim to a mother's heart-consuming grief.[A] Who then, after perusing her life, and that of how many other sovereigns, will refuse them, the meed of sympathy, because, raised so far above us in *outward* things, we deem the griefs and feelings of common humanity unknown and uncared for? To our mind, the destiny of the Sovereign, the awful responsibility, the utter loneliness of station, the general want of sympathy, the proneness to be condemned for faults or omissions of which they are, individually, as innocent as their contemners, present a subject for consideration and sympathy, and ought to check the unkind thoughts and hasty condemnation, excited merely because they are placed in rank and circumstances above us. A King of kings has placed them there, and a Universal Father calls them His children, even as ourselves.

[Footnote A: Isabella had been previously attacked by dangerous indisposition, from which, however, the natural strength of her constitution would have enabled her in some degree to rally; but the springs of life had been injured by previous bereavement. Her lungs became affected, and the symptoms of decline rapidly and fatally increased from continual affliction of mind.—*History of Spain*.]

Isabella had not seen Marie that morning; her trusty attendant, Donna Inez de Leon, had alone been with her, and had reported that she was calm and composed, and more like herself than she had been since her bereavement. Time passed but slowly, and Catherine Pas, the same high-spirited maiden mentioned in a former chapter, perceiving that the Queen's anxiety evidently increased as the hours waned, quietly left the chamber, unbidden, and even unseen. A brief interval saw her return, and with a countenance so expressive of horrified bewilderment, as to excite the astonishment of all.

"Oh, madam!" she exclaimed, as she flew to the Queen's seat, regardless of either decorum or rebuke; "Oh, madam, it has killed her; she is dying!"

"Dying!" repeated Isabella, and the whole strength of her character was put forth, to prevent her starting from her seat. "Dying!—who is dying? Speak out, in Santa Maria's name!"

"Donna Marie—the poor, unhappy Marie; she has been borne from the hall! Don Felix had her in his arms; I saw her; I followed them, and she looked dead, quite dead; they would not let me go to her at first, till I called them hard-hearted wretches! And I have tried to rouse her, but I could not. Oh, save her, gracious madam! Do not let her die!"

"And have they none with her?" demanded the Queen. "But whom can they have, save her own terrified women? Inez—Leonor—go to her at once! Your skill and tenderness will soon revive her; this silly child is terrified at shadows. 'Tis but a faint, such as followed the announcement of her husband's death. If any one dare refuse you entrance, tell them you go in your Queen's name. Foolish trembler," she added, in a tone of relief, as her commands were instantly obeyed, "why this excessive agitation, when thou hast seen a faint like this before?"

"Nay, but by your leave, gracious madam, I have not," replied Catherine, with emotion. "There is far more of horror in this; she is cold—cold, like stone; and they have planted a guard at the entrance of her apartments, and they tell a tale so wild and strange, I cannot give it credence!"

"Ha! what say they?" demanded the Queen hastily, her eyes flashing with light, as they always did when she was excited. "What can it be, too wild and strange for thy hair-brained fancy to believe? Marvellous it must be indeed!"

Isabella spoke jestingly, but her heart was not with her words: and Catherine replied with tears starting to her eyes, "Oh, do not speak thus, my liege. It is indeed no theme for jest." And she continued so rapidly, that to any but the quickened mind of Isabella, her words must have seemed unintelligible. "They say she is a heretic, royal madam! Nay, worse—a blaspheming unbeliever; that she has refused to take the oath, on plea of not believing in the Holy Catholic Church; that she has insulted, has trampled on the sacred cross! Nor is this all—worse, yet worse; they say she has proclaimed herself a JEWESS!—an abhorred, an unbelieving Jewess!"

A general start and loud exclamation of horror was the natural rejoinder to this unlooked-for intelligence; but not from Isabella, whose flashing eyes were still fixed on the young girl's face, as to read in her soul the confirmation of these strange words. "What dost thou say?" she said at length, and so slowly, a second might have intervened between each word. "Speak! let me hear again! A Jewess! Santa Maria! But no; it *cannot* be. They must have told thee false!"

So the Queen spoke; but ere Catherine had concluded a calmer repetition of the tale, Marie's words of the preceding evening rushed back on her mind, confirming it but too surely. "To-morrow all will be distinct and clear enough!" she had said; ay, distinct it was; and so engrossingly intense became the thoughts thronging in her mind, bewildering succession, that Isabella sat motionless, her brow leaning on her hand, wholly unconscious of the lapse of time.

A confusion in the gallery, and the words, "The King! the King!" roused her at length; and never was the appearance of Ferdinand more welcome, not only to Isabella, but to her attendants, as giving them the longed-for opportunity to retire, and so satisfy curiosity, and give vent to the wonderment which, from their compelled silence in Isabella's presence, had actually become intolerable.

Ferdinand speedily narrated the affairs of the morning, and concluded by inquiring if any thing had occurred in her interview with Marie to excite suspicion of her mad design. The Queen replied by relating, in her turn, all that had passed between them. The idea of madness could no longer exist; there was not the faintest hope that in a moment of frenzy she had spoken falsely.

"And yet, was it not madness," the King urged, "thus publicly to avow a determined heresy, and expose herself to all the horrors of the church's vengeance! 'Years of deception and fraud!' she told thee, 'would be disclosed.' By St. Francis! fraud enough. Who could have suspected the wife of Don Ferdinand Morales a Jewess? It was on this account he kept her so retired. How could he reconcile his conscience to a union with one of a race so abhorred, beautiful as she is? And where could he have found her? But this matters not: it is all wild conjecture, save the madness of the avowal. What cause could there have been for such self-sacrifice?"

"There was a cause," replied the Queen earnestly; "cause enough to render life to her of little moment. Do not ask me my meaning, dearest Ferdinand; I would not do her such wrong as to breathe the suspicion that, spite of myself, spite of incomprehensible mystery, will come, even to thee. Do not let us regret her secret is discovered. Let her but recover from the agony of these repeated trials, and with the help of our holy fathers, we may yet turn her from her abhorred faith, and so render her happy in this world, and secure her salvation in the next."

"The help of the holy fathers!" repeated the King. "Nay, Isabel, their sole help will be to torture and burn! They will accuse her of insulting, by years of deceit, the holy faith, of which she has appeared a member. Nay, perchance of using foul magic on Morales (whom the saints preserve), and then thou knowest what will follow!"

The Queen shuddered. "Never with my consent, my husband! From the first moment I beheld this unfortunate, something attracted me towards her; her misery deepened the feeling; and even now, knowing what she is, affection lingers. The Holy Virgin give me pardon, if 'tis sin!"

"For such sin I will give thee absolution, dearest," replied the King, half jestingly, half earnestly. "Do not look so grave. No one knows, or values thy sterling piety half so tenderly and reverentially as I do. But this is no common case. Were Marie one of those base and grovelling wretches, those accursed unbelievers, who taint our fair realm with their abhorred rites—think of nothing but gold and usury, and how best to cheat their fellows; hating us almost as intensely as we hate them—why, she should abide by the fate she has drawn upon herself. But the wife of my noble Morales, one who has associated so long with zealous Catholics, that she is already most probably one of us, and only avowed her descent from some mysterious cause—by St. Francis, she shall be saved!"

"But how?" inquired Isabella anxiously. "Wouldst thou deny her faith to Father Francis, and persuade him she has spoken falsely?"

The King shook his head. "That will never do, Isabel. I have had the holy man closeted with me already, insisting on the sanity of her words, and urging me to resign the unbeliever at once to the tender mercy of the church. All must depend on thee."

"On me?" repeated Isabella, in a tone of surprised yet anxious inquiry.

"On thee, love. Thy perfect humility is ignorant of the fact—yet it is nevertheless perfectly true—that thou art reverenced, well nigh canonized, by the holy church; and thy words will have weight when mine would be light as air. Refuse the holy fathers all access to her; say she is unfitted to encounter them; that she is ill; nay, mad, if thou wilt. Bring forward the state in which she was borne from the hall; her very laugh (by St. Francis, it rings in my ear still) to confirm it, and they will believe thee. The present excitement will gradually subside, and her very existence be forgotten. Let none but thy steadiest, most pious matrons have access to her; forbid thy young maidens to approach or hold converse with her; and her being under thy protection can do harm to none. Let her be prisoner in her own apartments, an thou wilt; she deserves punishment for the deception practised towards thee. Treat her as thou deemest best, only give her not up to the mercy of the church!"

"Talk not of it," replied the Queen earnestly. "Unbeliever though she be, offspring of a race which every true Catholic must hold in abhorrence, she is yet a *woman*, Ferdinand, and, as such, demands and shall receive the protection of her Queen. Yet, would there were some means of saving her from the eternal perdition to which, as a Jewess, she is destined; some method, without increase of suffering, to allure her, as a penitent and believing child, to the bosom of our holy mother church."

"And to do this, who so fitted as thyself, dearest Isabel?" answered the King with earnest affection. "Thou hast able assistants in some of thy older matrons, and may after a while call in the aid of Father Denis, whose kindly nature is better fitted for gentle conversion than either Francis, or thy still sterner chaplain, Torquemada. Thy kindness has gained thee the love of this misguided one; and if any one have sufficient influence to convert, by other than sharp means, it can only be thyself."

Isabella was not long undecided. Her heart felt that to turn Marie from blindness and perdition by kindness and affection would be indeed far more acceptable to the virgin (her own peculiar saint) than the heretic's blood, and she answered with animation, "Then so it shall be, Ferdinand; I fear me, alas! that there will be little reason to prevaricate, to deny all spiritual access to her. Thy report, combined with my terrified Catherine's, gives me but little hope for health or reason. But should she indeed recover, trust me she shall be happy yet."

Great was the astonishment of the guards as they beheld their Sovereign fearlessly enter the chamber of a proclaimed Jewess—a word in their minds synonymous with the lowest, most degraded rank of being; and yet more, to hear and perceive that she herself was administering relief. The attendants of Isabella—whose curiosity was now more than satisfied, for the tale had been repeated with the usual exaggerations, even to a belief that she had used the arts of sorcery on Morales—huddled together in groups, heaping every opprobrious epithet upon her, and accusing her of exposing them all to the horrors of purgatory by contaminating them with her presence. And as the Sovereign re-appeared in her saloon with the leech Benedicto, whose aid she had summoned, there were many who ventured to conjure her not to expose herself to such pollution as the tending of a Jewess—to leave her to the fate her fraud so merited. Even Catherine, finding to disbelieve the tale any longer was impossible, and awed and terrified at the mysterious words of her companions, which told of danger to her beloved mistress, flung herself on her knees before her, clasping her robe to detain her from again seeking the chamber of Marie. Then was the moment for a painter to have seized on the face and form of Isabella! Her eye flashed till its very color was undistinguishable, her lip curled, every feature—usually so mild and feminine—was so transformed by indignation into majesty and unutterable scorn as scarcely to have been recognized. Her slight and graceful form dilated till the very boldest cowered before her, even before she spoke; for never had they so encountered her reproof:—

"Are ye women?" she said at length, in the quiet, concentrated tone of strong emotion; "or are we deceived as to the meaning of your words? Pollution! Are we to see a young, unhappy being perish for want of sympathy and succor, because—forsooth—she is a Jewess? Danger to our soul! We should indeed fear it; did we leave her to die, without one effort to restore health to the frame, and the peace of Christ to the mind! Has every spark of woman's nature faded from your hearts, that ye can speak thus? If for yourselves you fear, tend her not, approach her not—we will ourselves give her the aid she needs. And as for thee," she continued severely, as she forced the now trembling Catherine to stand upright before her, "whose energy to serve Marie we loved and applauded; child as thou art, must thou too speak of pollution? but example may have done this. Follow me, minion; and then talk of pollution if thou canst!" And with a swift step Isabella led the way to the chamber of Marie.

"Behold!" she said emphatically, as she pointed to the unhappy sufferer, who, though restored to life, was still utterly unconscious where she was or who surrounded her; her cheek and brow, white and damp; her large eye lustreless and wandering; her lip and eyelid quivering convulsively; her whole appearance proving too painfully that reason had indeed, for the time, fled. The soul had been strong till the dread words were said; but the re-action had been too much for either frame or mind. "Catherine! thou hast seen her in her beauty, the cherished, the beloved of all who knew her—seen her when no loveliness could mate with hers. Thou seest now the wreck that misery has made, though she has numbered but few more years than thou hast! Detest, abhor, avoid her *faith*—for that we command thee; but her sex, her sorrow, have a claim to sympathy and aid, which not even her race can remove. Jewess though she be, if thou can look on her thus, and still speak of pollution and danger, thou art not what we deemed thee!"

Struck to the heart, alike by the marked display of a mistress she idolized and the sympathy her better nature really felt for Marie, Catherine sunk on her knees by the couch, and burst into tears. Isabella watched her till her unusual indignation subsided, and then said more kindly, "It is enough; go, Catherine. If we judge thee rightly thou wilt not easily forget this lesson! Again I bid thee abhor her faith; but seek to win her to the right path, by gentleness and love, not prejudice and hate."

"Oh! let me tarry here and tend her, my gracious Sovereign," implored Catherine, again clasping Isabella's robe and looking beseechingly in her face—but from a very different feeling to the prompter of the same action a few minutes before—"Oh, madam, do not send me from her! I will be so gentle, so active—watch, tend, serve; only say your Grace's bidding, and I will do it, if I stood by her alone!"

"My bidding would be but the promptings of thine own heart, my girl," replied the Queen, fondly, for she saw the desired impression had been made. "If I need thee—which I may do—I will call upon thee; but now, thou canst do nothing, but think kindly, and judge mercifully—important work indeed, if thou wouldst serve an erring and unhappy fellow-creature, with heart as well as hand. But now go: nay, not so sorrowfully; thy momentary fault is forgiven," she added, kindly, as she extended her hand towards the evidently pained and penitent maiden, who raised it gratefully and reverentially to her lips, and thoughtfully withdrew.

It was not, however, with her attendants only, this generous and high-minded princess had to contend—with them her example was enough; but the task was much more difficult, when the following day, as King Ferdinand had anticipated, brought the stern Sub-Prior of St. Francis to demand, in the church's name, the immediate surrender of Marie. But Isabella's decision once formed never wavered. Marie was under her protection, she said—an erring indeed, but an unhappy young creature, who, by her very confession, had thrown herself on the mercy of her Sovereign—and she would not deliver up the charge. In vain the Prior urged the abomination of a Jewess residing under her very roof—the danger to her soul should she be tempted to associate with her, and that granting protection to an avowed and blaspheming unbeliever must expose her to the suspicions, or, at least the censure of the church. Isabella was inexorable. To his first and second clause she quietly answered as she had done to her own attendants; his third only produced a calm and fearless smile. She knew too well, as did the Prior also, though for the time he chose to forget it, that her character for munificent and heartfelt piety was too well established, not only in Spain but throughout Europe, to be shaken even by the protection of a Jewess. Father Francis then solicited to see her; but even this point he could not gain. Isabella had, alas! no need to equivocate as to the reason of his non-admission to Marie. Reason had indeed returned, and with it the full sense of the dangers she had drawn upon herself; but neither frame nor mind was in a state to encounter such an interview as the Prior demanded.

The severity of Father Francis originated, as we have before remarked, neither in weak intellect nor selfish superstition. Towards himself indeed he never relented either in severity or discipline; towards others benevolence and humanity very often gained ascendency; and something very like a tear glistened in his eye as Isabella forcibly portrayed the state in which Marie still remained. And when she concluded, by frankly imparting her intention, if health were indeed restored, to leave no means untried—even to pursue some degree of severity if nothing else would do—to wean her from her mistaken faith, he not only abandoned his previous intentions, but commended and blessed the nobler purpose of his Sovereign. To his request that Marie might be restrained from all intercourse with the younger members of Isabella's female court—in fact, associate with none but strict and uncompromising Catholics—the Queen readily acceded; and moreover, granted him full permission to examine the mansion of Don Ferdinand Morales, that any books or articles of dangerous or heretical import might be discovered and destroyed.

With these concessions Father Francis left his Sovereign, affected at her goodness and astonished at her influence on himself. He had entered her presence believing nothing could change the severity of his intentions or the harshness of his feelings; he left her with the one entirely renounced, and the other utterly subdued.

Such was the triumph of prejudice achieved by the lofty-minded and generous woman, who swayed the sceptre of Castile.[A] And yet, though every history of the time unites in so portraying her; though her individual character was the noblest, the most magnanimous, the most complete union of masculine intellect with perfect womanhood, ever traced on the pages of the past; though under her public administration her kingdom stood forth the noblest, the most refined, most generous, ay, and the freest, alike in national position, as in individual sentiment, amongst all the nations of Europe, Isabella's was the fated hand to sign two edicts[B] whose consequences extinguished the lustre, diminished the virtues, enslaved the sentiments, checked the commerce, and in a word deteriorated the whole character of Spain.

[Footnote A: We are authorized to give this character to Isabella of Castile, and annex the lustre of such action to her memory; as we know that even when, by the persuasions and representations of Torquemada, the Inquisition was publicly established, Isabella constantly interfered her authority to prevent *zeal* from becoming *inhumanity*. Rendered unusually penetrating by her peculiarly feeling and gentle nature, she discovered, what was concealed from others, "That many enormities may be committed under the veil of religion—many innocent persons falsely accused; their riches being their only crime. Her exertions brought such things to light, and the suborners were punished according to their guilt."—WASHINGTON IRVING'S *Siege of Granada.*—Of Ferdinand too we are told, "*Respetó la jurisdiction ecclesiastica, y conservo la real*," he respected the ecclesiastical jurisdiction, but *guarded* or was *jealous*, for that of the crown. His determination, therefore, to refuse the church's interference in the case of Marie, though unusual to his *age*, is warranted by his larger mind and freer policy.]

[Footnote B: The establishment of the Inquisition, and expulsion of the Jews.]

For fourteen days affairs remained the same. At the end of that period the castle and city of Segovia were thrown anew into a state of the wildest excitement by a most mysterious occurrence—Marie had disappeared.

CHAPTER XXII.

"Meekly had he bowed and prayed,
As not disdaining priestly aid;
And while before the Prior kneeling,
His heart was weaned from earthly feeling:
No more reproach, no more despair—
No thought but heaven, no word but prayer."

BYRON.

Time passed slowly on, and no proof appeared to clear Arthur Stanley's fame. All that man's judgment could counsel, was adopted—secret measures were taken throughout Spain, for the apprehension of any individual suspected of murder, or even of criminal deeds; constant prayers offered up, that if Arthur Stanley were not the real murderer, proofs of his innocence might be made so evident that not even his greatest enemy could doubt any longer; but all seemed of no avail. Week after week passed, and with the exception of one most mysterious occurrence, affairs remained the same. So strong was the belief of the nobles in his innocence, that the most strenuous exertions were made in his favor; but, strong as Ferdinand's own wish was to save him, his love of justice was still stronger; though the testimony of Don Luis might be set aside, calm deliberation on all the evidence against him marked it as sufficiently strong to have sentenced any other so accused at once. The resolute determination to purge their kingdom from the black crimes of former years, which both sovereigns felt and unitedly acted upon, urged them to conquer every private wish and feeling, rather than depart from the line laid down. The usual dispensers of justice, the Santa Hermandad—men chosen by their brother citizens for their lucid judgment, clearness of perception, and utter absence of all overplus of chivalrous feeling, in matters of cool dispassionate reasoning—were unanimous in their belief in the prisoner's guilt, and only acquiesced in the month's reprieve, because it was Isabella's wish. Against their verdict what could be brought forward? In reality nothing but the prisoner's own strongly-attested innocence—an attestation most forcible in the minds of the Sovereign and the nobles, but of no weight whatever to men accustomed to weigh, and examine, and cross-examine, and decide on proof, or at least from analogy, and never from an attestation, which the greatest criminals might as forcibly make. The power and election of these men Ferdinand and Isabella had confirmed. How could they, then, interfere in the present case, and shackle the judgment which they had endowed with authority, dispute and deny the sentence they had previously given permission to pronounce? Pardon they might, and restore to life and liberty; but the very act of pronouncing pardon supposed belief in and proclamation of guilt. There was but one thing which could save him and satisfy justice, and that was the sentence of "not guilty." For this reason Ferdinand refused every petition for Stanley's reprieve, hoping indeed, spite of all reason, that even at the eleventh hour evidence of his innocence would and must appear.

Stanley himself had no such hope. All his better and higher nature had been called forth by the awful and mysterious death of Morales, dealt too by his own sword—that sword which, in his wild passions, he had actually prayed might shed his blood. The film of passion had dropped alike from mental and bodily vision. He beheld his irritated feelings in their true light, and knew himself in thought a murderer. He would have sacrificed life itself, could he but have recalled the words of insult offered to one so noble; not for the danger to himself from their threatening nature, but for the injurious injustice done to the man from whom he had received a hundred acts of little unobtrusive kindnesses, and whom he had once revered as the model of every thing virtuous and noble—services which Morales had rendered him, felt gratefully perhaps at the time, but forgotten in the absorption of thought or press of occupation during his sojourn in Sicily, now rushed back upon him, marking him ingrate as well as dishonored. All that had happened he regarded as Divine judgment on an unspoken, unacted, but not the less encouraged sin. The fact that his sword had done the deed, convinced him that his destruction had been connived at, as well as that of Morales. A suspicion as to the designer, if not the actual doer of the deed, had indeed taken possession of him; but it was an idea so wild, so unfounded, that he dared not give it words.

From the idea of death, and such a death, his whole soul indeed revolted; but to avert it seemed so utterly impossible, that he bent his proud spirit unceasingly to its anticipation; and with the spiritual aid of the good and feeling Father Francis, in some degree succeeded. It was not the horror of his personal fate alone which bade him so shrink from death. Marie was free once more; nay, had from the moment of her dread avowal—made, he intuitively felt, to save him—become, if possible, dearer, more passionately loved than before. And, oh! how terrible is the anticipation of early death to those that love!—the only trial which bids even the most truly spiritual, yet while on earth still *human* heart, forget that if earth is loved and lovely, heaven *must* be lovelier still.

From Don Felix d'Estaban, his friendly warder, he heard of Isabella's humane intentions toward her; that her senses had been restored, and she was, to all appearance, the same in health as she had been since her husband's death; only evidently suffering more, which might be easily accounted for from the changed position in which the knowledge of her unbelief had placed her with all the members of Isabella's court; that the only agitation she had evinced was, when threatened with a visit from Father Francis—who, finding nothing in the mansion of Don Ferdinand Morales to confirm the truth of her confession, had declared his conviction that there must be some secret chamber destined for her especial use. As if shrinking from the interview he demanded, Marie had said to the Senora, to whose care she had been intrusted—"He need not seek me to obtain this information. For my husband's sake alone I concealed the faith in which I glory. Let Father Francis remove a sliding panel beneath the tapestry behind the couch in my sleeping apartment, and he will find not only all he seeks, but the surest proof of my husband's care and tenderness for me, unbeliever though he might deem me."

The discovery of this secret closet, Don Felix continued, had caused much marvel throughout the court. Where Morales had found her, or how he could have reconciled his conscience not only to make her his wife, but permit her the free exercise of a religion accursed in the sight both of God and man, under his own roof, were questions impossible to solve, or reconcile with the character of orthodox Catholicism he had so long borne. The examination had been conducted with the church's usual secrecy; the volumes of heresy and unbelief (it did not signify that the word of God was amongst them) burnt; the silver lamps and other ornaments melted down, to enrich, by an image of the virgin, the church of St. Francis; the recess itself purified with incense and sprinkled with holy water; the sign of the cross deeply burnt in the walls; and the panel which formed the secret entrance firmly fastened up, that its very existence should be forgotten. The matter, however, Don Felix added, was not publicly spoken of, as both the King and Queen, in conjunction with the Sub-Prior, seemed to wish all that had passed, in which Donna Marie was concerned, should be gradually forgotten. Don Ferdinand's vast possessions had, in consequence of his widow's being an unbeliever, and so having no power to inherit, reverted to the crown; but in case of Marie's conversion, of which Don Felix appeared to entertain little doubt, the greater part would be restored to her. Till then, Marie was kept in strict confinement in the palace; but all harsher measures Isabella had resolved to avoid.

This intelligence relieved Stanley's mind of one painful dread, while it unconsciously increased his wish to live. Marie free! a Catholic! what could come between them then? Must she not love him, else why seek to save him? And then again the mystery darkened round her. A wild suspicion as to the *real reason* of her having wedded Ferdinand, had flitted across his mind; but the words of Estaban so minutely repeated, seemed to banish it entirely; they alluded but to her husband's forbearing tenderness, felt the more intensely from its being extended by a zealous Catholic to one of a race usually so contemned and hated. In vain he tried to reconcile the seeming inconsistency of her conduct; his thoughts only became the more confused and painful, till even the remembrance of her self-devotion lost its power to soothe or to allay them.

When Don Felix again visited his prisoner, his countenance was so expressive of consternation, that Stanley had scarcely power to ask what had occurred. Marie had disappeared from the castle so strangely and mysteriously, that not a trace or clue could be discovered of her path. Consternation reigned within the palace; the King was full of wrath at the insult offered to his power; the Queen even more grieved than angry. The guards stationed without the chamber had declared on oath that no one had passed them; the Senoras Leon and Pas, who slept in the room adjoining, could tell nothing wherewith to explain the mystery. In the first paroxysm of alarm they had declared the night had passed as usual; but on cooler reflection they remembered starting from their sleep with the impression of a smothered cry, which having mingled with their dreams, and not being repeated, they had believed mere fancy. And this faint sound was the only sign, the only trace that her departure was not a voluntary act.

"Father Francis! the arm of the church!" gasped Stanley, as Don Felix paused in his recital, astonished at the effect of his words on the prisoner, whose very respiration seemed impeded.

"Father Francis has solemnly sworn," he replied, "that neither he nor any of his brethren had connived at an act of such especial disrespect to the sovereign power, and of injustice towards the Queen. Torquemada is still absent, or suspicion night rest on him—he is stern enough even for such a deed; but how could even he have withdrawn her from the castle without discovery?"

"Can she not have departed voluntarily?" inquired Stanley, with sudden hope. "The cry you mention may indeed have been but fancy. Is it not likely that fear as to her fate may have prompted her to seek safety in flight?"

"Her Grace thinks not, else some clue as to her path must, ere this, have been discovered. Besides, escape was literally impossible without the aid of magic, which however her accursed race know well how to use. The guards must have seen her, had she passed her own threshold in any human form. The casement was untouched, remaining exactly as the Senora Leon secured it with her own hand the preceding evening; and, even had she thence descended to the ground, she could have gone no further from the high and guarded walls. It may be magic: if so, and the devil hides himself in so fair a form, the saints preserve us! for we know not in whom next he will be hid." So spoke, gravely, seriously, undoubtingly, a wise and thoughtful Spanish noble, of the fifteenth century; and so then thought the whole European world. Stanley scarcely heard the last words; for in his mind, however sorcery might be synonymous with *Judaism* it certainly was not with *Marie*; and he could only realize the fact of the utter impossibility of a voluntary flight.

"Had the Queen seen her since her trial?" he inquired.

"She had not; a fact which deepens her distress; for she fancies had Marie been nearer her person, and aware of the full extent of her merciful intentions, this might have been averted. She believes that the smothered cry alluded to was really Donna Marie's; but, if so, what the dark power is, which has so trampled on the royal prerogative, is plunged in as impenetrable mystery as every thing else, in which Donna Marie has been concerned."

"Even the same dark power which seeks my destruction, and laid Morales low," replied Stanley, more as if thinking aloud than addressing his companion; "and when the clue to one mystery is found, the rest will follow. Some fiend from hell is at work around us. Morales is gone. Marie has followed, and I shall be the next; and then, perhaps, the demon's reign will end, and the saints of heaven triumph."

"Would to heaven a Jewess had never come amongst us," was the rejoinder; "there is always evil in their train." And the blood rushed to Arthur's cheek, his hand involuntarily clenched, and his eye glanced defiance towards Don Felix, as if, even at such a moment, insult even in thought towards Marie should not pass unquestioned; but he restrained himself, and the emotion was unnoticed.

From that day so engrossed were the thoughts of the prisoner with vain speculations as to the fate of Marie, that the fact of his own position remaining the same, and his hours of life waning fast, seemed actually unheeded. From Don Felix, in various visits, he heard that Marie was no longer publicly spoken of; the excitement occasioned alike by her avowal and disappearance was fast fading from the imagination of the populace. The public jousts and festivals, intended to celebrate the visit of the sovereigns, but which Morales's death and the events ensuing had so painfully suspended, were recommencing, and men flocked to them, as glad to escape from the mourning and mystery which had held sway so long.

And now only three days intervened ere the expiration of the given month; and each day did the Sub-Prior of St. Francis pass with the prisoner, exhorting, comforting, and strengthening him for the dread passage through which it was now too evident his soul must pass to eternity. It was with difficulty and pain, that Stanley could even then so cease to think of Marie, as to prepare himself with fitting sobriety and humility for the fate impending; but the warm sympathy of Father Francis, whose fine feelings had never been blunted by a life of rigid seclusion, won him to listen and to join in his prayers, and, gradually weaning his thoughts from their earthly resting, raised them to that heaven which, if he truly repented of sin, the good father assured him, was fast opening for him. Under the inviolable seal of confession, Arthur acknowledged his deep and long-cherished love for Marie, his dislike to her husband, which naturally followed the discovery of her marriage, and the evil passions thence arising; but he never wavered in the reiteration of his innocence; adding, that he reproached no man with his death. The sentence was just according to the appearances against him. Had he himself been amongst his judges, his own sentence would have been the same. Yet still he was innocent; and Father Francis so believed him that, after pronouncing absolution and blessing, he hastened from the prisoner to the King to implore a yet longer reprieve. But Ferdinand, though more moved by the Prior's recital than he chose to display, remained firm; he had pledged his kingly word to the chief of the Santa Hermandad that the award of justice should not be waived without proof of innocence, and he could not draw back. One chance only he granted, urged to do so by an irresistible impulse, which how often comes we know not wherefore, till the event marks it as the whisper of some guardian angel, who has looked into the futurity concealed from us. The hour of the execution had been originally fixed for the sixth hour of the morning; it was postponed till noon.

The morning dawned, and with its first beams came Father Francis to the prisoner. He found him calm and resigned: his last thought of earth was to commend Marie, if ever found, to the holy father's care, conjuring him to deal gently and mercifully with a spirit so broken, and lead her to the sole fountain of peace by kindness, not by wrath; and to tell her how faithfully he had loved her to the last. Much affected, Father Francis promised—aye, even to protect, if possible, an unbeliever. And Stanley once mere knelt in prayer, every earthly thought at rest. The last quarter-bell had chimed; and ere it ceased, the step of Don Felix was heard in the passage, followed by the heavy tramp of the guard. The Prior looked eagerly in the noble's countenance as he entered, hoping even then to read reprieve; but the stern yet sad solemnity on Don Felix's face betrayed the hope was vain. The hour had indeed come, and Arthur Stanley was led forth to death!

CHAPTER XXIII.

"Oh! blissful days,
When all men worship God as conscience wills!
Far other times our fathers' grandsires knew.
What tho' the skeptic's scorn hath dared to soil
The record of their fame! What tho' the men
Of worldly minds have dared to stigmatize
The sister-cause Religion and the Law
With Superstition's name! Yet, yet their deeds,
Their constancy in torture and in death—
These on Tradition's tongue shall live; these shall
On History's honest page be pictur'd bright
To latest time."

GRAHAME.

Retrospection is not pleasant in a narrative; but, if Marie has indeed excited any interest in our readers, they will forgive the necessity, and look back a few weeks ere they again arrive at the eventful day with which our last chapter closed. All that Don Felix had reported concerning the widow of Morales was correct. The first stunning effects of her dread avowal were recovered, sense was entirely restored, but the short-lived energy had gone. The trial to passively endure is far more terrible than that which is called upon to *act* and *do*. She soon discovered that, though nursed and treated with kindness, she was a prisoner in her own apartments. Wish to leave them she had none, and scarcely the physical strength; but to sit idly down under the pressure of a double dread—the prisoner's fate and her own sentence—to have no call for energy, not a being for whom to rouse herself and live, not one for whose sake she might forget herself and win future happiness by present exertion; the Past, one yearning memory for the husband, who had so soothed and cherished her, when any other would have cast her from his heart as a worthless thing; the Present, fraught with thoughts she dared not think, and words she might not breathe; the very prayer for Stanley's safety checked— for what could he be to her?—the Future shrouded in a pall so dense, she could not read a line of its dark page, for the torch of Hope was extinguished, and it is only by her light we can look forward; Isabella's affection apparently lost for ever; was it marvel energy and hope had so departed, or that a deadening despondency seemed to crush her heart and sap the very springs of life?

But in the midst of that dense gloom one ray there was, feeble indeed at first as if human suffering had deadened even that, but brightening and strengthening with every passing day. It was the sincerity of her faith—the dearer, more precious to its followers, from the scorn and condemnation, in which it was held by man.

The fact that the most Catholic kingdom, of Spain, was literally peopled with secret Jews, brands this unhappy people, with a degree of hypocrisy, in addition to the various other evil propensities with which they have been so plentifully charged. Nay, even amongst themselves in modern times, this charge has gained ascendency; and the romance-writer who would make use of this extraordinary truth, to vividly picture the condition of the Spanish Jews, is accused of vilifying the nation, by reporting practices, opposed to the upright dictates of the religion of the Lord. It is well to pronounce such judgment *now*, that the liberal position which we occupy in most lands, would render it the height of dissimulation, and hypocrisy, to conceal our faith; but to judge correctly of the secret adherence to Judaism and public profession of Catholicism which characterized our ancestors in Spain, we must transport ourselves not only to the *country* but to the *time*, and recall the awfully degraded, crushing, and stagnating position which *acknowledged Judaism* occupied over the whole known world. As early as 600—as soon, in fact, as the disputes and prosecutions of Arian against Catholic, and Catholic against Arian, had been checked by the whole of Spain being subdued and governed by Catholic kings—intolerance began to work against the Jews, who had been settled in vast numbers in Spain since the reign of the Emperor Adrian; some authorities assert still earlier.[A] They were, therefore, nearly the original colonists of the country, and regarded it with almost as much attachment as they had felt towards Judea. When persecution began to work, "90,000 Jews were compelled to receive the sacrament of baptism," the bodies of the more obstinate tortured, and their fortunes confiscated; and yet—a remarkable instance of inconsistency—*they were not permitted to leave Spain*; and this species of persecution continued from 600 downwards. Once or twice edicts of expulsion were issued, but speedily recalled; the tyrants being unwilling to dismiss victims whom they delighted to torture, or deprive themselves of industrious slaves over whom they might exercise a lucrative oppression; and a statute was enacted, "that the Jews who had been baptized should be *constrained*, for the honor of the church, to persevere in the *external practice* of a religion which they *inwardly* disbelieved and detested."[B]

[Footnote A: Basnage asserts that the Jews were introduced into Spain by the fleet of Soloman, and the arms of Nebuchadnezzar, and that Hadrian transported *forty thousand* families of the tribe of Judah, and ten thousand of the tribe of Benjamin, etc.]

[Footnote B: "Gibbon's Decline and Fall," vol. 6, chap. xxxvii, from which all the previous sentences in inverted commas have been extracted.]

How, then, can compelled obedience to this statute be termed hypocrisy? Persecution, privation, tyranny, may torture and destroy the body, but they cannot force the mind to the adoption of, and belief in tenets, from which the very treatment they commanded must urge it to revolt. Of the 90,000 Jews forcibly baptized by order of Sisebut, and constrained to the external profession of Catholicism, not ten, in all probability, became actually Christians. And yet how would it have availed them to relapse into the public profession of the faith they so obeyed and loved in secret? To leave the country was utterly impossible. It is easy to talk now of such proceedings being their right course of acting, when every land is open to the departure and entrance of every creed; but it was widely different then, and, even if they could have quitted Spain, there was not a spot of ground, in the whole European and Asiatic world, where persecution, extortion, and banishment would not equally have been their doom. Constant relapses into external as well as internal Judaism, there were, but they were but the signal for increased misery to the whole nation; and by degrees they ceased. It was from the forcible baptism of the 90,000 Hebrews, by Sisebut, that we may trace the origin of the secret Jews. From father to son, from mother to daughter, the solemn secret descended, and gradually spread, still in its inviolable nature, through every rank and every profession, from the highest priest to the lowest friar, the general to the common soldier, the noble to the peasant, over the whole land. There were indeed some few in Spain, before the final edict of expulsion in 1492, who were Hebrews in external profession as well as internal observance; but their condition was so degraded, so scorned, so exposed to constant suffering, that it was not in human nature voluntarily to sink down to them, when, by the mere continuance of external Catholicism—which from its universality, its long existence, and being in fact a rigidly enforced statute of the state, *could* not be regarded either as hypocrisy or sin—they could take their station amongst the very highest and noblest of the land, and rise to eminence and power in any profession, civil, military, or religious, which they might prefer. The subject is so full of philosophical inquiry, that in the limits of a romance we cannot possibly do it justice; but to accuse the secret Jews of Spain of hypocrisy, of departing from the pure odinances of their religion, because *compelled* to simulate Catholicism, is taking indeed but a one-handed, short-sighted view of an extensive and intensely interesting topic. We may often hope for the *present* by considering the changes of the *past*; but to attempt to pronounce judgment on the sentiments of the *past* by reasoning of the *present*, when the mind is always advancing, is one of the weakest and idlest fallacies that ever entered the human breast.

Digression as this is, it is necessary clearly to comprehend the situation in which Marie's avowal of her religion had placed her, and her reason for so carefully wording her information as to the existence of the secret closet, that no suspicion might attach itself to the religion of her husband. Her confession sent a shock, which vibrated not only through Isabella's immediate court, but through every part of Spain. Suspicion once aroused, none knew where it might end, or on whom fall. In her first impulse to save Arthur, she had only thought of what such confession might bring to herself individually, and that was, comparatively, easy to endure; but as the excitement ceased, as the dread truth dawned upon her, that, if he must die at the expiration of the given month, her avowal had been utterly useless, the dread of its consequences, to the numerous secret members of her faith appalled her, and caused the firm, resolve under no circumstances to betray the religion of her husband. Him indeed it could not harm; but that one so high in rank, in influence, in favor with sovereigns and people, was only outwardly a Catholic, might have most fatal consequences on all his brethren. That he should have wedded a Jewess might excite surprise, but nothing more; and in the midst of her varied sufferings she could rejoice that all suspicion as to his race and faith had been averted. She felt thankful also at being kept so close a prisoner, for she dreaded the wrath of those whom her avowal might have unwittingly injured. Such an instance had never been known before, and she might justly tremble at the chastisement it might bring upon her even from her own people. As long as she was under Isabella's care she was safe from this; all might feel the vibration, but none dared evince that they did, by the adoption of any measures against her, further than would be taken by the Catholics themselves.

Knowing this, her sole prayer, her sole effort was to obtain mental strength sufficient under every temptation, either from severity or kindness, to adhere unshrinkingly to the faith of her fathers—to cling yet closer to the love of her Father in heaven, and endeavor, with all the lowly trust and fervid feelings of her nature, to fill the yearning void within her woman's heart with his image, and so subdue every human love. It seemed to her vivid fancy as if all the misfortunes she had encountered sprung from her first sin—that of loving a Nazarene. Hers was not the age to make allowances for circumstances in contradistinction to actual deeds. Then, as unhappily but too often now, all were sufferings from a misplaced affection—sprung, not from her fault, but from the mistaken kindness which it exposed her to without due warning of her danger. Educated with the strong belief, that to love or wed, beyond the pale of her own people was the greatest sin she could commit, short of actual apostacy, that impression, though not strong enough, so to conquer human nature, as to arm against love, returned with double force, as sorrow after sorrow gathered round her, and there were none beside her to whisper and strengthen, with the blessed truth that God afflicts yet more in mercy than in wrath; and that his decrees, however fraught with human anguish, are but blessings in disguise—blessings, sown indeed with tears on earth, to reap their deathless fruit in heaven.

But though firmly believing all her suffering was deserved, aware that when she first loved Arthur, the rebel-thought—"Why am I of a race so apart and hated?" had very frequently entered her heart, tempting her at times with fearful violence to give up all for love of man; yet Marie knew that the God of her fathers was a God of love, calling even upon the greatest sinner to return to him repentant and amending, and that even as a little child such should be forgiven. He had indeed proclaimed himself a jealous God, and would have no idol-worship, were it by wood or stone, or, far more dangerous, of human love; and she prayed unceasingly for strength to return to Him with an undivided heart, even if to do so demanded not only separation from Stanley—but a trial in her desolate position almost as severe—the loss of Isabella's confidence and love.

Few words passed between Marie and her guardians; their manner was kind and gentle, but intercourse between rigid Catholics and a proclaimed Jewess, could not be other wise than restrained. From the time that reason returned, the Queen had not visited her, doing actual violence to her own inclinations from tire mistaken—but in that age and to her character natural—dread that the affection and interest she felt towards Marie personally, would lessen the sentiments of loathing and abhorrence with which it was her duty to regard her faith. Isabella had within herself all the qualifications of a martyr. Once impressed that it was a religious duty, she would do violence to her most cherished wishes, sacrifice her dearest desires, her best affections, resign her most eagerly pursued plans—not without suffering indeed, but, according to the mistaken tenets of her religion, the greater personal suffering, the more meritorious was the deed believed to be. This spirit would, had she lived in an age when the Catholic faith was the persecuted, not the persecutor, have led her a willing martyr to the stake; as it was, this same spirit led to the establishment of the Inquisition, and expulsion of the Jews—deeds so awful in their consequences, that the actual motive of the woman-heart which prompted them, is utterly forgotten, and herself condemned. We must indeed deplore the mistaken tenets that could obtain such influence—deplore that man could so pervert the service of a God of love, as to believe and inculcate that such things could be acceptable to Him; but we should pause, and ask, if we ourselves had been influenced by such teaching, could we break from it? ere we condemn.

Isabella's own devoted spirit could so enter into the real reason of Marie's self abnegation for Arthur's sake, that it impelled her to love her more; while at the very same time the knowledge of her being a Jewess, whom she had always been taught and believed must be accursed in the sight of God, and lost eternally unless brought to believe in Jesus, urged her entirely to conquer that affection, lest its indulgence should interfere with her resolution, if kindness failed, by severity to accomplish her own version. She was too weak in health, and Isabella intuitively felt too terribly anxious as to young Stanley's fate, to attempt any thing till after the expiration of the month; and she passed that interval in endeavoring to calm down her own feelings towards her.

So fifteen days elapsed. On the evening of the fifteenth, Marie, feeling unusually exhausted, had sunk down, without disrobing, on her couch, and at length fell into a slumber so deep and calm, that her guardians, fearing to disturb it, and aware that her dress was so loose and light, it could not annoy her, retired softly to their own chamber without arousing her. How many hours this lethargic sleep lasted, Marie knew not, but was at length broken by a dream of terror, and so unusually vivid, that its impression lasted even through the terrible reality which it heralded. She beheld Arthur Stanley on the scaffold about to receive the sentence of the law—the block, the axe, the executioner with his arm raised, and apparently already deluged in blood—the gaping crowds—all the fearful appurtenances of an execution were distinctly traced, and she thought she sprung towards Stanley, who clasped her in his arms, and the executioner, instead of endeavoring to part them, smiled grimly as rejoicing in having two victims instead of one; and as he smiled, the countenance seemed to change from being entirely unknown to the sneering features of the hated Don Luis Garcia. She seemed to cling yet closer to Stanley, and knelt with, him to receive the blow; when, at that moment, the scaffold shook violently, as by the shock of an earthquake, a dark chashm yawned beneath their feet, in the centre of which stood the spectral figure of her husband, his countenance ghastly and stern, and his arm upraised as beckoning her to join him. And then he spoke; but his voice sounded unlike his own:—

"Marie Henriquez Morales! awake, arise, and follow!"

And with such extraordinary clearness did the words fall, that she started up in terror, believing they must have been spoken by her side—and they were! they might have mingled with, perhaps even created her dream. She still lay on her couch; but it seemed to have sunk down through the very floor of the apartment[A] she had occupied, and at its foot stood a figure, who, with upraised arm held before her a wooden cross. His cowl was closely drawn, and a black robe, of the coarsest serge, was secured round his waist by a hempen cord. Whether he had indeed spoken the words she had heard in her dream Marie could not tell, for they were not repeated. She saw him approach her, and she felt his strong grasp lift her from the couch, which sprung up, by the touch of some secret spring, to the place whence it had descended; and she heard no more.

[Footnote A: I may be accused in this scene, of too closely imitating a somewhat similar occurrence in Anne of Geirstein. Such seeming plagiarism was scarcely possible to be avoided, when the superstitious proceedings of the *vehmic* tribunal of Germany and the *secret* Inquisition of Spain are represented by history as so very similar.]

CHAPTER XXIV.

"Isabel.—Ha! little honor to be much believed,
And most pernicious purpose—seeming, seeming.
I will proclaim thee, Angelo! look for't;
Sign me a present pardon—
Or, with an outstretch'd throat, I'll tell the world
Aloud what man thou art.

"Angelo.—Who will believe thee?
My unsoil'd name, th' austereness of my life,
My vouch against you, and my place i' the State,
Will so your accusation overweigh
That you will stifle in your own report
The smile of Calumny."

SHAKSPEARE.

When Marie recovered consciousness, she found herself in a scene so strange, so terrific, that it appeared as if she must have been borne many miles from Segovia, so utterly impossible did it seem, that such awful orgies could be enacted within any short distance of the sovereigns' palace, or their subjects' homes. She stood in the centre of a large vaulted subterranean hall, which, from the numerous arched entrances to divers passages and smaller chambers that opened on every side, appeared to extend far and wide beneath the very bowels of the earth. It was lighted with torches, but so dimly, that the gloom exaggerated the horrors, which the partial light disclosed. Instruments of torture of any and every kind—the rack, the wheel, the screw, the cord, and fire—groups of unearthly-looking figures, all clad in the coarse black serge and hempen belt; some with their faces concealed by hideous masks, and others enveloped in the cowls, through which only the eyes could be distinguished, the figure of the cross upon the breast, and under that emblem, of divine peace, inflicting such horrible tortures on their fellow-men that the pen shrinks from their delineation. Nor was it the mere instruments of torture Marie beheld: she saw them in actual use; she heard the shrieks and groans of the hapless victims, at times mingled with the brutal leers and jests of their fiendish tormentors; she seemed to take in at one view, every species of torture that could be inflicted, every pain that could be endured; and yet, comparatively, but a few of the actual sufferers were visible. The shrillest sounds of agony came from the gloomy arches, in which no object could be distinguished.

Whatever suffering meets the sight, it does not so exquisitely affect the brain as that which reaches it through the ear. At the former the heart may bleed and turn sick; but at the latter the brain seems, for the moment, wrought into frenzy; and, even though personally in safety, it is scarcely possible to restrain the same sounds from bursting forth. How then must those shrill sounds of human agony have fallen on the hapless Marie, recognizing as she did with the rapidity of thought, in the awful scene around her, the main hall of that mysterious and terrible tribunal, whose existence from her earliest infancy had been impressed upon her mind, as a double incentive to guard the secret of her faith; that very Inquisition, from which her own grandfather, Julien Heuriquez, had fled, and in which the less fortunate grandfather of her slaughtered husband, had been tortured and burnt.

For a second she stood mute and motionless, as turned to stone; then, pressing both hands tightly on her temples, she sunk down at the feet of her conductor, and sought in words to beseech his mercy; but her white lips gave vent to no sound save a shriek, so wild that it seemed, for the moment, to drown all other sorrows, and startle even the human fiends around her. Her conductor himself started back; but quickly recovering—

"Fool!" he muttered, as he rudely raised her. "I have no power to aid thee; come before the Superior—we must all obey—ask him, implore him, for mercy, not me."

He bore her roughly to a recess, divided off at the upper end of the hall, by a thick black drapery, in which sat the Grand Inquisitor and his two colleagues. One or two familiars were behind them, and a secretary sat near a table covered with black cloth, and on which were several writing implements. All wore masks of black crape, so thick that not a feature could be discerned with sufficient clearness for recognition elsewhere; yet, one glance on the stern, motionless figure, designated as the Grand Inquisitor, sufficed to bid every drop of blood recede from the prisoner's heart with human terror, at the very same moment that it endowed the *woman* with such supernatural fortitude that her very form seemed to dilate, and her large eye and lovely mouth expressed—if it could be, in such a scene and such an hour—unutterable scorn. Antipathy, even as love, will pierce disguise; and that one glance, lit up with almost bewildering light, in the prisoner's mind, link after link of what had before been impenetrable mystery. Her husband's discovery of her former love for Arthur; his murder; the suspicion thrown on Stanley; her own summons as witness against him; her present danger; all, all were traced to one individual, one still working and most guilty passion, which she, in her gentle purity and holy strength, had scorned. She could not be deceived—the mystery that surrounded him was solved—antipathy explained; and Marie's earthly fate lay in Don Luis Garcia's hands! The Grand Inquisitor read in that glance that he was known; and for a brief minute a strange, an incomprehensible sensation, thrilled through him. It could scarcely have been fear, when one gesture of his hand would destine that frail being to torture, imprisonment, and death; and yet never before in his whole life of wickedness, had he experienced such a feeling as he did at that moment beneath a woman's holy gaze. Anger at himself for the sensation, momentary as it was, increased the virulence of other passions; but then was not the hour for their betrayal. In low, deep tones, he commenced the mockery of a trial. That her avowal of her faith would elude torture, by at once condemning her to the flames, was disregarded. She was formally accused of blasphemy and heresy, and threatened with the severest vengeance of the church which she had reviled; but that this case of personal guilt would be mercifully laid aside for the present, for still more important considerations. Was her late husband, they demanded, of the same blaspheming creed as herself? And a list of names, comprising some of the highest families of Spain, was read out and laid before her, with the stern command to affix a mark against all who, like herself, had relapsed into the foul heresy of their ancestors—to do this, or the torture should wring it from her.

But the weakness of humanity had passed; and so calm, so collected, so firm, was the prisoner's resolute refusal to answer either question, that the familiar to whom she had clung for mercy looked at her with wonder. Again and again she was questioned; instruments of torture were brought before her— one of the first and slightest used—more to terrify than actually to torture, for that was not yet the Grand Inquisitor's design; and still she was firm, calm, unalterable in her resolution to refuse reply. And then Don Luis spoke of mercy, which was to consist of imprisonment in solitude and darkness, to allow time for reflection on her final answer—a concession, he said, in a tone far more terrifying to Marie than even the horrors around her, only granted in consideration of her age and sex. None opposed the sentence; and she was conducted to a close and narrow cell, in which no light could penetrate save through a narrow chink in the roof.

How many days and nights thus passed the hapless prisoner could not have told, for there was nothing to mark the hours. Her food was delivered to her by means of a turn-screw in the wall, so that not even the sight of a fellow-creature could disturb her solitude, or give her the faintest hope of exciting human pity. Her sole hope, her sole refuge was in prayer; and, oh! how blessed was the calm, the confidence it gave.

So scanty was her allowance of food, that more than once the thought, crossed her, whether or not, death by famine would be her allotted doom; and human nature shuddered, but the spirit did not quail! Hour after hour passed, she knew not whether it was night or day, when the gloom of her dungeon was suddenly illumined; she knew not at first how or whence, so noiseless was the entrance of the intruder, but gradually she traced the light to a small lamp held in the hand of a shrouded individual, whom she recognized at once. There was one fearful thrill of mortal dread, one voiceless cry for strength from Heaven, and Marie Morales stood before Don Luis erect and calm, and firm as in her hour of pride.

Garcia now attempted no concealment. His mask had been cast aside, and his features gleamed without any effort at hypocritical restraint, in all the unholy passions of his soul. We will not pollute our pages with transcribing the fearful words of passions contending in their nature, yet united in their object, with which the pure ear of his prisoner was first assailed—still lingering desire, yet hate, wrath, fury, that she should dare still oppose, and scorn, and loathe him; rage with himself, that, strive as he might, even he was baffled by the angel purity around her; longing to wreak upon her every torture that his hellish office gave him unchecked power to inflict, yet fearing that, if he did so, death would release her ere his object was attained; all strove and raged within him, making his bosom a very hell, from which there was no retracting, yet whose very flames incited deeper fury towards the being whom he believed their cause.

"And solitude, darkness, privation—have they so little availed that thou wilt tempt far fiercer sufferings?" he at length demanded, struggling to veil his fury in a quiet, concentrated tone. "Thou hast but neared the threshold of the tortures which one look, one gesture of my hand, can gather around thee; tortures which the strongest sinew, the firmest mind, have been unable to sustain—how will that weakened frame endure?"

"It can but die," replied the prisoner, "as nobler and better ones have done before me!"

"Die!" repeated Garcia, and he laughed mockingly. "Thinkest thou we know our trade so little that such release can baffle us? I tell thee, pain of itself has never yet had power to kill; and we have learned the measure of endurance in the human form so well, that we have never yet been checked by death, ere our ends were gained. And so will it be with thee, boldly as now thou speakest. Thou hast but tasted pain!"

"Better the sharpest torture than thy hated presence," calmly rejoined Marie. "My soul thou canst not touch."

"Soul! Has a Jewess a soul? Nay, by my faith, thou talkest bravely! An thou hast, thou hadst best be mine, and so share my salvation; there's none for such as thee."

"Man!" burst indignantly from the prisoner. "Share thy salvation! Great God of Israel! that men like these have power to persecute thy children for their faith, and do it in thy name! And speak of mercy! Thou hast but given me another incentive for endurance," she continued, more calmly addressing her tormentor. "If salvation be denied to us, and granted thee, I would refuse it with my dying breath; such faith is not of God!"

"I came not hither to enter on such idle quibbles," was the rejoinder. "It matters not to me what thou art after death, but before it mine thou shalt be. What hinders me, at this very moment, from working my will upon thee? Who will hear thy cry? or, hearing, will approach thee? These walls have heard too many sounds of human agony to bear thy voice to those who could have mercy. Tempt me not by thy scorn too far. What holds me from thee now?"

"What holds thee from me? GOD!" replied the prisoner, in a tone of such, thrilling, such supernatural energy, that Garcia actually started as if some other voice than hers had spoken, and she saw him glance fearfully round. "Thou darest not touch me! Ay, villain—blackest and basest as thou art—thou darest not do it. The God thine acts, yet more than thy words blaspheme, withholds thee—and thou knowest it!"

"I defy him!" were the awful words that answered her; and Don Luis sprang forwards.

"Back!" exclaimed the heroic girl. "Advance one step nearer, and thy vengeance, even as thy passion, will alike be foiled—and may God forgive the deed I do."

She shook down the beautiful tresses of her long luxuriant hair, and, parting them with both hands around her delicate throat, stood calmly waiting in Don Luis's movements the signal for her own destruction.

"Fool!" he muttered, as involuntarily he fell back, awed—in spite of his every effort to the contrary—at a firmness as unexpected as it was unwavering. "Fool! Thou knowest not the power it is thy idle pleasure to defy; thou wilt learn it all too soon, and then in vain regret thy scorn of my proffer now. Thou hast added tenfold to my wild yearning for revenge on thy former scorn—tenfold! ay, twice tenfold, to thy own tortures. Yet, once more, I bid thee pause and choose. Fools there are, who dare all personal physical torment, and yet shrink and quail before the thought of death for a beloved one. Idiots, who for others, sacrifice themselves; perchance thou wilt be one of them. Listen, and tremble; or, sacrifice, and save! When in thy haughty pride, and zenith of thy power, thou didst scorn me, and bidding me, with galling contempt, go from thy presence as if I were a loathsome reptile, unworthy even of thy tread, I bade thee beware, and to myself swore vengeance. And knowest thou how that was accomplished? Who led thy doting husband where he might hear thine own lips proclaim thy falsity? Who poisoned the chalice of life, which had been so sweet, ere it was dashed from his lips by death? Who commanded the murderer's blow, and the weapon with which it was accomplished? Who laid the charge of his murder on the foreign minion, and brought thee in evidence against him? Who but I—even I! And if I have done all this, thinkest thou to elude my further vengeance? I tell thee, if thou refuse the grace I proffer, Arthur Stanley dies; accept it, and he lives!"

"And not at such a price would Arthur Stanley wish, to live," replied Marie calmly. "He would spurn existence purchased thus."

"Ay, perchance, if he knew it; but be it as thou wilt, he shall know thou couldst have saved him and refused."

"And thinkest thou he will believe thee? As little as I believed him my husband's murderer. How little knowest thou the trust of love! He will not die," she continued emphatically; "his innocence shall save him—thy crime be known."

"Ay!" replied Garcia, with a sneering laugh. "Give thyself wings as a bird, and still stone walls will encircle thee; dwindle into thin air, and gain the outer world, and tell thy tale, and charge Don Luis Garcia with the deed, and who will believe thee? Thinkest thou I would have boasted of my triumphant vengeance to aught who could betray me? Why my very tool, the willing minister of my vengeance—who slew Morales merely because I bade him— might not live, lest he should be tempted to betray me; I slew him with my own hand. What sayest thou now—shall Stanley live, if I say Let him die?"

There was no reply, but he looked in vain for any diminution in the undaunted resolution which still sustained her.

"I go," he continued, after a pause. "Yet, once more, I charge thee choose; accept the terms I proffer—be mine—and thou art saved from all further torture thyself, and Stanley lives. Refuse, and the English minion dies; and when thou and I next meet, it will be where torture and executioners wait but my nod to inflict such suffering that thou wilt die a thousand deaths in every pang. And, Jewess—unbeliever as thou art—who will dare believe it more than public justice, or accuse me of other than the zeal, which the service of Christ demands? Choose, and quickly—wilt thou accept my proffers, and be mine? Thou must, at last. What avails this idle folly of tempting torture first?"

"Thou mayest kill my body, but thou canst not pollute my soul," was the instant reply, and its tones were unchanged. "And as for Stanley, his life or death is not in thine hands; but if it were, I could not—nay, thus I *would* not— save him. I reject thy proffers, as I scorn thyself. Now leave me—I have chosen!"

Don Luis did not reply, but Marie beheld his cheek grow livid, and the foam actually gather on his lip; but the calm and holy gaze she had fixed upon him, as he spoke, quailed not, nor changed. The invisible door of her cell closed with a deep, sullen sound, as if her tormentor had thus, in some measure, given vent to the unutterable fury shaking his soul to its centre; and Marie was alone. She stood for many, many minutes, in the fearful dread of his return; and then she raised her hand to her brow, and her lip blanched and quivered, and, with a long, gasping breath, she sunk down upon the cold floor—all the heroine lost in an agonized burst of tears.

CHAPTER XXV.

"Hovers the steel above his head,
Suspended by a spider thread:
On, on! a life hangs on thy speed;
With lightning wing the gallant steed!
Buoy the full heart up! It will sink
If it but pause to feel and think.
There is no time to dread his fate:
No thought but one—too late, too late!"

MS.

Too soon did Marie realize the power of Don Luis to exercise his threatened vengeance! Two days after that terrible interview, she was again dragged to the hall of judgment: the same questions were proposed as before, whether or not she would denounce the secret followers of her own creed, and confess her late husband's real belief; and the same firm answers given. We shrink in loathing from the delineation of horrible tortures applied to that frail and gentle being—shrink, for we know that such things actually have been; and women—young, lovely, inoffensive as Marie Morales—have endured the same exquisite agony for the same iniquitous purpose! In public, charged to denounce innocent fellow-beings, or suffer; in private—in those dark and fearful cells—exposed to all the horror and terror of such persecution as we have faintly endeavored to describe. It is no picture of the imagination, delighting to dwell on horrors. Would that it were! Its parallel will be found, again and again repeated, in the annals—not of the Inquisition alone—but of every European state where the Romanists held sway.

But Marie's prayer for superhuman strength had been heard. No cry, scarcely a groan, escaped her. She saw Don Luis at her side; she heard his hissing whisper that there was yet time to retract and be released; but she deigned him no reply whatever. It was not his purpose to try her endurance to the utmost in the first, second, or third trial; though, so enraged at her calmness, as scarcely to be able to restrain it even before his colleagues, and with difficulty controlling his fiendish desire to increase the torture to its utmost at once, he remanded her to her dungeon till his further pleasure should be known. She had fainted under the intolerable pain, and lay for many successive hours, too exhausted even to raise to her parched lips the pitcher of water lying near her. And even the gradual cessation of suffering, the sensation of returning power, brought with them the agonized thought, that they did but herald increased and increasing torture.

One night—she knew not how long after she had been remanded to her cell, but, counting by suffering, it felt many weary nights and days—she sunk into a sleep or trance, which transported her to her early home in the Vale of Cedars. Her mother seemed again to stand before her; and she thought, as she heard her caressing voice, and met the glance of her dove-like eyes, she laid her head on her bosom, as she was wont to do in her happy childhood; and peace seemed to sink into her heart so blessedly, so deeply, that the very fever of her frame departed. A voice aroused her with a start; it was so like her mother's, that the dream seemed lingering still.

"Marie, my beloved one," murmured the voice, and a breath fanned her cheek, as if some one were leaning over her. She unclosed her eyes—the words, the voice, still so kept up the illusion, though the tones were deeper than a woman's, that even the hated dress of a familiar of the Inquisition could not create alarm. "Hast thou forgotten me, my child? But it matters not now. Say only thou wilt trust me, and safety lies before us. The fiends hold not their hellish court to-night; and the arch-fiend himself is far distant, on a sudden summons from the King, which, though the grand Inquisitor might scorn, Don Luis will obey. Wilt come with me, my child?"

"Ay, any where! That voice could not deceive: but 'tis all vain," she continued, the first accents of awakened hope lost in despondency—"I cannot rise."

"It needs not. Do thou hold the lantern, Marie; utter not a word—check even thy breath—and the God of thy fathers shall save thee yet."

He raised her gently in his arms; and the hope of liberty, of rescue from Don Luis, gave her strength to grasp the light to guide them. She could not trace their way, but she felt they left the dungeon, and traversed many long, damp, and narrow passages, seemingly excavated in the solid earth. All was silent, and dark as the tomb; now and then her guide paused, as if to listen; but there was no sound. He knew well the secret paths he trod.

The rapid motion, even the sudden change, almost deprived Marie of consciousness. She was only sensible, by a sudden change from the close, damp, passages to the free breezes of night, that she was in the open air, and apparently a much freer path; that still her guide pressed swiftly onwards, apparently scarcely feeling her light weight; that, after a lengthened interval, she was laid tenderly on a soft, luxurious couch—at least, so it seemed, compared with the cold floor of her cell; that the blessed words of thanksgiving that she was safe broke from that strangely familiar voice; and she asked no more—seemed even to wish no more—so completely was all physical power prostrated. She lay calm and still, conscious only that she was saved. Her guide himself for some time disturbed her not; but after changing his dress, and preparing a draught of cooling herbs, he knelt down, raised her head on his knee with almost woman's tenderness, and, holding the draught to her lips, said, gently—

"Drink, beloved child of my sainted sister; there is life and health in the draught."

Hastily swallowing it, Marie gazed wildly in his face.—The habiliments of the familiar had been changed for those of a Benedictine monk; his cowl thrown back, and the now well remembered countenance of her uncle Julien was beaming over her. In an instant, the arm she could still use was thrown round him, and her head buried in his bosom; every pulse throbbing with the inexpressible joy of finding, when most desolate, one relative to love and save her still. Julien left not his work of healing and of security incomplete; gradually he decreased, by the constant application of linen bathed in some cooling fluid, the scorching fire which still seemed to burn within the maimed and shrivelled limb; parted the thick masses of dishevelled hair from her burning temples, and bathed them with some cooling and reviving essence; gently removed the sable robes, and replaced them, with the dress of a young novice which he had provided; concealed her hair beneath the white linen hood, and then, administering a potion which he knew would produce deep and refreshing sleep, and so effectually calm the fevered nerves, she sunk down on the soft moss and heath which formed her couch, and slept calmly and sweetly as an infant for many hours.

Julien Morales had entered Segovia in his monkish garb, as was frequently his custom, on the evening of the trial.—The excitement of the whole city naturally called forth his queries as to its cause; and the information imparted—the murder of Don Ferdinand, and incomprehensible avowal of Judaism on the part of his niece—demanded a powerful exercise of self-control to prevent, by a betrayal of unusual grief and horror, his near relationship to both parties. Hovering about the palace, he heard of Isabella's merciful intentions towards Marie; and feeling that his presence might only agitate, and could in nothing avail her, he had resolved on leaving the city without seeing her, when her mysterious disappearance excited all Segovia anew.

Julien Morales alone, perhaps, amidst hundreds, in his own mind solved the mystery at once. Well did he know tire existence of the secret Inquisition. As we narrated in one of our early chapters, the fate of his father had so fixed itself upon his mind, that he had bound himself by a secret, though solemn oath, as his avenger. To accomplish this fully, he had actually spent ten years of his life as familiar in the Inquisition. The fate of Don Luis's predecessor had been plunged in the deepest mystery. Some whispered his death was by a subtle poison; others, that his murderer had sought him in the dead of night, and, instead of treacherously dealing the blow, had awakened him, and bade him confess his crimes—one especially; and acknowledge that if the mandate of the Eternal, "Whoso sheddeth man's blood, by man shall his blood be shed," were still to govern man, his death was but an act of justice which might not be eluded. Whether these whispered rumors had to do with Julien Morales or not, we leave to the judgment of our readers.—Suffice it, that not only was his vow accomplished, but, during his ten years' residence in these subterranean halls, he naturally became familiarized with all their secret passages and invisible means of egress and ingress—not only to the apparently private homes of unoffensive citizens, but into the wild tracts of country scattered round. By one of these he had, in fact, effected his own escape; and in the mild and benevolent Benedictine monk—known alike to the cities and solitudes of Spain—none would have recognized the former familiar of the Inquisition, and still less have imagined him the being which in reality he was—a faithful and believing Jew.

To him, then, it was easy to connect the disappearance of Marie with the existence of the Holy Office, even though he was entirely ignorant of Garcia's ulterior designs. In an agony of apprehension, he resolved on saving her if possible, even while he trembled at the delay which must necessarily ensue ere he could arrange and execute his plans, more especially as it was dangerous to associate a second person in their accomplishment. With all his haste and skill he was not in time to save her from the barbarity of her misnamed judges. His very soul was wrung, as he stood amongst the familiars a silent witness of her sufferings; but to interfere was impossible. One thing, however, was favorable. He knew she would not be again disturbed till a sufficient time had elapsed for the recovery of such strength as would enable her to endure further torture; and he had, therefore, some time before him for their flight.

Her voluntary avowal of her faith—aware too, as she was, of the existence of the Inquisition—had, indeed, perplexed the good uncle greatly; but she was in no state, even when partially recovered from physical weakness, to enter into explanation then. He saw she was unhappy, and the loss of her husband might well account for it. To the rumors which had reached him in Segovia, as to the suppositions of the real cause of Stanley's enmity to Morales, and Marie's self-sacrifice, he would not even listen, so completely without foundation did they seem to him.

The second evening after their escape, they left the cave to pursue their journey. Father Ambrose—for so, now he has resumed his monkish garb, we must term Julien—had provided a mule for the novice's use; and thus they leisurely traversed the desolate and mountainous tract forming the boundaries of the provinces now termed old and new Castile. Neither uncle nor niece spoke of their destined goal; Marie intuitively felt she was proceeding to the Vale of Cedars, the only place of safety now for her; but, so engrossed was her mind with the vain thought how to save Arthur, that for herself she could not frame a wish.

The second evening of their journey they entered a small, straggling village, so completely buried in mountains that its existence was unknown save to its own rustic inhabitants. The appearance of a monk evidently caused an unusual excitement, which was speedily explained. The chief of the villagers approached Father Ambrose, and, addressing him with the greatest respect, entreated him to follow him to his house, where, he said, lay a man at the point of death, who had, from the time he became aware of his dangerous position, incessantly called for a priest to shrive him from some deadly sin. He had been found, the villager continued. In a deep pit sunk in a solitary glen half way to Segovia, with every appearance of attempted murder, which, being supposed complete, the assassins had thrown him into the pit to conceal their deed; but chancing to hear his groans as he passed, he had rescued him, and hoped to have cured his wounds. For three weeks they seemed to progress favorably, but then fever—occurring, he thought, from great restlessness of mind—had rapidly increased, and, after ten days of fearful struggle between life and death mortification had ensued, and hope could exist no longer At first, Perez added, he seemed to shrink from the idea of priestly aid, only harping on one theme—to get strength enough to reach Segovia, and speak to the King. They had thought him mad, but humored him; but now he was almost furious in his wild cries for a priest, not only to shrive him, but to bear his message to the King. They had tried to gratify him, but their distance from any town or monastery had prevented it; and they now, therefore, hailed Father Ambrose almost as sent from heaven to save a sinner by absolution ere he died.

This tale was told as the monk and novice hastened with. Perez to his house. The poor inhabitants thronged his path to crave a blessing, and proffer every attention their simple means afforded. Fearing for Marie, Julien's only care was for the supposed novice; and therefore Perez, at his request, eagerly led her to a large comfortable chamber, far removed from the bustle of the house, and left her to repose. But repose was not at that moment possible, even though her slightly returning strength was exhausted, from the fatigue of a long day's travel. Fruit and cakes were before her; but, though her mouth was parched and dry, she turned from them in loathing; and interminable seemed the space till Father Ambrose returned. Ere he spoke, he carefully closed and secured the door, and exclaimed, in a low, cautious tone, "My child, this is indeed the finger of a righteous God—blessed be His name! The unhappy man to whose dying bed they brought me—"

"Is the murderer of my husband!" interposed Marie in a tone of almost unnatural calmness. "I knew it from the first moment Perez spoke. We have but to think of one thing now—Stanley is innocent, and must be saved!"

"And shall be, if possible, my child; but there are fearful difficulties in the way. The unhappy man conjures me not to leave him, and is in such a horrible state of mental and bodily agony that I fear if I do, he will commit some act of violence on himself, and so render his evidence of no avail. We are not much above sixty miles from Segovia, but the roads are cross and rugged; so that it will need steadiness and speed, and instant audience with the King."

"But time—have we time?" reiterated Marie. "Say but there is time, and every other difficulty shall be smoothed."

"There is full time: the execution is not till the second day after to-morrow. Nay, my child," he added, observing her look of doubting bewilderment, "suffering makes the hours seem longer than they are. Fear not for time, but counsel me whom to send. Who amongst these poor ignorant rustics will ever reach the King—or, failing him, the Chief Hermano—and make his tale so sufficiently clear as to release the prisoner, and send messengers here with the necessary speed to take down this man's confession? He cannot linger two days more. Would that I could go myself; but I can leave neither him nor thee."

"And it needs not," was the firm reply. "Father, I myself will do thy errand. There must be no delay, no chance of hesitation in its accomplishment. Ah! do not look upon me as if my words were wild and vain; were there other means I would not speak them—but he must be saved!"

"And again at the sacrifice of thy safety—perchance thy life! Marie, Marie! what hold has this young stranger upon thee that thou shouldest twice so peril thyself? Thy life is dearer to me than his—I cannot grant thy boon."

"Nay, but thou must. Listen to me, my second father! If Stanley dies, his blood is on my head!" And struggling with strong emotion, she poured forth her whole tale.

"And thou lovest him still—him, a Nazarene—thou, child, wife, of an unstained race! And is it for this, thy zeal to save him?" ejaculated Julien, retreating several paces from her—"Can it be?"

"I would save him because he is innocent—because he has borne more than enough for me; for aught else, thou wrongest me, father. He will never be to me more than he is now."

It was impossible to resist the tone of mournful reproach in which those simple words were said. Julien pressed her to his bosom, bade God bless her, and promised, if indeed there were no other means, her plan should be adopted; objection after objection, indeed, he brought forward, but all were overruled. She pledged herself to retain her disguise, and to return with Perez, without hesitation, and accompany her uncle to the vale, as intended. But that she should start at once, he positively refused. How could she hope to accomplish her journey without, at least, two hours' repose? It was then late in the evening. At six the next morning all should be ready for her journey, and there would be still more than twenty-four hours before her; Marie tried to be content, but the horrible dread of being too late did not leave her for a moment, even in sleep, and inexpressibly thankful was she when the morning dawned. Julien's provident care had been active while she slept. Perez, flattered at the trust reposed in him, had offered himself to accompany the young novice to Segovia: and at the appointed hour he was ready, mounted himself, and leading a strong, docile palfrey for brother Ernest's use. He knew an hostellerie, he said, about twenty miles from the city, where their steeds could be changed; and promised by two hours after noon, the very latest, the novice should be with the King. It could be done in less time, he said; but his reverence had told him the poor boy was unusually delicate, and had, moreover, lost the use of his left arm; and he thought, as there was so much time before them, it was needless to exhaust his strength before his errand was done. Julien expressed his entire satisfaction, gave them his blessing, and they were rapidly out of sight.

Once or twice they halted to give their horses rest and refresh themselves; but so absorbed were the senses of Marie, that she was unconscious of fatigue. Every mile they traversed seemed bearing a heavy load from her chest, and enabling her to breathe more freely; while the fresh breeze and exciting exercise seemed actually to revive her. It wanted rather more than an hour for noon when they reached the hostellerie mentioned by Perez. Two fleet and beautiful horses were speedily provided for them, bread and fruit partaken, and Perez, ready mounted, was tasting the stirrup cup, when his friend demanded—

"Is it to Segovia ye are bound?"

"Yes, man, on an important errand, charged by his reverence Father Ambrose himself."

"His reverence should have sent you two hours earlier, and you would have been in time for one of the finest sights seen since Isabella—God bless her!—begun to reign. They were common enough a few years back."

"What sight? and why am I not in time?"

"Now, art thou not the veriest rustic to be so entirely ignorant of the world's doings? Why, to-day is the solemn execution of the young foreigner whom they believe we have murdered Don Ferdinand Morales—the saints preserve him! He is so brave a fellow, they say, that had it not been for this confounded hostellerie I would have made an effort to be present: I love to see how a brave man meets death. It was to have been two hours after day-break this morning, but Juan here tells me it was postponed till noon. The King—"

He was proceeding, when he was startled by a sharp cry, and Perez, hastily turning, caught the novice as he was in the act of falling from his horse. In an instant, however, he recovered, and exclaiming, in a thrilling tone of excitement—

"Father Ambrose said life or death hung upon our speed and promptness; he knew not the short interval allowed us. This young foreigner is innocent—the real murderer is discovered. On—, on, for mercy, or we shall be too late!"—gave his horse the rein, and the animal started off at full speed. Perez was at his side in an instant, leaving his friend open-mouthed with astonishment, and retailing the marvellous news into twenty different quarters in as many seconds.

Not a word was spoken; not a moment did the fiery chargers halt in their headlong way. On, on they went; on, over wide moors and craggy steeps; on, through the rushing torrent and the precipitous glen; on, through the forest and the plain, with the same unwavering pace. Repeatedly did Marie's brain reel, and her heart grow sick, and her limbs lose all power either to guide or feel; but she neither spoke nor flagged—convulsively she grasped the reins, and closed her eyes, as the voice and hand of her companion urged their steeds swifter and yet swifter on.

An exclamation from Perez roused her. The turrets of Segovia were visible in the distance, glittering in the brilliant sun; but her blood-shot eye turned with sickening earnestness more towards the latter object than the former. It had not yet attained its full meridian—a quarter of an hour, perhaps twenty minutes, was still before them. But the strength of their horses was flagging, foam covered their glossy hides, their nostrils were distended, they breathed hard, and frequently snorted—the short, quick, sound of coming powerlessness. Their steady pace wavered, their heads drooped; but, still urged on by Perez's encouraging voice, they exerted themselves to the utmost—at times darting several paces suddenly forward, then stumbling heavily on. The cold dew stood on Marie's brow, and every pulse seemed stilled. They passed the outer gates—they stood on the brow of a hill commanding a view of the whole city. The castle seemed but a stone's throw from, them; but the sound of muffled drums and other martial instruments were borne towards them on the air. Multitudes were thronging in one direction; the Calle Soledad seemed one mass of human heads, save where the scaffold raised its frightful sign above them. Soldiers were advancing, forming a thin, glittering line through the crowds. In their centre stood the prisoner. On, again, dashed the chargers—scarcely a hundred yards separated them from the palace-gate. Wildly Marie glanced back once more—there were figures on the scaffold. And at that moment—borne in the stillness more loudly, more heavily than usual, or, at least, so it seemed to her tortured senses—the huge bell of the castle chimed the hour of noon!

CHAPTER XXVI.

"The outmost crowd have heard a sound,
Like horse's hoof on harden'd ground;
Nearer it came, and yet more near—
The very deathsmen pause to hear!"

SIR WALTER SCOTT.

In his private closet, far removed from the excitement stirring without, King Ferdinand was sitting, on the morning appointed for Stanley's execution: several maps and plans were before him, over which he appeared intently engaged; but every now and then his brow rested on his hand, and his eyes wandered from their object; Isabella was at work in a recess of the window near him, conversing on his warlike plans, and entering warmly into all his measures, as he roused himself to speak of them, or silent when she saw him sunk in thought. The history of the period dwells with admiration on the domestic happiness of Ferdinand and Isabella, and most refreshingly do such annals stand forth amid the rude and stormy scenes, both in public and private life, most usual to that age. Isabella's real influence on the far less lofty and more crafty Ferdinand was so silent, so unobtrusive, that its extent was never known, either to himself or to her people, till after her death, when in Ferdinand's rapid deterioration from the nobler qualities of earlier years, it was traced too clearly, and occasioned her loss to be mourned, yet more than at the moment of her death.

The hour of noon chimed, and Ferdinand, with unusual emotion, pushed the papers from him.

"There goes the knell of as brave and true a heart as ever beat," he said. "If he be innocent—as I believe him—may Heaven forgive his murderer! Hark! what is that?" he continued hurriedly, as the last chime ceased to vibrate; and, striding to the door of his cabinet he flung it open and listened intently.

"Some one seeks the King! follow me, Isabel. By St. Francis, we may save him yet!" he exclaimed, and rapidly threading the numerous passages, in less than a minute he stood within the hall.

"Who wills speech of Ferdinand?" he demanded. "Let him step forth at once and do his errand."

"I seek thee, King of Spain!" was the instant answer, and a young lad in the white garb of a Benedictine novice, staggered forwards. "Arthur Stanley is innocent! The real murderer is discovered; he lies at the point of death sixty miles hence. Send—take his confession; but do not wait for that. Fly, or it is too late. I see it—the axe is raised—is flashing in the sun; oh, stop it ere it falls!" And with the wild effort to loose the grasp of an old soldier, who more supported than detained him, his exhausted strength gave way, and they laid him, white, stiff, and speechless, on a settle near.

With his first word, however, Ferdinand had turned to a trusty soldier, and bade him "fly to stop the work of death;" and the man needed not a second bidding: he darted from the hall, flew through the castle-yard, repeated the words to the first individual he met, by whom it was repeated to another, and by him again on and on till it reached the crowds around the scaffold; where it spread like wildfire from mouth to mouth, reaching the ear of Don Felix, even before his eye caught the rapidly advancing soldier, whom he recognized at once as one of his Sovereign's private guards; impelling him, with an almost instinctive movement, to catch the upraised arm of the executioner at the very instant he was about to strike.

"Wherefore this delay, Don Felix? it is but a cruel mercy," sternly inquired the Chief Hermano, whose office had led him also to the scaffold.

"Behold, and listen: praised be the holy saints, he is saved!" was the rapid reply, as the voice of the soldier close by the foot of the scaffold, was distinguished bidding them "Hold! hold! the King commands it. He is innocent; the real murderer is discovered!" and then followed a shout, so loud, so exulting, that it seemed to have burst from those assembled hundreds at the same instant. The prisoner heard it, indeed; but to his bewildered senses—taking the place as it did of the expected blow—it was so utterly meaningless that he neither moved nor spoke; and even Don Felix's friendly voice charging him—"Up, Stanley! up, man! thou art saved—thine innocence made known!" failed to convince him of the truth. He rose from his knees; but his limbs shook, and his face—which had changed neither hue nor expression when he had knelt for the fatal blow—was colorless as marble. He laid his trembling hand on Father Francis's arm, and tried to speak, but he could not utter a sound.

"'Tis true, my beloved son: thy sinful thoughts have been sufficiently chastised; and the mercy of Heaven publicly revealed. Our prayers have not been said in vain; thine innocence is known—the guilty one discovered!"

To doubt these solemn accents was impossible, and though the effort was mighty to prevent it, Nature would have sway, and Stanley laid his head on the Prior's arm, and burst into tears. And the wild shout that again awoke, seemed to clarion forth a thrilling denial to the charge of weakness, which on such openly demonstrated emotion, some hearts dead to the voice of Nature might have pronounced.

King Ferdinand had not been idle while this exciting scene was enacting; questioning briefly but distinctly the villager who had accompanied the novice; the latter still remaining in a state of exhaustion precluding all inquiries from him. Perez, however, could only repeat the lad's words when informed that the execution of Senor Stanley was to take place that day. Father Ambrose had merely told him that he (Perez) had rendered a most important service to more than one individual by his compassionate care of the dying man, whose desire to communicate with the King was no idle raving. He had also charged him to take particular care of the young novice, who was ailing and weakly; that the emergency of the present case alone had compelled him to send the lad to Segovia, as his dress and ability, might gain him a quicker admission to the King or Queen, than the rude appearance and uncouth dialect of his companion. The father had also requested him to urge the officers, whom the King might send to take the dying man's confession, to travel at their utmost speed, for he thought death was approaching fast.

With his usual rapidity of thought and decision, Ferdinand's orders were given and so quickly obeyed, that even before the arrival of the Sub-Prior and Don Felix with the released prisoner, a band of men, headed by Don Alonzo and two of the chief officers of the Santa Hermandad, had already started for the village. The King still retained Perez, not only to reward him liberally, but that his tale might be repeated to the proper authorities, and compared with that of the novice, as soon as he had sufficiently recovered to give it. The entrance of Stanley effectually prevented his giving more than a pitying glance towards the poor boy, who had been raised on one of the benches, surrounded by the soldiers, who were doing all their rude kindness suggested to revive him.

Isabella had followed her husband to the hall, and been a quiet but penetrative observer of all that followed. She had started as the voice of the novice met her ear, and made a few hasty steps forward; but then checked herself, and quietly watched the proceedings of the soldiers. Perceiving how wholly ineffectual their efforts appeared, she advanced towards them. With the most reverential affection the men made way for her. They had been so accustomed to see her on the battle-field, tending the wounded and the dying, soothing their anguish and removing their cares, ay, and more than once doing the same kindly office in their rude and lowly homes, that her appearance and gentle tending of the boy, excited no surprise whatever. She motioned them all back, apparently to allow a free current of air—in reality, to prevent them from adopting her own suspicions; she did not remove the somewhat unusually tightly-secured hood; but for her, one glance on that white and chiselled face was sufficient. Her skill was at length successful, and with the first symptom of returning animation, she left him to the soldiers, and joined the throng around the King; but her eye, which from long use, appeared literally endowed with power to take in every desired object, however separated, at one glance, still watched him as he painfully endeavored to rise, and threw one searching glance towards the principal group. His eyes rested a full minute on the prisoner, with an expression which Isabella alone, perhaps, of all in that hall, could read. A momentary crimson flushed his cheek, and then his face was bowed in his spread hands, and his slight frame shook, with the fervor of the thanksgiving, which his whole soul outpoured.

Perceiving that the lad had recovered his senses, Perez referred all the eager questioners to him, feeling so bewildered at the marvellous transformation of himself, in his own opinion, from, an ignorant rustic, who had never seen the interior of a town, to the permitted companion of his sovereign and his nobles, and even of Isabella, and he received from her lips a few words of kindly commendation, that it was almost an effort to speak; and he longed to rush back to his village and astound them all, and still more, triumph over his friend, the hostellerie-keeper, who, lord it as he might, had never been so honored.

"Come hither, boy," said Ferdinand kindly; and the novice slowly and with evident reluctance obeyed. "We could almost wish thy tastes had pointed elsewhere than the church, that our acknowledgments of thy exertions in our service might be more substantial than mere thanks; however, thy patron saint shall not want a grateful offering. Nay, our presence is surely not so terrible that thou shouldst tremble thus, poor child! Hast thou aught more to communicate?—aught for our private ear, or that of her Highness our consort? If not, we will not exhaust thy little strength by useless questions."

In a tone so low and faltering, that Ferdinand was obliged to bend down his head to hear, the novice replied, that if messengers had been despatched to the village, his errand was sufficiently accomplished. Father Ambrose had merely charged him to say that the real murderer had himself confessed his crime, and that the sin had been incited, by such a horrible train of secret guilt, that all particulars were deferred till they could be imparted to the authorities of justice, and by them to the sovereigns themselves. For himself he only asked permission to return to the village with Perez, and rejoin his guardian, Father Ambrose, as soon as his Grace would please to dismiss him.

"Thou must not—shalt not—return without my poor thanks, my young preserver," exclaimed Stanley, with emotion. "Had it not been for exertions which have well nigh exhausted thee, exertions as gratuitous as noble—for what am I to thee?—my honor might have been saved indeed, but my life would have paid a felon's forfeit. Would that I could serve thee—thou shouldst not find me ungrateful! Give me thine hand, at least, as pledge that shouldst thou ever need me—if not for thyself, for others—thou wilt seek me without scruple."

The boy laid his hand on Stanley's without hesitation, but without speaking; he merely raised his heavy eyes a moment to his face, and vainly did Stanley endeavor to account for the thrill which shot through his heart so suddenly as almost to take away his breath, as he felt the soft touch of that little hand and met that momentary glance.

Who has not felt the extraordinary power of a tone—a look—a touch? which,

"Touching th' electric chain, wherewith we are darkly bound,"

fills the heart and mind with irresistible impulses, engrossing thoughts, and startling memories, all defined and united, and yet lasting for so brief a moment that we are scarcely able to realize their existence ere they are gone— and so completely, that we perplex ourselves again and again with the vain effort to recall their subject or their meaning. And so it was with Stanley. The thrill passed and he could not even trace its origin or flitting thought; he only saw a Benedictine novice before him; he only felt regret that there was no apparent means with which he could evince his gratitude.

On Father Francis offering to take charge of the boy, till his strength was sufficiently renovated to permit his safe return to the village, Isabella spoke, for the first time:—

"Reverend Father! We will ourselves take charge of this poor child. There are some questions we would fain inquire, ere we can permit his return to his guardian: if satisfactorily answered, a munificent gift to his patron saint shall demonstrate, how deeply we feel the exertions he has made; and if we can serve him better than merely allowing his return to his monastery, trust me we shall not fail. Follow me, youth!" she continued, as the Sub-Prior and the King, though surprised at her words, acquiesced. The novice shrunk back and clung to the side of Perez, as if most unwilling to comply; but neither the command, nor the look, with which it was enforced could be disobeyed, and slowly and falteringly he followed Isabella from the hall.

CHAPTER XXVII.

'Tis done! and so she droops. Oh, woman-heart!
How bold and brave to do thy destined part!
Thro' sorrow's waves press firmly, calmly on,
And pause not, sink not, till the goal is won!

MS.

Not a word passed between them, until they had reached Isabella's private cabinet; and even then the Queen—though she seated herself and signed to the boy to stand before her, as desirous of addressing him—asked not a question, but fixed her penetrating eyes on his pallid features, with a look in which severity was very evidently struggling, with commiseration and regard. To attempt to retain disguise was useless; Marie flung aside the shrouding hood, and sinking down at the Queen's feet, buried her face in her robe, and murmured in strong emotion—

"Gracious Sovereign—mercy!"

"Again wouldst thou deceive, again impose upon me, Marie? What am I to think of conduct mysterious as thine? Wherefore fly from my protection—reject with ingratitude the kindness I would have proffered—mistrust the interest which thou hadst already proved, and then return as now? I promised forgiveness, and continuation of regard, if the truth were revealed and mystery banished, and darker than ever has thy conduct drawn the veil around thee. What urged thy flight, and wherefore this disguise? Speak out, and truthfully; we will be tampered with no longer!"

But Marie vainly tried to obey; her brain was burning; the rapid ride, the sudden transition, from the sickening horror of being too late, to the assurance of Stanley's safety, the thought that she had indeed parted from him for ever, and now Isabella's evident anger, when her woman-heart turned to her as a child's to its mother's, yearning for that gentle sympathy which, at such a moment, could alone have soothed. Words seemed choked within her, and the effort to speak produced only sobs. Isabella's eyes filled with tears.

"Speak," she said, more gently; "Marie—say only why thou didst fly me, when I had given no evidence, that the boon thou didst implore me to grant, had become, by thy strange confession, null and void. What urged thy flight?"

"Not my own will. Oh, no—no, gracious Sovereign; I would have remained a contented prisoner with thee, but they bore me away to such scenes and sounds of horror that their very memory burns my brain. Oh, madam! do with me what thou wilt, but condemn me not to return to that fearful place again. Death, death itself—ay, even such a death as Arthur has escaped—were mercy in its stead!"

"Of what speakest thou, Marie? Who could have dared bear thee from our protection without thine own free will? Thy mind has been overwrought and is bewildered still; we have been harsh, perchance, to urge thee to speak now: repose may—".

"Repose! Oh, no—no; let me remain with thee!" she sobbed, as forgetful of either state or form, her head sunk on Isabella's knee. "He has borne me from your highness' power once; he can, he may, I know he will again. Oh, save me from him! It was not because of my faith he bore me there, and tempted and tortured and laughed at my agony; he taunted me with his power to wreak the vengeance of a baffled passion upon me—for, as a Jewess, who would protect me? Oh, mighty Sovereign! send me not from thy presence. Don Luis will take me from thy very roof again."

"Don Luis!" repeated Isabella, more and more convinced that Marie's sufferings had injured her brain. "What power can he have, so secret and so terrible? Marie, thou ravest!"

"Do I rave?" replied the unhappy girl, raising her right hand to her throbbing brow. "It may be so; perhaps it has all been a dream—a wild and fearful dream!—and I am awakened from it now; and yet—yet how can it be; how came my arm thus if it had not been reality—horrible, agonizing reality!" And as she spoke she removed the covering from her left arm. Painfully Isabella started: the beautiful limb hung powerless from wrist to shoulder, a dry and scorched and shrievelled bone.

"And couldst thou think thy Sovereign would ordain, or even permit, such suffering?" she exclaimed, after a moment's pause, passing her arm fondly round Marie, whom she had raised from the ground to a cushion by her side. "My poor unhappy child, what is this dark mystery? Who can have dared to injure thee, and call it justice, zeal—religion, perchance! Mother of Mercy! pardon the profanation of the word! Try and collect thy thoughts, and tell me all. Who has dared thus insult our power?"

"Don Luis!—Don Luis!" repeated Marie, clinging like an infant to the Queen, and shuddering with terror at the very recollection of a power which she had faced so calmly. "Oh, save me from him! torture itself I could bear, but not his words."

"Don Luis!" reiterated the astonished Queen. "What has he to do with torture? Who is he—what is he, my poor child, that his very name should thus appal thee? He may indeed have dared speak insulting words, but what power has he thus fearfully to wreak his vengeance?"

"Who is he—what is he?" repeated Marie, looking with surprise in the Queen's pitying face. "Does not your highness know—and yet how shouldst thou?—his very office is as secret as his own black nature? Has your highness never heard men whisper of a secret Inquisition, hiding itself even in thy domains? Oh, my Sovereign, it was there they dragged me! [her voice sunk to a low shuddering whisper] and he was grand master there; he—even Don Luis! And he will bear me there again. Oh, save me from those fearful sounds—those horrid sights: they glare before me now!"

"And I will save thee, my child! ay, and root out these midnight horrors from my kingdom," exclaimed Isabella, indignation flashing in her eye, and flushing on her cheek. "Once we have been insulted—once deceived; but never to us can such occur a second time. Fearfully shall this deed of infamy recoil upon its perpetrators! Tremble not thus, my poor girl, no one shall injure thee; no one can touch thee, for we are warned, and this fearful tale shall be sifted to the bottom! Child of a reprobate faith, and outcast race as thou art, thinkest thou that even to thee Isabella would permit injury and injustice? If we love thee too well, may we be forgiven, but cared for thou shalt be; ay, so cared for, that there shall be joy on earth, and in heaven for thee yet!"

At another moment, those words would have been understood in their real meaning; but Marie could then only feel the consoling conviction of security and love. It was not merely personal kindness which had so bound her to her Sovereign; it was the unacknowledged but felt conviction, that Isabella had penetrated her secret feelings, with regard to Arthur Stanley; and yet not a syllable of this had ever passed the Queen's lips. Oh, true sympathy seldom needs expression, for its full consolation to be given and received! The heart recognizes intuitively a kindred heart, and turns to it in its sorrow or its joy, conscious of finding in it, repose from itself. But only a woman can give to woman this perfect sympathy; for the deepest recesses, the hidden sources of anguish in the female heart no man can read.

Engrossed as Isabella was by the mysterious information imparted by Marie, indefinitely yet forcibly confirmed by her, then unusual, knowledge of the past history of Spain, she was more easily satisfied with Marie's hurried and hesitating account of her escape, than she might otherwise have been. To proclaim her relationship with Father Ambrose was ruin to him at once. He had been one, she said with truth, who had received great obligations from her family, and had vowed to return them whenever it should be in his power so to do; he had, therefore, made the exertion to save her, and was about taking her to her childhood's home on the frontiers of Castile, the only place, it appeared to him, sufficiently secret to conceal her from Don Luis's thousand spies; but that on the providential discovery of the real murderer, and the seeming impossibility of ever seeing the King himself in time—she paused.

"Could he send thee on such a rapid errand, my child, and suffering thus?" gently inquired Isabella.

"No, gracious madam," was the unhesitating rejoinder, though a burning blush mounted to her very temples; "it was my own voluntary choice. It was my unhappy fate to have been the actual cause of his arraignment; it was but my duty to save him if I could."

"And thou wouldst have returned with Perez had we not penetrated thy disguise?"

"Yes, gracious Sovereign." And the flush faded into paleness, ashy as before; but the tone was calm and firm.

The Queen looked at her intently, but made no further observation; and speedily summoning her before trusted attendants, placed the widow of Morales once more in their charge; imparted to them as much of Marie's tale as she deemed requisite, and the consequent necessity for her return to the Queen's care; nay, her very existence was to be kept secret from all save those to whom she herself should choose to impart it. Gratified by her confidence, they were eager to obey; and so skilfully did they enter into her wishes, that their very companions suspected not the identity of the prisoner, in whom, they were told, their Sovereign was so much interested. Curiosity might have been busy with very many, but their vague conjectures fell far short of the truth; Catharine Pas was the only one of Isabella's younger maidens to whom the real fact was imparted.

CHAPTER XXVIII.

'Twas a dark tale of crime, and awed and chilled
E'en indignation seeming horror still'd,
Men stood beside a murd'rer's couch of death,
Watching-the glazing-eye and flickering-breath—
Speaking with look and hurried sign alone,
Their thoughts, too terror-fraught for word or tone.—MS.

The indignation excited in the Queen's mind against Don Louis was destined, very speedily, to be increased. Ferdinand had had time to become half angry, and quite impatient, ere his messengers dispatched to the village returned. Stanley had been released—was regarded by all as innocent; but this was literally only from a peasant's word and the half broken intelligence of an exhausted boy: he wanted proof, and a vague dread would take possession of him that his fate was but temporarily suspended. At an early hour the next day, however, Don Alonzo returned; and Ferdinand's impatient anger was averted, when he found the delay had been occasioned by their determination, to convey the dying man to Segovia, and the caution necessary for its accomplishment. The Hermanos had already noted down his confession; but it was so fraught with extended and dangerous consequences, that they felt, they dared not act on their responsibility: all suppressing measures must proceed from the sovereigns themselves. Perez was again summoned, and at once swore to the identity of the dying man as the individual he had rescued from a deep pit, in a lonely mountain-pass, about twenty miles from his village; and the man, whose eagerness to speak was evident, though his voice was so faint, as scarcely to be intelligible, commenced his dark and terrible tale.

The indignation of the Sovereign, and of those whom he had chosen to be present, was excited to the utmost, mingled with horror as the mysterious fates of many a loved companion were thus so fearfully solved; but none felt the recital with the same intensity of emotion as the Sub-Prior, who, with, head bowed down upon his breast, and hands tightly clenched, knelt beside the penitent. It was not indignation, it was not horror; but agony of spirit that a religion which he loved better than himself, whose purity and honor he would have so jealously guarded, that he would have sacrificed life itself for its service, should have been made the cover for such unutterable villany. Few imagined the deeds of painful mortification and bodily penance which, in his solitude, the Sub-Prior afterwards inflicted on himself; as if his individual sufferings should atone for the guilt of his brethren, and turn from them the wrath of an avenging God.

Horrible as were the details imparted, incomprehensible as it seemed that so extended and well-organized a power, should exist so secretly throughout Spain, as to hide itself even from the sovereigns and ministers of justice themselves, yet none doubted what they heard. Sovereigns and nobles well knew that the Inquisition had been established both in Castile and Arragon centuries before, and that the annals of those kingdoms, though mentioning the resistance of the people against this awful power, had been silent as to its entire extirpation.

In the first part of his narrative the man had spoken shrinkingly and fearfully, as if still in dread of vengeance on his betrayal; but his voice became bolder when he confessed his own share in the late atrocious crime. Accustomed by the strictest and most rigid training, to obey as familiars, the will of their superiors without question—to be mere mindless and feelingless tools, to whom death itself was awarded, if by word or hint, or even sign, they dared evince themselves to be as other men—he had, at the command of the Grand Inquisitor, deeply drugged Senor Stanley's evening draught, and, while under its potent influence, had purloined his sword; waylaid Don Ferdinand in the Calle Soledad, effectually done the deed, and—aware that it would be many hours ere the English Senor could arouse himself from the stupifying effects of the draught—had intended returning to his chamber still more effectually to throw on him the suspicion of the murder. It happened, however, that it was the first time he had ever been chosen by his superiors as their tool for actual murder, and the magnitude of the crime, from the greatness of, and universal love borne towards the victim, had so appalled him, that, combined with the raging storm and pitchy darkness, he had felt utterly bewildered. Not well acquainted with Segovia, he had found himself, after more than an hour's wandering—instead of, as he expected, again near the Senor's lodgings—in the self-same spot whence he had started, and close by the body of his victim. The sight horrified and bewildered him yet more, and he crept behind a low wall, resolved on remaining there till the tempest had at least partially subsided, and then fulfil the remainder of his instructions; knowing that to fail in any one point, would be the signal of his own destruction. Fortune, however, so far favored him, as to send the young English Senor to the very spot, and there was therefore no occasion for his further interference. He tarried till he had seen Stanley's arrest, and had heard the loud execrations of all proclaiming him the murderer—and then returned to his employers.

The education of the familiars had so far failed with him, that, though aware of its danger, thoughts would enter his mind, as to how Don Ferdinand Morales could have offended the dread power which he served, and why the foreign Senor should be thus implicated in the deed. He hoped to have concealed these doubts; but from the issue, he imagined that some unguarded word spoken to a companion, must have betrayed him. He was chosen by the Grand Inquisitor as his companion, on some secret expedition two days after the trial, unsuspicious of the danger awaiting him, till the desolate scene on which they unexpectedly entered flashed terror on his mind. His superior had there paused, told him that from the witness of Beta, the servant girl, it was quite evident he had disobeyed part of the instructions given, or his *return* to Arthur's lodgings would have been heard by her as well as his *departure* and thus at once have implicated the Englishman as the real murderer; that though chance had thrown equal suspicion upon him, it did net remove his disobedience, and so he was doomed to death; and the blow, instantaneously given, felled him insensible to the ground. When he recovered his senses, he found himself lying in a deep pit, where he had evidently been thrown as dead. The wounds and contusions received in the fall, as far as he could recollect, by producing a most excruciating sense of pain, roused him from temporary insensibility, and he was convinced he heard his murderer's voice—though he could not see him—exclaim distinctly, as if he were leaning over the mouth of the pit, "There goes my last doubt: other men might call it their last fear, but I know not the word! Three victims for the possession of one—and who will now dare to brand me? I had slain that faltering craven without his disobedience, he dared to *think* upon his deed."

Almost insensible from agony as he was, these words had impressed themselves indelibly; causing the burning desire to live and be revenged. And the opportune succors of the villager, Perez, with a party of woodmen; the completely hidden site of the village to which, he had been conveyed; and the, at first, favorable healing of his wounds, appeared to give him every hope of its accomplishment. He had resolved on communicating his tale to none save to Ferdinand himself, or to the Chief Hermano, under strict promise to reveal it to the Sovereign: but his intense anxiety had evidently prevented the attainment of his desire, by producing fever; and thence arose his wild and almost maniac cravings to make confession, and bind some holy monk, by a solemn vow, to convey it to the King.

It was not till the conclusion of this momentous narration, that the King permitted any questions to be asked; and those he then demanded were so concise and clear, that but few words were needed in which to couch the reply.

"And the designer of this hellish plot, the real murderer—through thy hand, of one brave friend, and almost another—is the same who has murdered thee!" he inquired, after learning the exact sites of these mysterious halls; information which caused some of the bravest hearts to shudder, from their close vicinity.

The man answered at once in the affirmative.

"And he dares assume, in this illegal tribunal, the rank of Grand Inquisitor?"

"Ay, gracious liege."

"And his name?—that by which he is known to man? Speak! And as thy true confession may be the means of bringing a very fiend to justice, so may thy share in his deeds be pardoned."

An indescribable expression passed over the fast stiffening features of the dying. He half raised himself, and, laying his clammy hand on Ferdinand's robe, whispered, in clear and thrilling tones—

"Bend low, my liege; even at this moment I dare not speak it loud; but, oh! beware of those who affect superior sanctity to their fellows: there is one who in the sunshine stands forth wisest, and purest, and strictest; and at midnight rules arch-fiend—men call him DON LUIS GARCIA. *He* is Don Ferdinand's murderer! *He* sought Senor Stanley's death and mine; but instead of a victim, he has found an accuser! His web has coiled round himself—flee him! avoid him as ye would a walking pestilence, or visible demon! Minister as he may be of our holy father, the Pope, he is a villain—his death alone can bring safety to Spain. Ha! what is this? Mother of mercy! save me! The cross! the cross! Absolution! The flames of hell! Father, bid them avaunt! I—a true confession." The words were lost in a fearful gurgling sound, and the convulsion which ensued was so terrible, that some of the very bravest involuntarily turned away; but Stanley, who had listened to the tale with emotions too varied and intense for speech, now sprung forward, wildly exclaiming—

"Three victims for one! Where is that one? Speak—speak in mercy! Oh, God! he dies and says no word!"

The eyes of the dying man glared on him, but there was no meaning in their gaze; they rolled in their sockets, glazed, and in another minute all was stiff in death.

CHAPTER XXIX.

"Doth Heaven
Woo the free spirit for dishonored breath
To sell its birthright? Doth Heaven set a price
On the clear jewel of unsullied faith
And the bright calm of conscience?"

MRS. HEMANS.

A private council immediately followed the confession received; but though it continued many hours, no active measures could at once be decided upon. Secret and illegal, according to Spanish laws, as this tribunal was, it was yet an instrument of the Pope, acknowledging his supremacy alone, and, in consequence, always receiving his protection. Civil justice, it appeared, could not reach those who were protected by; the head of the church; but Ferdinand's mind was far too capacious to admit this plea. Rooted out of his dominions—in its present form, at least—he resolved it should be, and Isabella confirmed the resolve. Not only was its secret existence fraught with the most awful crimes and injustice, regarded generally, but it was derogatory and insulting to that sovereign power, which Ferdinand and Isabella had both determined on rendering supreme. Father Francis, whose usual energy of thought and counsel appeared completely annihilated from the fearful tale he had heard, strenuously urged the sovereigns to wait the arrival of Torquemada, the Queen's confessor, who was now every hour expected, and whose sterner and more experienced mind would give them better counsel. To this both sovereigns agreed, but one measure they adopted at once. As Grand Inquisitor, the principal actor in this atrocious drama might be servant of and solely answerable to the Pope; as Don Luis Garcia, he was subject to Ferdinand and Isabella, and as such amenable to the laws of Spain. A schedule was therefore drawn up, stating that whereas the man commonly known as Don Luis Garcia, had been convicted of many atrocious and capital crimes, and, amongst the gravest, of having instigated and commanded the murder of Don Ferdinand Morales, and done to death his own tool, the real committer of the deed, that Arthur Stanley might be charged with, and executed for, the same; the sovereigns of Spain called upon their loving subjects—of every rank and every degree, in all and every part of the realm—to unite in endeavoring to discover, and deliver up the said Don Luis Garcia, to the rigor of the law. An enormous reward was offered for delivering him alive into the hands of justice, and half the sum, should he have resisted to the death. The proclamation was made by sound of trumpet in various parts of Segovia, and copies sent, with all possible speed, to every city, town, and even village, over Spain. A correct description of his person accompanied the schedule, and every possible measure was adopted that could tend to his apprehension. So strong was the popular feeling against him that every class, almost every individual, felt it a personal duty to assist, in this case, the course of justice. He had deceived all men, and all men in consequence leagued themselves against him. So secretly, and yet so judiciously, were the plans for his seizure carried on, and so universal the popular ferment, that it appeared marvellous how he could have escaped; and yet weeks merged into months, and, though the measures of the Santa Hermandad in no way relaxed, Don Luis was still at large, and effectually concealed. We may here state at once— though it carries us much in advance of our present scene—that Father Francis resolved at all costs to purge the church of Spain from this most unholy member; and, authorized by the sovereigns, made a voluntary pilgrimage to the court of St. Peter's, obtained an audience with the Pope, laid the case before him, and besought the penalty of excommunication to be fulminated against the hypocrite who had dared to use, as cover for most atrocious villany, the pure and sacred ordinances of the church. Alexander the Sixth, himself a worker of such awful crimes that he was little capable of entering into the pure and elevated character of the Sub-Prior, heard him calmly, smiled sneeringly, and then informed him, he was too late. The worthy and zealous servant of Rome, known to men as Don Luis Garcia, had been before him, made confession of certain passions as exciting erring deeds, to which all men were liable, had done penance, received absolution, and was in a fair way of rising to the highest eminence in the church.

Father Francis remonstrated, urged, dared to speak bolder truths than had ever before reached the papal ear but all without effect: and this truly good and spiritual man returned to Spain stricken to the dust. He reported the failure of his mission; heard, with bowed head and aching soul, the natural indignation of Ferdinand, and the quieter, but to him, still more expressive sorrow, at this fearful abuse of her holy religion from Isabella; and then, with an earnestness impossible to be resisted, conjured the royal permission to retire entirely from all interference in public life. He could not, he said, support the weight of shame, which, falling on his church, had affected him individually. Vain were the royal solicitations, vain the love of the people, vain the entreaties of the abbot and brethren of his convent; he resigned the office of Sub-Prior, relinquished every religious and secular honor, and buried himself in the most impenetrable solitude, fraught with austerity and mortification, personal penance, and yet devoted to such extraordinary acquirements, that, though for long years his very existence was well nigh forgotten, when next he burst upon the astonished eyes of the world, it was no longer as Father Francis, the Sub-Prior of a Franciscan monastery, a good and benevolent monk, but as the learned priest, the sagacious statesman, the skilful general, ay, and gallant warrior—the great and good CARDINAL XIMENES!

To wait the arrival of Torquemada, the sovereigns and their council unanimously resolved. It was but a very brief delay, and would permit a more effectual extermination of the secret office than could be decided upon by the laity alone. Ere the day closed, and in presence of the sovereigns, of all the nobles, officers of state, the Santa Hermandad and principal citizens, Arthur Stanley was formally pronounced INNOCENT of the crime with which he had been charged. The golden spurs, which had been ignominiously hacked from his heels, were replaced by the aged Duke of Murcia; knighthood again bestowed by the King; and Isabella's own hand, with winning courtesy, presented him a sword, whose real Toledo blade, and richly jewelled hilt, should replace the valued weapon, the loss of which had caused him such unmerited suffering, and shame.

"May it be used for us, as faithfully and nobly as its predecessor," were Isabella's concluding words; "and its associations, Senor Stanley, be nought but those of joy."

The young man's cheek burned, but there was a deep shadow on his countenance, which neither the honors he received, nor his own urgent efforts had power to remove. He looked wistfully after the sovereigns as they quitted the church, then with an irresistible impulse, broke from the throng with whom he had been endeavoing to join in animated converse, and, suddenly kneeling before Isabella, exclaimed in low, agitated tones—

"*She*—she may still be in the villain's power. Oh, my liege, wait not for Torquemada's arrival and leave her to die! He will wreak his full vengeance upon her."

"Trust me for her safety, my young friend; measures have been already taken to secure it," was Isabella's instant reply, in a tone so full of sympathy, that Arthur caught her robe, and pressed it to his lips.

She smiled kindly and passed on, still accompanied by Ferdinand, not a little astonished at her words, and still more so when Marie's whole tale was imparted to him.

On retiring to rest that night, his thoughts still engrossed with vain speculations as to the destined fate of Marie,—Arthur, half unconsciously, unsheathed Isabella's magnificent gift, to judge of the temper of the blade; and, as he did so, a scroll, which had been twisted round the steel, fell to the ground. He raised it with hasty curiosity, but his heart throbbed as he recognized the handwriting of the Queen, and deciphered the following words:—

"To Senor Stanley, in secrecy and confidence, these: The eye of love is said to pierce through all disguises. In this instance it has proved less discriminative than woman's sympathy, and woman's penetration. She in whom we believe Senor Stanley interested, and to whose exertions he owes the publication of his innocence in time to save life as well as honor, is safe, and under the protection of her Queen. Let this suffice for present peace, and speak of it to none. ISABELLA R."

Arthur's first impulse was to press the precious letter to his lips, and gaze upon it till every letter seemed transferred from the paper to his heart; his next was to sit down on the nearest seat, and bury his face in his hands, actually bewildered by the flash of light, which with those brief words came. Disguise—exertion—could it be possible? Nay, it must be! The soft touch of that little hand, the speaking look of those lovely eyes, again thrilled through his very soul, and he knew their meaning now. Mysterious, bewildering as it was, the novice, the poor, exhausted, seeming boy—was Marie! Again he owed his life to her, and the wild yearning to gaze on her again, to clasp her to his bosom, to pour forth his gratitude, to soothe and shield, became so painfully intense, as almost to banish the joy, which her rescue from danger ought to have occasioned. Had it not been for her refusal to bear witness against him, not even the month's grace would have been allowed him; he would have been executed at once. She had saved him then—she had saved him now! And his heart so swelled he knew not how to contain its fulness, how to calm it down, to wait till the Queen's further pleasure should be known. But hope sprung up to give him comfort; Isabella would accomplish her intention of conversion; Marie could never resist her, and then—then, oh! she would be all, all his own, and life shine, for both the brighter, for its former tempest clouds. Meanwhile, he had such sweet thoughts, such lovely images, to rest on. He owed his life, his honor, to her; and he thought that it was his devoted gratitude which so deepened love. How sweet is such illusion! how refreshingly soothing to be grateful, when the object of that gratitude has been, and is still, the dear object of our love! How often we deceive ourselves, and imagine we are experiencing the strongest emotions of gratitude, when, had an indifferent person conferred the same benefit, we might feel it indeed, but it would more pain than pleasure; and be an obligation, so heavy that we should never rest, till in some measure, at least, it was returned. How contrary the impression of benefits from those we love!

Never before had the appearance of the Queen's confessor, the stern, and some said cruel, Torquemada, been hailed with such excitement. He was speedily informed of the late transactions, and his counsel most earnestly demanded by both sovereigns. He required some days to deliberate, he said, so momentous and important was the affair; and when he did reply, his counsel was entirely opposed to what many hoped, and Ferdinand expected. Indignant as he declared himself to be, at the abuses in religion, he yet put a strong and most decided negative on the royal proposition, of utterly exterminating this unlawful tribunal. With all his natural eloquence, and in most forcible language, he declared that, if kept within proper bounds, restrained by due authority, and its proceedings open to the inspection of the Sovereign, and under him, the archbishops and other dignitaries of the church, the Inquisition would be a most valuable auxiliary to the well-doing and purifying of the most Catholic kingdom. He produced argument after argument of most subtle reasoning, to prove that every effort to abolish the office in Spain had been entirely useless: it would exist, and if not publicly acknowledged, would always be liable to abuse and desecration; that the only means of exterminating its secret, and too arrogant power, was to permit its public establishment, and so control it, that its measures should be open to the present, and to every successive sovereign. He allowed the necessity, the imperious necessity of rooting out the *secret* office; but he was convinced this could not be done, nor in fact would the church allow it, unless it should be recognized in the face of all Europe, as based on alike the civil and religious laws of Spain.

On Ferdinand the wily churchman worked, by proving that his royal prerogative would be insured rather than injured by this proceeding; that by publicly establishing the Inquisition, he proved his resolution to control even this power, and render it a mere instrument in his sovereign hand; that his contemplated conquest of the Moors could not be better begun than by the recognition of a holy office, whose glory it would be to bring all heathens to the purifying and saving doctrines of the church of Rome. Ferdinand, though wary and politic himself, was no match for Torquemada's Jesuitical eloquence; he was won over to adopt the churchman's views with scarcely an effort to resist them. With Isabella the task was much more difficult. He appealed guardedly and gently to her tender regard for the spiritual welfare of her people, sympathized with her in her indignant horror of the crimes committed under religion's name, but persisted that the evil of a secret Inquisition would never be remedied, save by the measure he proposed. He pledged himself never to rest, till the present halls and ministers of darkness were exterminated from every part of Spain; but it could only be on condition of her assent to his counsel. He used all his eloquence; he appealed to her as a zealous Catholic, whose first duty was to further and purify her faith; but for four days he worked in vain; and when she did give her consent, it was with such a burst of tears, that it seemed as if her foreboding eye had indeed read the shrouded annals of the future, and beheld there, not the sufferings of individuals alone, but of the decline and dishonor of that fair and lovely land, which she had so labored to exalt. Ere another year from that day had passed, the Inquisition was publicly established throughout the kingdom; and Torquemada, as first Grand Inquisitor, reaped the reward of his persevering counsel, and sealed, with blood, the destiny of Spain.

To her confessor, Isabella revealed the story of Marie, and her own intentions. Torquemada heard the tale with a stern severity, little encouraging to the Queen's ideas of mercy; he insisted that her conversion *must* be effected; if by kindness and forbearance, well and good; but if she were obstinate, harshness must be resorted to; and only on that condition would he grant Isabella the desired blessing on her task. He did not fail to bring forward the fact of a zealous Catholic, such as Don Ferdinand Morales, wedding and cherishing one of the accursed race, and conniving at her secret adherence to her religion, as a further and very strong incentive for the public establishment of the Inquisition, whose zealous care would effectually guard the sons of Spain from such unholy alliances in future. He urged the supposition of Marie's having become the mother of children by Ferdinand; was it not most probable, nay, certain, that she would infuse her own unbelief in them; and then how mixed and defiled a race would take the place of the present pure Castilians. Isabella could reply nothing satisfactory to this eloquent reasoning. The prejudices of education are strong in every really earnest heart; and though her true woman's nature revolted at every thought of severity, and towards one so suffering as Marie, she acknowledged its necessity, in case of kindness failing. Under the seal of confession, she imparted her full plan to Torquemada, entering more into minute particulars than she had done even to her husband, or in words to herself. It was so fraught with mercy and gentleness that Torquemada gave his consent, believing it utterly impossible, if Marie really loved, as Isabella fancied, that she could resist.

On the departure of her confessor, the Queen communed, as was her frequent custom, long and severely with her own heart. What was the cause of her extreme dislike to using harshness? With any other member of that detested race, she felt Torquemada's counsel would have been all-powerful; she would have left it all to him. It was then mere personal regard, fear of the suffering which, did she cause Marie increase of pain, she should inflict upon herself, and this must not be. She was failing in the duty she owed her religion, if she could not summon resolution to sacrifice even affection at its shrine. And so she nerved herself, to adopt Torquemada's stern alternative, if indeed it were required. How strange is self-delusion! how difficult, even to the noblest, most unselfish natures, to read another spirit by their own! Isabella felt it might be a duty to sacrifice affection for religion, and nerved herself to its performance at any cost. And yet that Marie should do so, she could not believe; and if she did, harshness and suffering were to be her sole reward! Oh, that in religion, as in every thing else, man would judge his brother man by his own heart; and as dear, as precious, as his peculiar creed may be to him, believe so it is with the faith of his brother! How much of misery, how much of contention, of cruelty and oppression, would pass away from this lovely earth, and give place for Heaven's own unity and peace, and harmony and love.

CHAPTER XXX.

"Oh, bear me up
Against the unutterable tenderness
Of earthly love, my God! In the sick hour
Of dying human hope, forsake me not!"

MRS. HEMANS.

For some months all was gayety and rejoicing in Segovia, not a little heightened by the exciting preparations for the much desired war. The time had now come when Ferdinand could, with safety to the internal state of his kingdom, commence the struggle for which he had so impatiently waited, since the very first hour of the union of Arragon and Castile. Troops were marshalling secretly all over Spain; the armorers and smiths were in constant requisition. The nobles were constantly flitting from their hereditary domains to the court, eager and active to combine all the pomp and valor of a splendid chivalry with the more regular force; standing armies, which in almost every European land were now beginning to take the place of the feudal soldiery, so long their sole resource. It was necessary for Ferdinand, ere he commenced operations, to visit his own dominions; a measure he did not regret, as it effectually concealed his ulterior plans from the Moors, who were also at that time too much disturbed by internal dissensions, to give more than a cursory glance on the movements and appearances of their Christian foes.

In the festivals of the palace the young Englishman was naturally the hero of the day; the best feelings of the Spanish character had been called into play towards him: he had been unjustly accused and seriously injured; been subject to dishonor and shame; and many might say it had all sprung from prejudice against him as a foreigner. The very failing of the Spaniards in this case also operated in his favor; their national jealousy called upon them to make publicly manifest the falsity of such a supposition, and he was courted and fêted by all, brought forward on every occasion, and raised and promoted both to civil and military distinction, by those very men who, before the late events, would have been the first to keep him back, yielding him but the bare and formal courtesy, which, however prejudiced, no true-born Spaniard could refuse.

Amongst Isabella's female train, Arthur Stanley was ever gladly welcomed, and his presence might have proved dangerous to more than one of Isabella's younger attendants, had not his manner been such as to preclude even the boldest and most presuming from any thought of love. One alone he certainly singled out to talk with, and treat with more attention than any other; and that one was the maiden we have more than once had occasion to mention, Catherine Pas. Rallied as she was by her companions, the young girl herself imagined there could be no danger to her peace in associating thus with the handsome young Englishman; for *she* knew, though her companions did not, the real reason of his preference for her society. Isabella had once slightly hinted from which of her attendants Stanley might hear of Marie, and giving them permission to answer his queries. It was a dangerous ordeal for Catherine, but she laughed at the idea of permitting her heart to pass into the possession of one who cared nothing for her, save as she could speak of Marie.

Great was the surprise and many the conjectures of the Queen's female court, when rather more than six months after her strange disappearance, the widow of Morales re-appeared amongst them; not publicly indeed, for at the various fêtes and amusements of the palace, and elsewhere, Marie was never seen. Her existence, however, and safety, under Isabella's especial protection, were no longer kept secret; and her recent loss was in itself quite sufficient reason for her strict retirement. Her identity with brother Ernest, the supposed novice, never transpired; he was supposed to have returned with Perez to his guardian, Father Ambrose, who, though seen and questioned by Don Alonzo at the village, did not accompany his dying penitent to Segovia, nor, in fact, was ever seen in that city again.

The tender care and good nursing which had been lavished on Marie, had restored her sufficiently to health as to permit returning elasticity of mind. All morbid agony had passed, all too passionate emotions were gradually relaxing their fire-bands round her heart; and strength, the martyr strength, for which she unceasingly prayed, to give up all if called upon for her God, seemed dawning for her. That she was still under some restraint, a sort of prisoner in the palace, Marie herself was not aware; she had neither wish nor energy to leave the castle, and therefore knew not that her egress, save under watchful guardianship, would have been denied. She had no spirits to mingle with the light-hearted, happy girls, in her Sovereign's train, and therefore was unconscious that, with the sole exception of Catherine whose passionate entreaties had obtained her this privilege, all intimacy with them would have been effectually prevented. It was enough, more than enough (for the foreboding dread was ever present, that such a blissful calm, such mental and bodily repose, were far, far too sweet for any long continuance) to be employed in little services for and about the person of the Queen, and to know that Arthur Stanley was restored to even more than former favor, and fast rising to eminence and honor.

Before the sovereigns quitted Segovia, Stanley left the court to march southward with Pedro Pas, to occupy a strong fortification on the barrier line, dividing the Spanish from the Moorish territories, and commanding a very important post, which Ferdinand was anxious to secure, and where he intended to commence his warlike operations, as speedily as he could settle affairs at Saragossa. Twice before Stanley's departure did Isabella contrive an apparently accidental meeting between him and Marie, permitting them, though in her presence, ample opportunity for mutual explanation; but not with much evident success. Stanley, indeed, was painfully and visibly agitated, finding it difficult, almost impossible to speak the feelings which had so long filled heart and mind, and been in fancy so often thrown into eloquent words, that he could not understand why in her presence words were frozen up, and he could only *feel*. Marie's cheek and lip had indeed blanched as she beheld him, but the deep and quiet calm she had so earnestly sought, even then did not forsake her; once only her voice faltered, when she conjured him to allude no longer to the past, that the exertions she had made for him demanded no such gratitude as he expressed. He would have answered with his usual passionate impetuosity, but there was something in her manner which restrained him; it was no longer the timid, yielding girl, who, even while she told him of the barrier between them, had yet betrayed the deep love she felt: it was the woman whose martyr spirit was her strength. And yet, spite of himself, he hoped. Isabella, in parting with him, had spoken such words as sent a thrill of delight over his whole being, and he quitted Segovia buoyant and glad-hearted, to wait weeks, months, he thought even years: so certain did he feel of success at last.

Isabella accompanied Ferdinand to Arragon, and determined on remaining at Saragossa during the commencement of his Moorish campaign; but she did not part from him without demanding and receiving his solemn promise to send for her as soon as the residence of females in the camp was practicable. She well knew the inspiring power of her presence in similar scenes, and the joy and increased ardor which the vicinity of near and dear relations, composing her court, would excite in the warrior camp of Ferdinand. The promise was given, and the annals of the Moorish war tell us how faithfully it was kept, and how admirably Isabella performed the part she had assigned herself.

Months glided slowly and peacefully on; as each passed, the trembling heart of Marie foreboded change and sorrow; but it was not till she had been eight months a widow that aught transpired which could account for such strange fears. Then, indeed, the trial came: she thought she was prepared, but the aching heart and failing strength with which she listened to the Queen's commands, betrayed how little our best endeavors can pave the way for sorrow. Isabella spoke gently and kindly indeed, but so decisively, there was no mistaking the meaning of her words: she had waited, she said, till time had restored not only health and strength, but some degree of tranquillity to the heart, and elasticity to the mind. That, as a Jewess, Marie must have long known, the Queen could not continue favor; that she was, in fact, acting without a precedent in thus permitting the attendance of an unbeliever on her person, or appearance in her court; but that she had so acted, believing that when perfectly restored to sense and energy, Marie would herself feel the necessity, and gladly embrace the only return she required—a calm deliberation of the Catholic faith, and, as a necessary consequence, its acceptance. She therefore desired that Marie would devote herself to the instructions of a venerable monk (Father Denis by name), whom she had selected for the task. That from that day Marie would not be called upon for either service or attendance on the Queen, but to devote her whole mind and energies to the task proposed; and that when Father Denis brought her information that Marie accepted the cross, that very hour she should resume her place in Isabella's court, and be the dearest, most cherished there!—be publicly acknowledged as the inheritrix of her husband's vast possessions, and a future of love and joy would shine before her, so bright as to banish even the memories of the stormy past.

Marie would have replied, but Isabella, with gentle firmness, refused to hear her. "I demand nothing now," she said, "but obedience. A willing heart, and open mind, are all you need bring with you to your task: the father's holy lessons, blessed with God's grace, will do the rest. I cannot believe that all the kindness and affection I have shown have been so utterly without effect, that thou too wilt evince the ungrateful obstinacy, so unhappily the characteristic of thy blinded people. If banishment from our presence be a source of sorrow, which I do believe it is, the term of that banishment rests entirely with thyself. The sooner we can hail the child of the Virgin, even as thou art now of our affections, the greater share of happiness wilt thou bestow upon us and upon thyself. We have heard that nought but harshness and severity can have effect on thy hardened race. It may be, but with thee, at least, we will not use it, unless—" and her voice and her look grew sufficiently stern for Marie to feel her words were no idle threat—"unless obduracy and ingratitude so conquer affection that we can see no more in the Marie Morales we have loved than a hardened member of her own stiff-necked race; then—, but we will not pain ourself or thee, by imagining what thine own will may avert. Go, and the holy Virgin bless thee. Not a word; I know what will be thine answer now; but a month hence thou wilt thank me for this seeming severity."

And Isabella turned somewhat hastily away; for her lip quivered and her eye swelled. Marie did not see these indications of emotion, and silently withdrew.

CHAPTER XXXI.

"I have lost for that Faith more than thou canst bestow,
As the God who permits thee to prosper doth know.
In His hand is my heart, and my hope; and in thine
The land, and the life, which for Him I resign."

BYRON.

Marie Morales had had many trials. Her life had been one of those painful mysteries, as to why such a being should have been thus exposed to scorn, which while on earth we vainly try to solve. Yet it is no imaginary picture: hundreds, aye thousands, of Israel's devoted race have thus endured; in every age, in every clime, have been exposed to martyrdom—not of the frame alone, but of the heart; doomed but to suffer, and to die. And how may we reconcile these things with the government of a loving father, save by the firm belief, which, blessed—thrice blessed—are those who feel; that, for such sufferers on earth, a future of blessedness is laid up in another and lovelier world—where there is no more sorrow, no more tears!

Her former trials had been sharp agony and strong excitement. Her present had neither the one nor the other; yet it was fraught with as heavy suffering, as any that had gone before it; even though she knew not, guessed not, *all* that depended upon her conversion. It would have been comparatively easy to have endured, for her faith's sake, harshness and contempt; in such a case, self-respect rises to sustain us, and we value our own tenets the more, from their startling contrast with those which could command the cruelty we endure; but Father Denis used harshness neither of manner nor of words. Firmly impressed in his own mind, that it was utterly vain for a soul to hope for salvation unless it believed in Jesus, the Virgin, the saints and holy martyrs; he brought heart and soul to his task; and the more he saw of Marie, the more painfully did he deplore her blind infatuation, and the more ardently desire, to save her from the eternal perdition which, as a Jewess, must await her. He poured forth such soul-breathing petitions, for saving grace to be vouchsafed to her, in her hearing, that Marie felt as if she would have given worlds, only to realize the belief for which he prayed; but the more her heart was wrung, the more vividly it seemed that her own faith, the religion of her fathers through a thousand ages, impressed itself upon her mind and heart, rendering it more and more impossible for her to forswear it, even at the very moment that weak humanity longed to do it, and so purchase peace. Naturally so meek and yielding, so peculiarly alive to the voice of sympathy and kindness, it was inexpressibly and harrowingly distressing to be thus compelled to resist both; to think also of all Isabella's gentle, cherishing, and manifested affection; and to know that the only return she demanded, she dared not, might not give. To some dispositions these considerations would have been of no weight whatever; to Marie they were so exquisitely painful, that she could scarcely understand how it was that, feeling them thus acutely, she could yet so clearly, so calmly, reply to Father Denis, bring argument for argument, and never waver in her steadfast adherence to, and belief in her own creed. The very lessons of her youth, which she had thought forgotten in the varied trials which had been her portion since, returned with full—she fancied superhuman—force and clearness to her mind, rendering even the very wish to embrace the Catholic religion, futile. There was a voice within her that *would* be heard, aye above every human feeling, every strong temptation. She could not drown its clear ringing tones; even where her mental sufferings seemed to cloud and harrow up the brain, to the exclusion of every distinct idea, that voice would breathe its thrilling whisper, telling her it was vain to hope it, she could not be in heart a Catholic; and so she dared not be in words.

A romance is no place for polemical discussion, and we will therefore leave those painful arguments unrecorded. Suffice it, that Marie's intimate acquaintance with the Holy Scriptures in their original tongue—the language of her own people—gave her so decided an advantage over the old monk, that, after nearly three months' trial, he sought his Sovereign, and, with the most touching humility, acknowledged his utter incapacity, for the conversion of Donna Marie, and implored her to dismiss him, and select one more fitted for the task.

Astonished, and bitterly disappointed, Isabella cross-questioned him as to the cause of this sudden feeling of incapacity, and his answers but increased her desire to compel Marie to abandon Judaism, and become—in semblance at least, a Catholic; believing fully that, this accomplished, the Holy Spirit would do the rest, and she would at least have saved her soul. She retained the father in the palace; desiring him to inform his charge that one fortnight's grace would be allowed her, to ponder on all the solemn truths he had advanced, and on her own decision whether she would not rather yield to kindness, than tempt the severity her obstinacy demanded; but, save this enjoyment, he was to commune with her no further. With a trembling spirit the Queen again sought the counsel of her confessor, and reported the information of the holy father. Torquemada listened, with a curling lip and contracted brow. He was not surprised, he said, for it was exactly what he had expected. It was a part of their blaspheming creed, to blind by sorcery, the eyes and minds of all those who had ever attempted to win them over by kind and reasonable argument. Father Denis had been bewitched, as all were, who ever attempted to convert, by other than the harshest means. Her grace must see the necessity of severity, and surely could not refuse the using it any longer. But Isabella did refuse, till her last resource had been tried; and all she asked was, if she might hold forth a powerful temporal temptation to obtain the end she so earnestly desired? Torquemada hesitated; but at length, on being told the severe alternative which Isabella would enforce, if her first proposal were rejected, reluctantly acceded; still persisting that nothing but the rack and the flame, or fatal expulsion, would ever purge Spain from the horrible infection of so poisonous a race. Isabella heard him with a shudder; but, thankful even for this ungracious sanction, waited, with, trembling impatience, the termination of the given fourteen days; hoping, aye praying in her meek, fervid piety, that the mistaken one might be softened to accept the proffered grace, or her own heart strengthened to sacrifice all of personal feeling for the purifying by fire and consequent salvation, of that immortal soul now so fearfully led astray.

It was with little hope that the father again sought Marie. Bewitched he might be, but he was so impressed with the fervid earnestness of her gentle spirit; with the lofty enthusiasm that dictated her decision; so touched with the uncomplaining, but visible suffering, which it cost her to argue with, and reject the voice of kindness—that it required a strong mental effort in the old man, to refrain from conjuring his Sovereign, to permit that misguided one to remain unmolested, and wait, till time, and prayer, from those so interested in her, should produce the desired effect. But this feeling was so contrary to the spirit of the age, that it scarcely needed Torquemada's representations to convince him, that he was experiencing the effect of the invisible sorcery with which the race of Israel always blinded the eyes of their opponents. The kind old man was awed and silenced by his stern superior. Liberty of conscience was then a thing unheard of; and therefore it was, that so much of the divine part of our mingled nature was so completely concealed, that it lost alike effect or influence. It was not even the subjection of the weak to the strong; but the mere superiority of clerical rank. The truest and the noblest, the most enlarged mind, the firmest spirit would bend unresistingly to the simple word of a priest; and the purest and kindest impulses of our holier nature be annihilated, before the dictates of those, who were supposed to hold so infallibly, in their sole keeping, the oracles of God. The spiritual in man was kept in rigid bondage; the divinity worshipped by the Catholics of that age, represented to the mass like the Egyptian idol, with a key upon his lips—his attributes, as his law, hid from them, or imparted by chosen priests, who explained them only as suited their individual purposes. Is it marvel, then, that we should read of such awful acts committed in Religion's name by man upon his brother? or that we should see the purest and loveliest characters led away by priestly influence to commit deeds, from which now, the whole mind so recoils, that we turn away disappointed and perplexed at the inconsistency, and refuse the meed of love and admiration to those other qualities, which would otherwise shine forth so unsullied? The inconsistency, the seeming cruelty and intolerance, staining many a noble one in the middle ages, were the effects of the fearful spirit of the time; but their virtues were their own. Truth if sought, must triumph over prejudice. By inspection and earnest study of facts—of *causes*, as well as of *events*, the mind disperses the mists of educational error, and enables us to do justice, even to the injurer; and enlarges and ennobles our feelings towards one another; till we can attain that perfection of true, spiritual charity, which would look on all men as children of one common parent. Liable, indeed, to be led astray by evil inclination, and yet more by evil circumstances; but still our brethren, in the divine part of our nature; which, however crushed, hidden, lost to earth, is still existing—still undying. For such is the immortal likeness of our universal Father; in which He made man, and by which He marked mankind as brethren!

Marie's answer was as Father Denis feared. She had pondered on all he had said, and the dread alternative awaiting her; but the impossibility of embracing Catholicism was stronger than ever. The unfeigned distress of the old monk pained and alarmed her, for it seemed to her as if he were conscious that some dreadful doom was hanging over her, which he shrunk from revealing. She had not long to remain in that torturing suspense: a few hours later in the same day, she was summoned to Isabella's presence. The sensation of terror was so intense as to render obedience, for the minute, utterly impossible. Every limb shook, and again came the wild longing for power to believe as they desired; for a momentary cessation of the voice of conscience, to embrace the proffered cross, and be at rest. But it *would not* cease; and, scarcely able to support herself, she stood before the dread Princess in whose hand was her earthly fate.

CHAPTER XXXII.

"She clasped her hands"!—the strife
Of love—faith—fear, and the vain dream of life,
Within her woman-heart so deeply wrought—
It seemed as if a reed, so slight and weak,
Must, in the rending storm, not quiver only—break!

MRS. HEMANS.

Isabella's expressive countenance was grave and calm; but it was impossible to doubt the firmness of her purpose, though what that purpose might be, Marie had no power to read. She stood leaning against the back of one of the ponderous chairs; her head bent down, and her heart so loudly and thickly throbbing that it choked her very breath.

"We have summoned thee hither, Marie," the Queen said at length, gravely, but not severely, "to hear from thine own lips the decision which Father Denis has reported to us; but which, indeed, we can scarcely credit. Wert thou other than thou art—one whose heavy trials and lovable qualities have bound thee to us with more than common love—we should have delivered thee over at once to the judgment of our holy fathers, and interfered with their sentence no farther. We are exposing ourselves to priestly censure even for the forbearance already shown; but we will dare even that, to win thee from thine accursed creed, and give thee peace and comfort. Marie canst *thou* share the ingratitude—the obstinacy—of thy benighted race, that even with thee we must deal harshly? Compel me not to a measure from which my whole heart revolts. Do not let me feel that the charge against thy people is true, without even one exception, and that kindness shown to them, is unvalued as unfelt."

A convulsive sob was the sole reply. Marie's face was buried in her hands; but the tears were streaming through her slender fingers, and her slight figure shook with the paroxysm.

"Nay, Marie, we ask not tears. We demand the proof of grateful affection on thy part; not its weak display. And what is that proof? The acceptance of a faith without which there can be no security in this life, nor felicity hereafter! The rejection of a fearfully mistaken—terribly accursed—creed; condemning its followers to the scorn and hate of man, and abiding wrath of God."

"'To the scorn and hate of man?' Alas, gracious Sovereign, it is even so; but not to the 'abiding wrath of God,'" answered Marie, suppressing with a desperate effort, her painful emotion. "The very scorn and loathing we encounter confirms the blessed truth, of our having been the chosen children of our God, and the glorious promise of our future restoration. We are enduring now on earth the effects of the fearful sins of our ancestors; but for those who live and die true to His law, there is a future after death laid up with Him; that, how may we forfeit for transitory joy?"

"If it were indeed so, we would be the last to demand such forfeit," answered the Queen; "but were it not for the blinding veil of wilful rejection cast over the eyes and hearts of thy people, thou wouldst know and feel, that however thy race were *once* the chosen of God, the distinction has been lost for ever, by their blaspheming rejection of Jesus and his virgin mother; and the misery—its consequence—on earth, is but a faint type of that misery which is for everlasting. It is from this we would save thee. Father Denis has brought before thee the solemn truths which our sainted creed advances, in reply to the mystifying fallacies of thine; and, he tells me, wholly without effect. My arguments, then, can be of such little weight, that I have pledged myself to my confessor to attempt none. We summoned thee merely to tell our decision in this matter; of too vital importance to be left to other lips. Once more let me ask—and understand thee rightly!—have all the Holy Father's lessons failed to convince, even as all our affection has failed to move, thee?"

"Would—would to Heaven I could believe as thou demandest!" answered Marie. "Would that those lessons had brought conviction! The bitter agony of your Grace's displeasure—of feeling that, while my heart so throbs and swells with grateful devotion that I would gladly die to serve thee, yet the proof thou demandest I *cannot* give; and I must go down to an early grave, leaving with thee the sole impression that thou hadst cherished a miserable ingrate, whom, even as thou hast loved, so thou must now hate and scorn. Oh, madam! try me by other proof! My creed may be the mistaken one it seems to thee; but, oh! it is no garment we may wear and cast off at pleasure. Have mercy, gracious Sovereign! condemn me not as reprobate—hardened—more insensible than the veriest cur, who is grateful for the kindness of his master!—because I love my faith better even than thy love—the dearest earthly joy now left me."

"Methinks scarcely the dearest," replied Isabella, affected, in spite of her every effort for control; "but of that here after. Marie, I have pledged myself to my confessor, not to let this matter rest. He has told me that my very affection for thee is a snare, and must be sacrificed if it interfere with my duty; not alone as member of Christ's church, but as Sovereign of a Catholic realm, whose bounden duty it is to purge away all heresy and misbelief. I feel that he is right, and, cost what it may, Christ's dictates must be obeyed. The years of fraud—of passing for what thou wert not—I forgive, for thy noble husband's sake; but my confessor has told me, and I feel its truth, that if we allow thy return to thy people as thou art now, we permit a continuance of such unnatural unions, encourage fraud, and expose our subjects to the poisonous taint of Jewish blood and unbelief. A Christian thou must become. The plan we have decided upon must bring conviction at last; but it will be attended with such long years of mental and physical suffering, that we shrink from the alternative, and only thine own obstinacy will force us to adopt it."

She paused for above a minute; but though Marie's very lips had blanched, and her large eyes were fixed in terror on the Queen's face, there was no answer.

"Thou hast more than once alluded to death," Isabella continued, her voice growing sterner; "but, though such may be the punishment demanded, we cannot so completely banish regard as to expose thy soul, as well as body, to undying flames. Thou hast heard, perchance, of holy sisterhoods, who, sacrificing all of earthly joys and earthly ties, devote themselves as the willing brides of Christ, and pass their whole lives in acts of personal penance, mortification, self-denial, and austerity; which to all, save those impelled try this same lofty enthusiasm, would be unendurable. The convent of St. Ursula is the most strictly rigid and unpitying of this sternly rigid school; and there, if still thou wilt not retract, thou wilt be for life immured, to learn that reverence, that submission, that belief, which thou refusest now. Ponder well on all the suffering which this sentence must comprise. It is even to us—a Christian—so dreadful, that we would not impose it, could we save thy deluded spirit by any other means. The Abbess, from the strict and terrible discipline of long years, has conquered every womanly weakness; and to a Jewess placed under her charge, to be brought a penitent to the bosom of the Virgin, is not likely to decrease the severity of treatment and discipline, the portion even of her own. Once delivered to her charge, we interfere no further. Whatever she may command—short of actual torture, or death— thou must endure. Marie! wilt thou tempt a doom like this? In mercy to thyself, retract ere it be too late!"

"If I can bear the loss of thy favor, my Sovereign, I can bear this," replied Marie, slowly and painfully. "There is more suffering in the thought, that your Grace's love is lost for ever; that I shall never see your Highness more; and thou must ever think of me as only a wretched, feelingless ingrate, than in all the bodily and mental anguish such a life may bring."

"Marie!" exclaimed Isabella, with an irrepressible burst of natural feeling. And Marie had darted forwards, and was kneeling at her feet, and covering her hand with tears and kisses, ere she had power to forcibly subdue the emotion and speak again.

"This must not be," she said at length; but she did not withdraw the hand which Marie still convulsively clasped, and, half unconsciously it seemed, she put back the long, black tresses, which had fallen over her colorless cheek, looked sadly in that bowed face, and kissed her brow. "It is the last," she murmured to herself. "It may be the effects of sorcery—it may be sin; but if I do penance for the weakness, it must have way."

"Thou hast heard the one alternative," she continued aloud; "now hear the other. We have thought long, and watched well, some means of effectually obliterating the painful memories of the past, and making thy life as happy as it has been sad. We have asked and received permission from our confessor to bring forward a temporal inducement for a spiritual end; that even the affections themselves may be made conducive to turning a benighted spirit from the path of death into that of life; and, therefore, we may proceed more hopefully. Marie! is there not a love thou valuest even more than mine? Nay, attempt not to deny a truth, which we have known from the hour we told thee that Arthur Stanley was thy husband's murderer. What meant those wild words imploring me to save him? For what was the avowal of thy faith, but that thy witness should not endanger him? Why didst thou return to danger when safety was before thee?—peril thine own life but to save his? Answer me truly: thou lovest Stanley, Marie?"

"I have loved him, gracious Sovereign."

"And thou dost no longer? Marie, methinks there would be less wrong in loving now, than when we first suspected it," rejoined the Queen, gravely.

"Alas! my liege, who may school the heart? He was its first—first affection! But, oh! my Sovereign, I never wronged my noble husband. He knew it all ere he was taken from me, and forgave and loved me still; and, oh! had he been but spared, even memory itself would have lost its power to sting. His trust, his love, had made me all—all his own!"

"I believe thee, my poor child; but how came it that, loving Stanley, thy hand was given to Morales?"

For the first time, the dangerous ground on which she stood flashed on the mind of Marie; and her voice faltered as she answered—"My father willed it, Madam."

"Thy father! And was he of thy faith, yet gave his child to one of us?"

"He was dying, Madam, and there was none to protect his Marie. He loved and admired him to whom he gave me; for Ferdinand had never scorned nor persecuted us. He had done us such good service that my father sought to repay him; but he would accept nothing but my hand, and swore to protect my faith—none other would have made such promise. I was weak, I know, and wrong; but I dared not then confess I loved another. And, once his wife, it was sin even to think of Arthur. Oh, Madam! night and day I prayed that we might never meet, till all of love was conquered."

"Poor child," replied Isabella, kindly. "But, since thou wert once more free, since Stanley was cleared of even the suspicion of guilt, has no former feeling for him returned! He loves thee, Marie, with such faithful love as in man I have seldom seen equalled; why check affection now?"

"Alas! my liege, what may a Jewess be to him; or his love to me, save as the most terrible temptation to estrange me from my God?"

"Say rather to gently lure thee to Him, Marie," replied Isabella, earnestly. "There is a thick veil between thy heart and thy God now; let the love thou bearest this young Englishman be the blessed means of removing it, and bringing thee to the sole source of salvation, the Saviour Stanley worships. One word—one little word—from thee, and thou shalt be Stanley's wife! His own; dearer than ever from the trials of the past. Oh! speak it, Marie! Let me feel I have saved thee from everlasting torment, and made this life—in its deep, calm joy—a foretaste of the heaven that, as a Christian, will await thee above. Spare Stanley—aye, and thy Sovereign—the bitter grief of losing thee for ever!"

"Would—would I could!" burst wildly from the heart-stricken Marie; and she wrung her hands in that one moment of intense agony, and looked up in the Queen's face, with an expression of suffering Isabella could not meet. "Would that obedience, conviction, could come at will! His wife?—Stanley's. To rest this desolate heart on his? To weep upon his bosom?—feel his arm around me?—his love protect me? To be his—all his? And only on condition of speaking one little word? Oh! why can I not speak it? Why will that dread voice sound within, telling me I dare not—cannot—for I do not believe? How dare I take the Christians's vow, embrace the cross, and in my heart remain a Jewess still?"

"Embrace the cross, and conviction will follow," replied the Queen. "This question we have asked of Father Tomas, and been assured that the vows of baptism once taken, grace will be found from on high; and to the *heart*, as well as *lip*, conversion speedily ensue. Forswear the blaspheming errors of thy present creed—consent to be baptized—and that very hour sees thee Stanley's wife!"

"No, no, no!—Oh! say not such words again! My liege, my gracious liege, tempt not this weak spirit more!" implored Marie, in fearful agitation. "Oh! if thou hast ever loved me, in mercy spare me this!"

"In mercy is it that we do thus speak, unhappy girl." replied Isabella, with returning firmness; for she saw the decisive moment had come. "We have laid both alternatives before thee; it rests with thee alone to make thine own election. Love on earth and joy in Heaven, depends upon one word: refuse to speak it, and thou knowest thy doom!"

It was well, perhaps, for Marie's firmness, that the Queen's appealing tone had given place to returning severity; it recalled the departing strength—the sinking energy—the power once more to *endure!* For several minutes there was no sound: Marie had buried her face in her hands, and remained—half kneeling, half crouching—on the cushion at the Queen's feet, motionless as stone; and Isabella—internally as agitated as herself—was, under the veil of unbending sternness, struggling for control. The contending emotions sweeping over that frail woman-heart in that fearful period of indecision we pretend not to describe: again and again the terrible temptation came, to say but the desired word, and happiness was hers—such intense happiness, that her brain reeled beneath its thought of ecstasy; and again and again it was driven back by that thrilling voice—louder than ever in its call—to remain faithful to her God. It was a fearful contest; and when she did look up, Isabella started; so terribly was its index inscribed on those white and chiselled features.

She rose slowly, and stood before the Sovereign, her hands tightly clasped together, and the veins on her forehead raised like cords across it. Three times she tried to speak; but only unintelligible murmurs came, and her lips shook as with convulsion. "It is over," she said at length, and her usually sweet voice sounded harsh and unnatural. "The weakness is conquered, gracious Sovereign, condemn, scorn, hate me as thou wilt, thou must: I must endure it till my heart breaks, and death brings release; but the word thou demandest I *cannot* speak! Thy favor, Arthur's love, I resign them all! 'Tis the bidding of my God, and he will strengthen me to bear it. Imprison, torture, slay, with the lingering misery of a broken heart, but I cannot deny my faith!"

Disappointed, grieved, as she was at this unexpected reply, Isabella was too much an enthusiast in religion herself not to understand the feeling which dictated it; and much as she still abhorred the faith, the martyr spirit which could thus immolate the most fervid, the most passionate emotions of woman's nature at the shrine of her God, stirred a sympathetic chord in her own heart, and so moved her, that the stern words she had intended to speak were choked within her.

"We must summon those then to whose charge we are pledged to commit thee," she said with difficulty; and hastily rung a silver bell beside her. "We had hoped such would not have been needed; but, as it is—"

She paused abruptly; for the hangings were hastily pushed aside, and, instead of the stern figure of Torquemada, who was to have obeyed the signal, the Infanta Isabella eagerly entered; and ran up to the Queen, with childish and caressing glee at being permitted to rejoin her. The confessor—not imagining his presence would be needed, or that he would return to his post in time—

had restlessly obeyed the summons of a brother prelate, and, in some important clerical details, forgot the mandate of his Sovereign.

Marie saw the softened expression of the Queen's face; the ineffectual effort to resist her child's caresses, and retain her sternness: and, with a sudden impulse, she threw herself at her feet.

"Oh! do not turn from me, my Sovereign!" she implored, wildly clasping Isabella's knees. "I ask nothing—nothing, but to return to my childhood's home, and die there! I ask not to return to my people; they would not receive me, for I have dared to love the stranger; but in my own isolated home, where but two aged retainers of my father dwell, I can do harm to none—mingle with none; let me bear a breaking heart for a brief—brief while; and rest beside my parents. I will swear to thee never to quit that place of banishment—swear never more to mingle with either thy people or with mine—to be as much lost to man, as if the grave had already closed over me, or convent walls immured me! Oh, Madam! grant me but this! Will it not be enough of suffering to give up Arthur?—to tear myself from thy cherishing love?—to bear my misery alone? Leave me, oh! leave me but my faith—the sole joy, sole hope, now left me! Give me not up to the harsh, and cruel father—the stern mother of St. Ursula! If I can sacrifice love, kindness—all that would make earth a heaven—will harshness gain thine end? Plead for me," she continued, addressing the infant-princess, who, as if affected by the grief she beheld, had left her mother to cling round Marie caressingly; "plead for me, Infanta! Oh, Madam! the fate of war might place this beloved and cherished one in the hands of those who regard thy faith even as thou dost mine; were such an alternative proffered, how wouldst thou she should decide? My Sovereign, my gracious Sovereign, oh, have mercy!"

"Mamma! dear Mamma!" repeated the princess at the same moment, and aware that her intercession was required, though unable to comprehend the wherefore, she clasped her little hands entreatingly; "grant poor Marie what she wishes! You have told me a Queen's first duty is to be kind and good; and do all in her power to make others happy. Make her happy, dear Mamma, she has been so sad!"

The appeal to Isabella's nature was irresistible; she caught her child to her heart, and burst into passionate tears.

CHAPTER XXXIII.

"I will have vengeance!
I'll crush thy swelling pride! I'll still thy vaunting!
I'll do a deed of blood!
            Now all idle forms are over—
Now open villany, now open hate—
Defend thy life!"

JOANNA BAILLIE.

"Let me but look upon 'her' face once more—
Let me but say farewell, my soul's beloved,
And I will bless thee still."

MRS. HEMANS.

Some time had elapsed since King Ferdinand and his splendid army had quitted Saragossa. He himself had not as yet headed any important expedition, but fixing his head-quarters at Seville, dispatched thence various detachments under experienced officers, to make sallies on the Moors, who had already enraged the Christian camp by the capture of Zahara. Arthur Stanley was with the Marquis of Cadiz, when this insult was ably avenged by the taking of Albania, a most important post, situated within thirty miles of the capital. The Spaniards took possession of the city, massacred many of the inhabitants, placed strong restrictions on those who surrendered, and strongly garrisoned every tower and fort. Nor were they long inactive: the Moors resolved to retake what they considered the very threshold of their capital; hastily assembled their forces, and regularly entered upon the siege.

While at Seville, the camp of Ferdinand had been joined by several foreign chevaliers, amongst whom was an Italian knight, who had excited the attention and curiosity of many of the younger Spaniards from the mystery environing him. He was never seen without his armor. His helmet always closed, keeping surlily aloof, he never mingled in the brilliant jousts and tournaments of the camp, except when Arthur Stanley chanced to be one of the combatants: he was then sure to be found in the lists, and always selected the young Englishman as his opponent. At first this strange pertinacity was regarded more as a curious coincidence than actual design; but it occurred so often, that at length it excited remark. Arthur himself laughed it off, suggesting that the Italian had perhaps some grudge against England, and wished to prove the mettle of her sons. The Italian deigned no explanation, merely saying that he supposed the Spanish jousts were governed by the same laws as others, and he was therefore at liberty to choose his own opponent. But Arthur was convinced that some cause existed for this mysterious hostility. Not wishing to create public confusion, he contended himself by keeping a watch upon his movements. He found, however, that he did not watch more carefully than he was watched, and incensed at length, he resolved on calling his enemy publicly to account for his dishonorable conduct. This, however, he found much easier in theory than practice. The wily Italian, as if aware of his intentions, skilfully eluded them; and as weeks passed without any recurrence of their secret attacks. Stanley, guided by his own frank and honorable feelings, believed his suspicions groundless, and dismissed them altogether. On the tumultuary entrance of the Spaniards, however, these suspicions were re-excited. Separated by the press of contending warriors from the main body of his men, Stanley plunged headlong into the thickest battalion of Moors, intending to cut his way through them to the Marquis of Cadiz, who was at that moment entering the town. His unerring arm and lightness of movement bore him successfully onward. A very brief space divided him from his friends: the spirited charger on which he rode, cheered by his hand and voice, with one successful bound cleared the remaining impediments in his way, but at that moment, with a piercing cry of suffering, sprung high in the air and fell dead, nearly crushing his astonished master with his weight. Happily for Stanley, the despairing anguish of the Moors at that moment at its height, from the triumphant entry of the Spaniards into their beloved Albania, aggravated by the shrieks of the victims in the unsparing slaughter, effectually turned the attention of those around him from his fall. He sprung up, utterly unable to account for the death of his steed: the dastard blow had been dealt from behind, and no Moor had been near but those in front. He looked hastily round him: a tall figure was retreating through the thickening *melée*, whose dull, red armor, and deep, black plume, discovered on the instant his identity. Arthur's blood tingled with just indignation, and it was with difficulty that he restrained himself from following, and demanding on the instant, and at the sword's point, the meaning of the deed.

The sudden start, and muttered execration of the Italian, as Stanley joined the victorious group around the Marquis, convinced him that his reappearance, and unhurt, was quite contrary to his mysterious enemy's intention. The exciting events of the siege which followed, the alternate hope and fear of the Spaniards, reduced to great distress by the Moors having succeeded in turning the course of a river which supplied the city with water, and finally, the timely arrival of succors under the Duke of Medina Sidonia, which compelled the Moors to raise the siege and disperse—the rejoicing attendant on so great and almost unexpected a triumph, all combined to prevent any attention to individual concerns. The Italian had not crossed Arthur's path again, except in the general attack or defence; and Stanley found the best means of conquering his own irritation towards such secret machinations, was to treat them with indifference and contempt.

The halls of Alhama were of course kept strongly manned; and a guard, under an experienced officer, constantly occupied the summit of a lofty tower, situated on a precipitous height which commanded a view of the open country for miles, and overlooked the most distant approach of the Moors. As was usual to Moorish architecture, the tower had been erected on a rock, which on one side shelved down so straight and smooth, as to appear a continuance of the tower-wall, but forming from the battlements a precipice some thousand feet in depth. The strongest nerve turned sick and giddy to look beneath, and the side of the tower overlooking it was almost always kept unguarded.

It was near midnight when Stanley, who was that night on command, after completing his rounds, and perceiving every sentinel on duty, found himself unconsciously on the part of the tower we have named. So pre-occupied was his mind, that he looked beneath him without shrinking; and then retracing his steps some twenty or thirty yards from the immediate and unprotected edge, wrapped his mantle closely round him, and lying down, rested his head on his arm, and permitted the full dominion of thought. He was in that dreamy mood, when the silence and holiness of nature is so much more soothing than even the dearest sympathy of man; when every passing cloud and distant star, and moaning wind, speaks with a hundred tongues, and the immaterial spirit holds unconscious commune with beings invisible, and immaterial as itself. Above his head, heavy clouds floated over the dark azure of the heavens, sometimes totally obscuring the mild light of the full moon; at others merely shrouding her beams in a transparent veil, from which she would burst resplendently, sailing majestically along, seeming the more light and lovely from the previous shade. One brilliant planet followed closely on her track, and as the dark masses of clouds would rend asunder, portions of the heavens, studded with glittering stars, were visible, seeming like the gemmed dome of some mighty temple, whose walls and pillars, shrouded in black drapery, were lost in the distance on either side. Gradually, Stanley's thoughts became indistinct; the stars seemed to lose their radiance, as covered by a light mist; a dark cloud appearing, in his half dormant fancy, to take the gigantic proportions of a man, hovered on the battlement. It became smaller and smaller, but still it seemed a cloud, through which the moonlight gleamed; but a thrill passed through him, as if telling of some impalpable and indefinable object of dread. With a sudden effort he shook off the lethargy of half sleep, and sprung to his feet, at the very moment a gleaming sword was pointed at his throat. "Ha, villain! at thy murderous work again!" he exclaimed, and another moment beheld him closed in deadly conflict with his mysterious foe. A deep and terrible oath, and then a mocking laugh, escaped his adversary; and something in those sounds, nerved Stanley's arms with resistless power: he was sure he could not be mistaken, and he fought, not with the unguarded desire of one eager to obtain satisfaction for personal injury—but he was calm, cool, collected, as threefold an avenger. For once, the demon-like caution of the supposed Italian deserted him: discovery was inevitable, and his sole aim was to compass the death of the hated foreigner with his own. He tried gradually to retreat to the very edge of the precipice, and Stanley's calm and cautious avoidance of the design lashed him into yet fiercer desperation. Thick and fast, fell those tremendous blows. The Italian had the advantage in height and size, Stanley in steady coolness and prudent guard; the Italian sought only to slay his adversary, caring not to defend himself; Arthur evidently endeavored merely to unhelm the traitor, and bring him but slightly wounded to the ground. For several minutes there was no cessation in that fearful clash of steel; the strokes were so rapid, so continued, a hundred combatants might have seemed engaged. A moment they drew back, as if to breathe; the Italian, with a despairing effort, raised his weapon and sprung forwards; Arthur lightly leaped aside, and the murderous stroke clove but the yielding earth. Another second, and ere the Italian had regained his equilibrium, Arthur's sword had descended with so true and sure a stroke that the clasp of the helmet gave way, the dark blood bubbled up from the cloven brow, he reeled and fell; and a long, loud shout from the officers and soldiers, who, at the sound of arms, had flocked round, proclaimed some stronger feeling than simply admiration of Stanley's well-known prowess.

"Seize him! seize him! or by Heaven he will escape us yet!" were among the few words intelligible. "The daring villain, to come amongst us! Did he think for ever to elude Heaven's vengeance? Bind, fetter, hold him; or his assistant fiends will release him still!"

Fiercely the fallen man had striven to extricate himself; but Stanley's knee moved not from his breast, nor his sword from his throat, until a strong guard had raised and surrounded him: "but the horrible passions imprinted on those lived features were such, that his very captors turned away shuddering.

"Hadst thou not had enough of blood and crime, thou human monster, that thou wouldst stain thy already blackened soul with, another midnight murder?" demanded Stanley, as he sternly confronted his baffled foe. "Don Luis Garcia, as men have termed thee, what claim have I on thy pursuing and unchanging hate? With what dost thou charge me? What wrong?"

"Wrong!" hoarsely and fiercely repeated Don Louis. "The wrong of baffled hate; of success, when I planned thy downfall; of escape, when I had sworn thy death! Did the drivelling idiots, who haunted, persecuted, excommunicated me from these realms, as some loathed reptile, dream that I would draw back from my sworn vengeance for such as they? Poor, miserable fools, whom the first scent of danger would turn aside from the pursuit of hate! I staked my life on thine, and the stake is lost; but what care

I? My hate shall follow thee; wither thy bones with its curse; poison every joy; blight every hope; rankle in thy life blood! Bid thee seek health, and bite the dust for anguish because it flies thee! And for me. Ha, ha! Men may think to judge me—torture, triumph, slay! Well, let them." And with a movement so sudden and so desperate, that to avert it was impossible, he burst from the grasp of his guards; and with one spring, stood firm and triumphant on the farthest edge of the battlement. "Now follow me who dares!" he exclaimed; and, with a fearful mocking laugh; flung himself headlong down, ere the soldiers had recovered his first sudden movement. Stanley alone retained presence of mind sufficient to dart forward, regardless of his own imminent danger, in the vain hope of arresting the leap; but quick as were his movements, he only reached the brink in time to see the wretched man, one moment quivering in air, and lost the next in a dark abyss of shade.

A cry of mingled disappointment, horror, and execration, burst from all around; and several of the soldiers hastened from the battlements to the base of the rock, determined on fighting the arch-fiend himself, if, as many of them firmly believed, he had rendered Don Luis invulnerable to air, and would wait there to receive him. But even this heroic resolution was disappointed: the height was so tremendous, and the velocity of the fall so frightful, that the action of the air had not only deprived him of life, but actually loosed the limbs from the trunk, and a fearfully mangled corpse was all that remained to glut the vengeance of the infuriated soldiers.

The confusion and excitement attending this important event, spread like wildfire; not only over Albania, but reaching to the Duke's camp without the city. To send off the momentous information to the King, was instantly decided upon; and young Stanley, as the person principally concerned, selected for the mission.

Ferdinand was astonished and indignant, and greatly disappointed that justice had been so eluded; but that such a monster, whose machinations seemed, in their subtlety and secrecy, to prevent all defeat, no longer cumbered Spain, was in itself a relief so great both to monarch and people, as after the first burst of indignation to cause universal rejoicings.

It so happened that Ferdinand had been desirous of Stanley's presence for some weeks; letters from Isabella, some little time previous, had expressed an earnest desire for the young man's return to Saragossa, if only for a visit of a few days. This was then impossible. Three months had elapsed since Isabella's first communication; within the last two she had not again reverted to Stanley; but the King, thinking she had merely refrained from doing so, because of its present impossibility, gladly seized the opportunity of his appearance at Seville, to dispatch him, as envoy extraordinary, on both public and private business, to the court of Arragon.

Isabella was surrounded by her ministers and nobles when Stanley was conducted to her presence; she received him with cordiality and graciousness, asked many and eager questions concerning her husband and the progress of his arms, entered minutely into the affair of Don Luis, congratulated him on his having been the hand destined to unmask the traitor and bring him low; gave her full attention on the instant to the communications from the King, with which he was charged; occupied some hours in earnest and thoughtful deliberation with her counsel, which, on perusal of the King's papers, she had summoned directly. And yet, through all this, Arthur fancied there was an even unusual degree of sympathy and kindliness in the tone and look with which she addressed him individually; but he felt intuitively it was sympathy with sorrow, not with joy. He was convinced that his unexpected presence had startled and almost grieved her; and why should this be, if she had still the hope with which she had so infused his spirit, when they had parted. His heart, so full of elasticity a few hours previous, sunk chilled and pained within him, and it was with an effort impossible to have been denied, had it not been for the Queen's *unspoken* but real sympathy; he roused himself sufficiently to execute his mission.

But Isabella was too much the true and feeling woman, to permit the day to close without the private interview she saw Stanley needed; reality, sad as it was, she felt would be better than harrowing suspense; and, in a few kindly words, the tale was told.

"I should have known it!" he exclaimed, when the first shock of bitter disappointment permitted words. "My own true, precious Marie! How dared I dream that for me thou wouldst sacrifice thy faith; all, all else—joy, hope, strength; aye, life itself—but not thy God! Oh, Madam," he continued, turning passionately to the Queen, "thou hast not condemned her to misery for this! Thou hast not revoked thy former heavenly mercy, and delivered her over to the stern fathers of our holy church? No, no! Isabella could not have done this!"

"Nor have we," replied the Queen, so mildly that Arthur flung himself at her feet, conjuring her to pardon his disrespectful words. "Give her to thee, without retracting her fearful misbelief, indeed we dared not, but further misery has not been inflicted. We have indeed done penance for our weakness, severe penance; for Father Tomas asserts that we have most grievously sinned; and more, have pledged ourselves most solemnly, that what he may counsel for the entire uprooting of this horrible heresy, and accursed race, shall be followed, cost what it may, politically or privately; but to refuse the last boon of the unhappy girl, who had so strangely, perchance so bewilderingly, wound herself about my heart—Stanley, I must have changed my nature first!"

"Her last boon! Gracious Sovereign—"

"Nay, her last to her Sovereign, my friend. It may be that even yet her errors may be abjured, and grace be granted in her solitude, to become in this world as the next, what we have prayed for; but we dare not hope it; nor must thou. She besought permission to return to the home of her childhood, pledging herself never to leave it, or mingle with her people or ours more."

"And she is there! God in Heaven bless, reward your Highness for the mercy!" burst impetuously from Arthur. "I trust she is, nay, I believe it; for Jewess as she is, she would not pledge me false. In the garb of the novice, as she saved thee, Father Denis conducted her to the frontiers of Castile. More we know not, for we asked not the site of her home."

There was a few minutes' pause, and then, with beseeching eloquence, Arthur conjured the Sovereign to let him see her once, but once again. He asked no more, but he felt as if he could not sustain the agony of eternal separation, without one last, last interview. He pledged his honor, that no temptation of a secret union should interfere with the sentence of the Queen; that both would submit; only to permit them once more to meet again.

Isabella hesitated, but not for long. Perhaps the secret hope arose that Stanley's presence would effect that for which all else had failed; or that she really could not resist his passionate pleadings.

"One word of retraction, and even now she is thine.—And I will bless thee that thou gavest her to me again," she said in parting; but her own spirit told her the hope was vain.

Half an hour after this agitating interview Arthur Stanley was again on horseback, a deep hectic on either cheek; his eye bloodshot and strained, traversing with the speed of lightning the open country, in the direction of Castile.

CHAPTER XXXIV.

"Oh! love, love, strong as death—from such an hour
Pressing out joy by thine immortal power;
Holy and fervent love! Had earth but rest
For thee and thine, this world were all too fair:
How could we thence be weaned to die without despair!

"But woe for him who felt that heart grow still
  Which with its weight of agony had lain
Breaking on his. Scarce could the mortal chill
  Of the hushed bosom, ne'er to heave again,
And all the curdling silence round the eye,
Bring home the stern belief that she could die."

MRS. HEMANS.

The glowing light of a glorious sunset lingered on the Vale of Cedars, displaying that calm and beautiful retreat in all the fair and rich luxuriance of former years. Reuben and Ruth, the aged retainers of the house of Henriquez, had made it their pride and occupation to preserve the cherished retreat, lovely as it had been left. Nor were they its only inmates; their daughter, her husband, and children, after various struggles in the Christian world, had been settled in the Vale by the benevolence of Ferdinand Morales—their sole duty, to preserve it in such order, as to render it a fitting place of refuge for any who should need it. Within the last twelve months, another inmate had been added to them. Weary of his wanderings, and of the constant course of deception which his apparent profession of a monk demanded, Julien Morales had returned to the home of his childhood, there to fix his permanent abode; only to make such excursions from it, as the interests of his niece might demand. Her destiny was his sole anxious thought. Her detention by Isabella convinced him that her disguise had been penetrated, and filled him with solicitude for her spiritual, yet more than her temporal welfare. Royal protection of a Jewess was so unprecedented, that it could only argue the hope—nay, perhaps conviction—of her final conversion. And the old man actually tried to divorce the sweet image of his niece from his affections, so convinced was he that her unhappy love for Arthur, combined with Isabella's authority, and, no doubt, the threat of some terrible alternative should she refuse, would compel her acceptance of the proffered cross, and so sever them for ever. How little can man, even the most gentle and affectionate, read woman!

It was the day completing the eleventh month after Don Ferdinand's murder, when Julien Morales repaired earlier than usual to the little temple, there to read the service for the dead appointed for the day, and thence proceeded to his nephew's grave. An unusual object, which had fallen on, or was kneeling beside the grave, caught his eye, and impelled him to quicken his pace. His heart throbbed as he recognized the garb of a novice, and to such a degree as almost to deprive him of all power, as in the white, chiselled features, resting on the cold, damp sod, he recognized his niece, and believed, for the first agonizing moment, that it was but clay resting against clay; and that the sweet, pure spirit had but guided her to that grave and flown. But death for a brief interval withdrew his grasp; though his shaft had reached her, and no human hand could draw it back. Father Denis had conducted her so carefully and tenderly to the frontiers of Castile, that she had scarcely felt fatigue, and encountered no exposure to the elements; but when he left her, her desire to reach her home became stronger, with the seeming physical incapacity to do so. Her spirit gave way, and mental and bodily exhaustion followed. The season was unusually damp and tempestuous, and, though scarcely felt at the time, sowed the seeds of cold and decline, from which her naturally good constitution might, in the very midst of her trials, otherwise have saved her. Her repugnance to encounter the eyes or speech of her fellows, lest her disguise should be penetrated, caused her to shrink from entering any habitation, except for the single night which intervened, between the period of the father's leaving her and her reaching the secret entrance to the Vale. Her wallet provided her with more food than her parched throat could swallow; and for the consuming thirst, the fresh streams that so often bubbled across her path, gave her all she needed. The fellowship of man, then, was unrequited, and, as the second night fell, so comparatively short a distance lay between her and her home, that buoyed up by the desire to reach it, she was not sensible of her utter exhaustion, till she stood within the little graveyard of the Vale; and the moon shining softly and clearly on the headstones, disclosed to her the grave of her husband. She was totally ignorant that he had been borne there; and the rush of feeling which came over her, as she read his name—the memories of their happy, innocent, childhood, of all his love for her—that had he been but spared, all the last year's misery might have been averted, for she would have loved him, ay, even as he loved her; and he would have guarded, saved—so overpowered her, that she had sunk down upon the senseless earth which covered him, conscious only of the wild, sickly longing, like him to flee away and be at rest. She had reached her home; exertion no longer needed, the unnatural strength, ebbed fast, and the frail tenement withered, hour by hour, away. And how might Julien mourn! Her work on earth was done. Young, tried, frail as she was, she had been permitted to show forth the glory, the sustaining glory, of her faith, by a sacrifice whose magnitude was indeed apparent, but whose depth and intensity of suffering, none knew but Him for whom it had been made. She had been preserved from the crime—if possible more fearful in the mind of the Hebrew than any other—apostasy:

and though the first conviction, that she was indeed "passing away" even from his affection, was fraught with absolute anguish, yet her uncle could not, dared not pray for life on earth. And in the peace, the calm, the depth, of quietude which gradually sunk on her heart, infusing her every word and look and gentle smile, it was as if her spirit had already the foretaste of that blissful heaven for which its wings were plumed. As the frame dwindled, the expression of her sweet face became more and more unearthly in its exquisite beauty, the mind more and more beatified, and the heart more freed from earthly feeling. The reward of her constancy appeared in part bestowed on earth, for death itself was revealed to her—not as the King of Terrors, but as an Angel of Light, at whose touch the lingering raiment of mortality would dissolve, and the freed soul spring up rejoicing to its home.

It was the Feast of the Tabernacle and the Sabbath eve. The tent—formed of branches of thick trees and fragrant shrubs—was erected, as we have seen it in a former page, a short distance from the temple. Marie's taste had once again, been consulted in its decorations; her hand, feeble as it was, had twined the lovely wreaths of luscious flowers and arranged the glowing fruit. With some difficulty she had joined in the devotional service performed by her uncle in the little temple—borne there in the arms of old Reuben, for her weakness now prevented walking—and on the evening of the Sabbath in the Festival, she reclined on one of the luxurious couches within the tent, through the opening of which, she could look forth on the varied beauties of the Vale, and the rich glorious hues dyeing the western skies. The Sabbath lamps were lighted, but their rays were faint and flickering in the still glowing atmosphere. A crimson ray from the departing luminary gleamed through the branches, and a faint glow—either from its reflection, or from that deceiving beauty, which too often gilds the features of the dying—rested on Marie's features, lighting up her large and lustrous eyes with unnatural brilliance. She had been speaking earnestly of that life beyond the grave, belief in which throughout her trials had been her sole sustainer. Julien had listened, wrapt and almost awe-struck, so completely did it seem as if the spirit, and not the mortal, spoke.

"And thine own trials, my beloved one," he said,—"Has the question never come, why thou shouldst thus have been afflicted?"

"Often, very often, my father, and only within the last few weeks has the full answer come; and I can say from my inmost heart, in the words of Job, 'It is good that I have been afflicted,' and that I believe all is well. While *on* earth, we must be in some degree *of* earth, and bear the penalty of our earthly nature. The infirmities and imperfections of that nature in others, as often as in ourselves, occasion human misery, which our God, in his infinite love, permits, to try our spirit's strength and faith, and so prepare us for that higher state of being, in which the spirit will move and act, when the earthly shell is shivered, and earthly infirmities are for ever stilled. In the time of suffering we cannot think thus; but looking back as I do now—when the near vicinity of another world bids me regard my own past life almost as if it were another's—I feel it in my inmost heart, and bless God for every suffering which has prepared me thus early for his home. There is but one feeling, one wish of earth, remaining," she continued, after a long pause of utter exhaustion. "It is weak, perhaps, and wrong; but if—if Arthur could but know that fatal secret which made me seem a worse deceiver than I was—I know it cannot be, but it so haunts me. If I wedded one Christian, may he not think there needed not this sacrifice—sacrifice not of myself, but of his happiness. Oh! could I but—Hush! whose step is that?" she suddenly interrupted herself; and with the effort of strong excitement, started up, and laid her hand on her uncle's arm.

"Nay, my child, there is no sound," he replied soothingly, after listening attentively for several moments.

"But there is. Hark, dost thou not hear it now? God of mercy! thou hast heard my prayer—it is *his*!" she exclaimed, sinking powerlessly back, at the moment that even Julien's duller ear had caught a rapid step; and in another minute the branches were hastily pushed aside, and Stanley indeed stood upon the threshold.

"Marie—and thus!" he passionately exclaimed; and flinging himself on his knees beside her, he buried his face on her hand, and wept in agony.

* * * * *

Nearly an hour passed ere Marie could rally from the agitation of Arthur's unexpected presence sufficiently to speak. She lay with her hand clasped in his, and his arm around her—realizing, indeed, to the full, the soothing consolation of his presence, but utterly powerless to speak that for which she had so longed to see him once again. The extent of her weakness had been unknown till that moment either to her uncle or herself, and Julien watched over her in terror lest the indefinable change which in that hour of stillness was perceptibly stealing over her features should be indeed the dim shadow of death. To Arthur speech was equally impossible, save in the scarcely articulate expressions of love and veneration which he lavished on her. What he had hoped in thus seeking her he could not himself have defined. His whole soul was absorbed in the wild wish to see her again, and the thoughts of death for her had never entered his heart. The shock, then, had been terrible, and to realize the infinite mercy which thus bade sorrow cease, was in such a moment impossible. He could but gaze and clasp her closer and closer, yet, as if even death should be averted by his love.

"Uncle Julien," she murmured, as she faintly extended her hand towards him, "thou wilt not refuse to clasp hands with one who has so loved thy Marie! And thou, Arthur, oh! scorn him not. Without him the invisible dungeons of the Inquisition would have been my grave, and thine that of a dishonored knight and suspected murderer."

The eyes of her companions met, and their hands were grasped in that firm pressure, betraying unity of feeling, and reciprocal esteem, which need no words.

"Raise me a little, dearest Arthur; uncle Julien" put back that spreading bough. I would say something more, and the fresher air may give me strength. Ah! the evening breeze is so fresh and sweet; it always makes me feel as if the spirits of those we loved were hovering near us. We hold much closer and dearer communion with the beloved dead in the calm twilight than in the garish day. Arthur, dearest, thou wilt think of me sometimes in an hour like this."

"When shall I not think of thee?" he passionately rejoined. "Oh, Marie, Marie! I thought separation on earth the worst agony that could befall me; but what—what is it compared to the eternal one of death?"

"No, no, not eternal, Arthur. In heaven I feel there is no distinction of creed or faith; we shall all love God and one another there, and earth's fearful distinctions can never come between us. I know such is not the creed of thy people, nor of some of mine; but when thou standest on the verge of eternity, as I do now, thou wilt feel this too."

"How can I gaze on thee, and not believe it?" he replied. "The loudest thunders of the church could not shake my trust in the purity of heaven, which is thine."

"Because thou lovest, Arthur. Thy love for Marie is stronger than thy hatred of her race; and, oh! if thou lovest thus, I know thou hast forgiven."

"Forgiven!" he passionately reiterated.

"Yes, dearest Arthur. Is the past indeed so obliterated that the wrong I did thee is forgotten even as forgiven? But, oh, Arthur! it was not so unjustifiable as it seemed then. I dared not breathe the truth in Isabella's court. I dare not whisper it now save to thee, who would die rather than reveal it. Arthur, dearest Arthur, it was no Christian whom I wedded. We had been betrothed from early childhood, though I knew it not; and when the time came, I could not draw down on me a father's curse, or dash with agony a heart that so cherished, so loved me, by revelation of a truth which could avail me nothing, and would bring him but misery. Ferdinand was my cousin—a child of Israel, as myself."

"Now heaven bless thee for those words, my own, true, precious Marie!" exclaimed Stanley, in strong emotion, and clasping her still closer, he pressed his quivering lips to her forehead, starting in agony as he marked the cold, damp dews which had gathered upon it, too truly the index of departing life. He besought her to speak no more—the exertion was exhausting her; she smiled faintly, drank of the reviving draught which Julien proffered, and lay for a few minutes calm and still.

"I am better now," she said, after an interval. "It was only the excitement of speaking that truth, which I have so long desired to reveal—to clear my memory from the caprice and inconstancy with which even thy love must have charged me; and now, Arthur, promise me that thou wilt not mourn me too long: that thou wilt strive to conquer the morbid misery, which I know, if encouraged, will cloud thy whole life, and unfit thee for the glorious career which must otherwise be thine. Do not forget me wholly, love, but deem it not a duty to my memory never to love again. Arthur, dearest, thou canst bestow happiness on another, and one of thine own faith, even such happiness as to have been thy wife would have given me. Do not reject the calm rest and peacefulness, which such love will bring to thee, though now thou feelest as if the very thought were loathing. She will speak to thee of me; for Jewess as she knew me, she has loved and tended me in suffering, and so wept my banishment, that my frozen tears had well nigh flowed in seeing hers. Seek her in Isabella's court, and try to love her, Arthur—if at first merely for my sake, it will soon, soon be for her own."

Impressively and pleadingly, these words fell on Arthur's aching heart, even at that moment when he felt to comply with them was and must ever be impossible. When time had done its work, and softened individual agony, they returned again and yet again; and at each returning, seemed less painful to obey.

"And Isabella, my kind, loving, generous mistress," she continued, after a very long pause, and her voice was so faint as scarcely to make distinguishable the words, save for the still lingering sweetness, and clearness of her articulation—"Oh! what can I say to her? Arthur, dearest Arthur, thou must repay the debt of gratitude I owe her. Her creed condemns, but her heart loves me—aye, still, still! And better (though she cannot think so) than had I for earthly joy turned traitor to my God. Oh, tell her how with my last breath I loved and blessed her, Arthur; tell her we shall meet again, where Jew and Gentile worship the same God! Oh that I could but have proved—proved— How suddenly it has grown dark! Uncle Julien, is it not time for the evening prayer?"

And her lips moved in the wordless utterance of the prayer for which she had asked, forgetting it had some time before been said; and then her head sunk lower and lower on Arthur's bosom, and there was no sound. Twilight lingered, as loth to disappear, then deepened into night, and the silver lamps within the tents brighter and more brightly illumined the gloom; but Arthur moved not, suppressing even his breath, lest he should disturb that deep and still repose. It was more than an hour ere Julien Morales could realize the truth, and then he gently endeavored to unclasp Arthur's almost convulsive hold, and with, kindly force to lead him from the couch. The light of the lamp fell full upon that sweet, sweet face; and, oh! never had it seemed so lovely. The awful stillness of sculptured repose was indeed there; the breath of life and its disturbing emotions had passed away, and nought but the shrine remained. But like marble sculptured by God's hand, that sweet face gleamed—seeming, in its perfect tracery, its heavenly repose, to whisper even to the waves of agony, "Be still—my spirit is with God!"

* * * * *

Julien Morales and Arthur Stanley—the aged and the young—the Jewish recluse and Christian warrior—knelt side by side on the cold earth, which concealed the remains of one to both so inexpressibly dear. The moonlit shrubs and spangled heaven alone beheld their mutual sorrow, and the pale moon waned, and the stars gleamed paler and paler in the first gray of dawn ere that vigil was concluded. And then both arose and advanced to the barrier wall; the spring answered to the touch, and the concealed door flew back. The young Christian turned, and was folded to the heart of the Jew. The blessing of the Hebrew was breathed in the ear of the Englishman, and Stanley disappeared.

Oh, love! thou fairest, brightest, most imperishable type of heaven! what to thee are earth's distinctions? Alone in thy pure essence thou standest, and every mere earthly feeling crouches at thy feet. And art thou but this world's blessing? Oh! they have never loved who thus believe. Love is the voice of God, Love is the rule of Heaven! As one grain to the uncounted sands, as one drop to the unfathomed depths—is the love of earth to that of heaven; but when the mortal shrine is shivered, the minute particle will re-unite itself with its kindred essence, to exist unshadowed and for ever.

CHAPTER XXXV.

"Why then a final note prolong,
Or lengthen out a closing song,
Unless to bid the gentles speed
Who long have listened to my rede?"

SIR WALTER SCOTT.

The fickle sun of "merrie England" shone forth in unusual splendor; and, as if resolved to bless the august ceremony on which it gazed, permitted not a cloud to shadow the lustrous beams, which, darted their floods of light through the gorgeous casements of Westminster Abbey, in whose sacred precincts was then celebrating the bridal of the young heir of England, with a fair and gentle daughter of Spain. It was a scene to interest the coldest heart—not for the state and splendor of the accoutrements, nor the high rank of the parties principally concerned, nor for the many renowned characters of church, state, and chivalry there assembled; it was the extreme youth and touching expression, impressed on the features, of both bride and bridegroom.

Neither Arthur, Prince of Wales, nor Catherine, Infanta of Arragon, had yet numbered eighteen years, the first fresh season of joyous life; but on neither countenance could be traced the hilarity and thoughtlessness, natural to their age. The fair, transparent brow of the young Prince, under which the blue veins could be clearly seen, till lost beneath the rich chestnut curls, that parted on his brow, fell loosely on either shoulder; the large and deep blue eye, which was ever half concealed beneath the long, dark lash, as if some untold languor caused the eyelid to droop so heavily; the delicate pink of his downless cheek, the brilliant hue on his lips, even his peculiar smile, all seemed to whisper the coming ill, that one so dear to Englishmen would not linger with them to fulfil the sweet promise of his youth.

Beauty is, perhaps, too strong a word to apply to the youthful bride. It was the pensive sadness of her mild and pleasing features that so attracted— natural enough to her position in a strange land, and the thoughts of early severance from a mother she idolized, but recalled some twenty years afterwards as the dim shadow of the sorrowing future, glooming through the gay promise of the present. And there, too, was Prince Henry, then only in his twelfth year, bearing in his flashing eye and constantly varying expression of brow and mouth, true index of those passions which were one day to shake Europe to the centre; and presenting in his whole appearance a striking contrast to his brother, and drawing around him, even while yet so young, the hottest and wildest spirits of his father's court, who, while they loved the person, scorned the gentle amusements of the Prince of Wales.

Henry the Seventh and his hapless consort, Elizabeth of York, were, of course, present—the one rejoicing in the conclusion of a marriage for which he had been in treaty the last seven years, and which was at last purchased at the cost of innocent blood; the other beholding only her precious son, whose gentle and peculiarly domestic virtues, were her sweetest solace for conjugal neglect and ill-concealed dislike.

Amongst the many noble Spaniards forming the immediate attendants of the Infanta, had been one so different in aspect to his companions as to attract universal notice; and not a few of the senior noblemen of England had been observed to crowd round him whenever he appeared, and evince towards him the most marked and pleasurable cordiality. His thickly silvered hair and somewhat furrowed brow bore the impress of some five-and-fifty years; but a nearer examination might have betrayed, that sorrow more than years, had aged him, and full six, or even ten years might very well be subtracted from the age which a first glance supposed him. Why the fancy was taken that he was not a Spaniard could not have been very easily explained; for his wife was the daughter of the famous Pedro Pas, whose beauty, wit, and high spirits were essentially Spanish, and was the Infanta's nearest and most favored attendant; and he himself was constantly near her person, and looked up to by the usually jealous Spaniards as even higher in rank and importance that many of themselves. How, then, could he be a foreigner? And marvel merged into the most tormenting curiosity, when, on the bridal day of the Prince of Wales, though he still adhered to the immediate train of the Princess, he appeared in the rich and full costume of an English Peer. The impatience of several young gallants could hardly by restrained even during the ceremony; at the conclusion of which they tumultuously surrounded Lord Scales, declaring they would not let him go, till he had told them who and what was this mysterious friend: Lord Scales had headed a gallant band of English knights in the Moorish war, and was therefore supposed to know every thing concerning Spain, and certainly of this Anglo-Spaniard, as ever since his arrival in England they had constantly been seen together. He smiled good-humoredly at their importunity, and replied—

"I am afraid my friend's history has nothing very marvellous or mysterious in it. His family were all staunch Lancastrians, and perished either on the field or scaffold; he escaped almost miraculously, and after a brief interval of restless wandering, went to Spain and was treated with such consideration and kindness by Ferdinand and Isabella, that he has lived there ever since, honored and treated in all things as a child of the soil. On my arrival, I was struck by his extraordinary courage and rash disregard of danger, and gladly hailed in him a countryman. I learned afterwards that this reckless bravery had been incited by a wish for death, and that events had occurred in his previous life, which would supply matter for many a minstrel tale."

"Let us hear it, let us hear it!" interrupted many eager voices, but Lord Seales laughingly shook his head.

"Excuse me, my young friends: at present I have neither time nor inclination for a long story. Enough that he loved, and loved unhappily; not from its being unreturned, but from a concatenation of circumstances and sorrows which may not be detailed."

"But he is married; and he is as devoted to Donna Catherine as she is to him. I heard they were proverbial for their mutual affection and domestic happiness. How could he so have loved before?" demanded, somewhat skeptically, a very young man.

"My good friend, when you get a little older, you will cease to marvel at such things, or imagine, because a man has been very wretched, he is to be for ever. My friend once felt as you do (Lord Seales changed his tone to one of impressive seriousness); but he was wise enough to abide by the counsels of the beloved one he had lost, struggle to shake off the sluggish misery which was crushing him, cease to wish for death, and welcome life as a solemn path of usefulness and good, still to be trodden, though its flowers might have faded. Gradually as he awoke to outward things, and sought the companionship of her whom his lost one had loved, he became sensible that, spiritless as he had thought himself, he could yet, did he see fit, win and rivet regard; and so he married, loving less than he was loved, perchance at the time but scarcely so now. His marriage, and his present happiness, are far less mysterious than his extraordinary interference in the event which followed the conquest of the Moors—I mean the expulsion of the Jews."

"By the way, what caused that remarkable edict?" demanded one of the circle more interested in politics than in individuals. "It is a good thing indeed to rid a land of such vermin; but in Spain they had so much to do with the successful commerce of the country, that it appears as impolitic as unnecessary."

"Impolitic it was, so far as concerned the temporal interests of the kingdom; but the sovereigns of Spain decided on it, from the religious light in which it was placed before them, by Torquemada. It is whispered that Isabella would never have consented to a decree, sentencing so many thousands of her innocent subjects to misery and expulsion, had not her confessor worked on her conscience in an unusual manner; alluding to some unprecedented favor shown to one of that hated race, occasioned, he declared, by those arts of magic which might occur again and yet again, and do most fatal evil to the land. Isabella had, it appears, when reproached by Torquemada for her act of mercy, which he termed weakness, pledged herself, not to interfere with his measures for the extermination of the unbelief, and on this promise of course he worked, till the edict was proclaimed."

"But this stranger, what had he to do with it?" demanded many of the group, impatient at the interruption.

"What he had to do with it I really cannot tell you, but his zeal to avert the edict lost him, in a great measure the confidence of Ferdinand. When he found to prevent their expulsion was impossible, he did all in his power to lessen their misfortune, if such it may be called, by relieving every unbeliever that crossed his path."

An exclamation of horrified astonishment escaped his auditors. "What could such conduct mean? did he lean towards unbelief himself—"

"That could hardly be," replied Lord Scales. "Unless he had been a Catholic, earnest and zealous as herself, Isabella would never have so esteemed him, as to give him as wife her especial favorite, Catherine Pas, and place him so near the person of her child. When I left Spain, I entreated my friend to accompany me, and resume his hereditary title and estate, but I pleaded in vain. Some more than common tie seemed to devote him to the interests of the Queen of Castile, whom he declared he would never leave unless in England he could serve her better than in Spain. At that time there was no chance of such an event. He now tells me, that it was Isabella's earnest request that he should attend the Princess; be always near her, and so decrease the difficulties, which in a foreign land must for a time surround her. The Queen is broken in health, and dispirited, from many domestic afflictions; and it was with tears, she besought him to devote his remaining years, to the service of her child, and be to the future Queen of England true, faithful, and upright, as he had ever been to the Queen of Spain. Need I say the honorable charge was instantly accepted, and while he resumes his rank and duties as a Peer of his native land, the grateful service of an adopted son of Spain will ever be remembered and performed."

"But his name, his name?" cried many eager voices.

"ARTHUR STANLEY, EARL OF DERBY."

Milton Keynes UK
Ingram Content Group UK Ltd.
UKHW030740071024
449371UK00006B/693

9 789362 092939